Sexual Harassment and the Law in Africa

Written by a team of experts from legal, forensic, and policy backgrounds, this book presents new research into sexual violence and harassment across Africa.

This first of its kind book foregrounds the work of African scholars and presents careful research analysis and case studies that consider sexual harassment from legal, socio-economic, and cultural realities. It highlights the importance of laws around sexual harassment in Africa, the intersectional challenges it poses to women in the workplace, and the role of the feminist movement in Africa to hold perpetrators accountable and give voice to survivors of sexual harassment. The book forms part of a broader African-driven research initiative on sexual harassment and the law and is written in partnership with the Africa End Sexual Harassment Initiative (AESHI). It also explores the need to focus on best-practice benchmarks for Africa whilst gleaning from developments in Africa.

Timely and relevant, the book will be of great interest to legal and policy academic scholars, professionals, and activists working in the fields of gender policy, forensic psychology, and NGOs. It will also be useful reading for postgraduate students of law, gender studies, political science, and African studies.

Furaha-Joy Sekai Saungweme is Founder of Africa End Sexual Harassment Initiative (AESHI) and is a Georgetown Law LAWA Fellow specialising in women's rights in Africa. Furaha sits on the Editorial Board of the Berkeley University Centre on Comparative Equality and Anti-Discrimination Law (BCCE) and is an LLM Advisory Committee member of the Georgetown Journal of International Law (GJIL).

Carol Chi Ngang is Senior Lecturer at the Department of Public Law, National University of Lesotho, Research Fellow at the Free State Centre for Human Rights, University of the Free State and a Guest Lecturer at the Centre for Human Rights, University of Pretoria. He is the UNDP Human Rights Research Chair for Lesotho and a National Research Foundation of South Africa Category C2-rated Researcher.

Graham Towl is Professor of Forensic Psychology at Durham University, UK. He was the Pro Vice Chancellor Chair of the influential Durham University Sexual Violence Task Force in 2015/2016 and has co-written several books addressing sexual violence at universities in the UK. As a practitioner psychologist, he has worked with sex offenders and victim survivors of sexual violence.

Sexual Harassment and the Law in Africa

Country and Regional Perspectives

Edited by Furaha-Joy Sekai Saungweme, Carol Chi Ngang and Graham Towl

Routledge
Taylor & Francis Group
LONDON AND NEW YORK

Designed cover image: © Getty

First published 2024
by Routledge
4 Park Square, Milton Park, Abingdon, Oxon OX14 4RN

and by Routledge
605 Third Avenue, New York, NY 10158

Routledge is an imprint of the Taylor & Francis Group, an informa business

British Library Cataloguing-in-Publication Data
A catalogue record for this book is available from the British Library

Library of Congress Cataloging-in-Publication Data
Names: Saungweme, Furaha-Joy Sekai, editor, author. | Ngang, Carol Chi, editor, author. | Towl, Graham J., editor, author.
Title: Sexual harassment and the law in Africa : country and regional perspectives / edited by Furaha-Joy Sekai Saungweme, Carol Chi Ngang and Graham Towl.
Description: Abingdon, Oxon [UK] ; New York, NY : Routledge, 2024. | Includes bibliographical references and index.
Identifiers: LCCN 2023047642 (print) | LCCN 2023047643 (ebook) | ISBN 9781032446691 (hardback) | ISBN 9781032446684 (paperback) | ISBN 9781003373308 (ebook)
Subjects: LCSH: Sexual harassment—Law and legislation—Africa. | Women—Crimes against—Law and legislation—Africa. | Violence in the work place—Law and legislation—Africa. | Sex discrimination against women—Law and legislation—Africa. | Sexual harassment—Africa. | Women's rights—Africa. | African Charter on Human and Peoples' Rights (1981 June 27). Protocols, etc. (2003 July 11)
Classification: LCC KQC982.W66 S49 2024 (print) | LCC KQC982.W66 (ebook) | DDC 344.601/4133—dc23/eng/20231011
LC record available at https://lccn.loc.gov/2023047642
LC ebook record available at https://lccn.loc.gov/2023047643

ISBN: 978-1-032-44669-1 (hbk)
ISBN: 978-1-032-44668-4 (pbk)
ISBN: 978-1-003-37330-8 (ebk)

DOI: 10.4324/9781003373308

Typeset in Sabon
by Apex CoVantage, LLC

Contents

Acknowledgements

A special thank you to Professor David B. Oppenheimer, Deborah Byron, Megan E. Cistulli, and Julianna Bass.

For guidance and collaboration, thank you, Dr. Josephine Jarpa Dawuni of the Institute of African Women in Law, Dr. Wycliffe Nyachoti Otiso, Roseline Odede, Ana Daniela Pabón Ortiz, Caroline Kioko, Gladys Mbuyah, Maja Lundqvist, Dr. Ziona Tanzer, and Ann Noel.

For organisational support, thank you, John Senabulya.

For volunteer support, thank you, Berkeley Centre on Comparative Equality & Anti-Discrimination Law and your extraordinary members.

For your vision, mission, and team's support, thank you, Africa End Sexual Harassment Initiative (AESHI).

Thank you to the resilient, inspiring, and brilliant people across Africa and to our contributing authors. This book is just the beginning.

Editors and Authors Biographies

Editors

Furaha-Joy Sekai Saungweme

Furaha-Joy Sekai Saungweme is a lawyer and the founder of Africa End Sexual Harassment Initiative (AESHI). She is a Georgetown Law LAWA fellow specialising in women's rights in Africa. Furaha sits on the Editorial Board of the Berkeley University Centre on Comparative Equality and Anti-Discrimination Law (BCCE) and is an LLM Advisory Committee member of the Georgetown Journal of International Law (GJIL). In addition, she also serves as an Advisory Board member of the Decolonising Sexual and Gender Based Violence (SGBV) in Higher Education (HE): Innovations in Theory, Policy and Practice, a project which is funded by UK Research and Innovation (UKRI) Future Leaders Fellowship at the University of Westminster. She is a fellow of Women Leaders for the World, a project of How Women Lead based in the USA, in the state of California, which is a champion for promoting women in leadership. She is also a former company secretary, trainer, and advocate in GBV issues. Furaha has written widely on democracy, gender, and socio-economic rights in Africa, presenting research papers and discussions at academic institutions in Africa, Europe, and the USA.

Carol Chi Ngang

Carol Chi Ngang (LLD, LLM, IDHA, SUSTLAW, LLB) is a senior lecturer at the Department of Public Law, National University of Lesotho; research fellow at the Free State Centre for Human Rights, University of the Free State; and a guest lecturer at the Centre for Human Rights, University of Pretoria. He is the UNDP Human Rights research chair for Lesotho and a National Research Foundation of South Africa Category C2-rated researcher. He was a visiting researcher at the Van Vollenhoven Institute, Leiden University in

2022; Law and Development Research Group, University of Antwerp in 2016; and Cegla Centre for Interdisciplinary Research in Law, University of Tel-Aviv in 2015. His research interest combines human rights and development with a niche focus on the right to development and socio-economic and cultural rights wherein. He has published extensively, including books, book chapters, and journal articles. He is a member of the Law and Society Association (LSA), Law and Development Research Network (LDRN); associate editor of the *Lesotho Law Journal (LLJ)* and of *Turf Law Journal (TLJ);* and an advisory board member of the *International Journal of Ethiopia Legal Studies* (*IJELS*). He has also previously worked within the NGO sector in Cameroon and South Africa.

Graham Towl

Graham Towl is a professor of forensic psychology at Durham University, UK. He is co-author of two books on addressing sexual violence at universities in the UK (2019 and 2020) and co-editor of 'Stopping Gender-based Violence in Higher Education' (2023). He was the pro vice chancellor chair of the influential Durham University Sexual Violence Task Force in 2015/2016. Formerly, he was the chief psychologist at the Ministry of Justice, London, UK. As a practitioner psychologist, he has worked with sex offenders and victim survivors of sexual violence. He has published various blogs and articles on tackling sexual violence at universities and is committed to learning from and contributing to the work of others to more effectively tackle the problem of sexual violence.

Chapter Contributors

Wubrest F. Adamu

Wubrest F. Adamu is a legal officer working for the UNHCR where she focuses on the protection and assistance of internally displaced persons in Ethiopia. Wubrest obtained her first degree from Addis Ababa University School of Law in 2017 and is currently studying towards an LLM, advanced legal research studies at Georgetown University Law Center. In addition, she is a fellow of the McCain Global Leaders Institute, Arizona, focusing on peace, security, and reconciliation. Wubrest has also gained notable experience as a human rights investigator and a gender-focal person for both the Ethiopian Human Rights Council and the UN Human Rights Office (OHCHR). Her expertise includes conducting discussion papers and research on the Women, Peace, and Security Agenda, as well as the localisation of the peace and security agenda in Ethiopia.

Oluwatoyin Adejonwo-Osho

Oluwatoyin is a senior lecturer at the Department of Public Law, Faculty of Law, University of Lagos. She is a solicitor and advocate of the Supreme Court of Nigeria, and the founder and executive director of the Centre for Climate Change and Sustainable Development (3CSD). She holds a PhD in international environmental law from the School of Law, University of Dundee, United Kingdom. She teaches environmental law, human rights and civil liberties, and administrative law at undergraduate and postgraduate levels, and she supervises PhD theses. Dr. Adejonwo has taught environmental law at both undergraduate and postgraduate levels at universities in Scotland and South Africa, including at the Center for Human Rights, University of Pretoria, and Stellenbosch University. She serves on the Committee of Experts providing legal, advisory, and technical support on climate change to the Department of Climate Change (DCC) of the Federal Ministry of Environment, Nigeria. Dr. Adejonwo is the co-editor of the book *Climate Change Justice and Human Rights: An African Perspective* published by Pretoria University Law Press (PULP, 2022). She has, at various times, consulted for international environmental organisations including the Heinrich Böll Foundation and the Federal and State Ministry of Environment.

Veronica Fynn Bruey, PhD

Veronica Fynn Bruey is a multi-award winner and a passionate academic-advocate. Holding six academic degrees from four continents, she has researched, taught, consulted, and presented at conferences in over 30 countries. She's authored five books, several book chapters, and journal articles. In 2002, she founded Africa Awareness, a student-driven initiative responsible for instituting the first and only African Studies Program at the University of British Columbia. She is the founder/editor-in-chief of the *Journal of Internal Displacement*; co-editor of the *Migration, Displacement, and Development Book Series* with Rowman and Littlefield; the co-lead of the Law and Society's Collaborative Research Network (CRN-11), 'Displaced Peoples'; lead of the Law and Society Association's International Research Collaboration (IRC-10), 'Disrupting Patriarchy and Masculinity in Africa'; and founder of the Voice of West African Refugees in Ghana at the Buduburam Refugee Settlement in Ghana. Veronica is also the Australian National University International alumna of the year 2021, president of the International Association for the Study of Forced Migration, and co-chair of the Africa Interest Group, American Society of International Law. Currently, she is the director of Flowers School of Global Health Sciences and an assistant professor of legal studies at Atha.

Megan E. Cistulli

Megan E. Cistulli graduated from the University of California, Berkeley, in spring 2022 with highest distinction and earned a Bachelor of Arts in political science with specialisations in international relations and American politics while minoring in human rights. She is now pursuing her Juris Doctor Degree at the University of Chicago Law School. She continues to work on her STEM nonprofit based in Nairobi, Kenya, Technology & Entrepreneurship Ladder. As a postgraduate research fellow at the Berkeley Center on Comparative Equality and Anti-Discrimination Law, Megan participated in numerous research and fellowship projects including: an amicus brief for the Harvard/UNC affirmative action case; creating edX courses, including one on the Global #MeToo Movement; co-founding the Generation Professionale project supporting second-generation Italian students; maintaining a global membership and partnership network of over 1,000 activists, advocates, and academics; and conducting LGBTQIA+ research on Kenya, Botswana, and Uganda. In addition, Megan received the Muir Leadership Award, founded UC Berkeley's nationally ranked moot court team, is a member of Phi Beta Kappa and the Political Science Honor Society, a researcher at the Africa End Sexual Harassment Initiative, has worked as an editor for the UC Berkeley pre-law review, and presented her research at the London School of Economics.

Victoria Melkisedeck Lihiru

Victoria Melkisedeck Lihiru is a lawyer from Tanzania and a lecturer of law at the Open University of Tanzania. Dr. Lihiru has 12 years of extensive experience practising as a lawyer in Tanzania and across the region on issues pertaining to inclusive and democratic governance. She has contributed significantly to the national dialogue on the delivery of inclusive elections, gender and social inclusion, and the participation of women in the political, electoral, and decision-making processes. Dr. Lihiru holds a Ph.D. from the University of Cape Town and is currently a postdoctoral fellow at the Department of Public Law of the University of Pretoria.

Labila Sumayah Musoke

Labila is a health and human rights lawyer, social justice activist, and an advocate of the High Court of Uganda. She is also the program officer on the Right to Health at the Initiative for Social and Economic Rights. Her role allows her to actively work towards ensuring equitable access to healthcare for all. Additionally, Labila serves on the board of Medicus Mundi International Network and the Kampala Initiative, where she contributes to global advocacy efforts aimed at decolonising international corporations, access to medicines, and meaningful participation of the Global South in international spaces. Labila also coordinates the Reclaim Public Service Coalition in Uganda, a space that strives to revamp and enhance the quality public service delivery in critical sectors like education, health, and social protection. She has a postgraduate diploma in sustainable development and global justice from Antwerp University, Belgium; postgraduate in international contracts from Aalborg University, Denmark; and bachelor of laws from Makerere University, Uganda.

Yondela Ndema

Dr. Yondela Ndema is a lawyer and advocate of the High Court of South Africa and serves as the executive for compliance and ethics on behalf of Barloworld. Prior to this, she was the vice president, spearheading group compliance and ethics governance and assurance for SA multinational, Sasol. Dr. Ndema is also the vice chairperson and a ministerial appointee, University Council at the University of Johannesburg. In 2018, she was seconded at Shearman & Sterling in Washington DC and New York before proceeding to Boston to complete the General Management Program at Harvard Business School. Furthermore, Dr. Ndema holds seven post-graduate certificates in money laundering (Rand Afrikaans University); advanced corporate law and securities law (University of South Africa); compliance management (University of Cape Town); legal writing (University of Witwatersrand); international leadership development programme (Gordon Institute of Business Science); supply chain management (Smeal College of Business, Pennsylvania) and leading women (Gordon Institute of Business Science). She is a member of the International Women's Forum, Compliance Institute of South Africa, and Ethics SA. She volunteers with the Africa End Sexual Harassment Initiative (AESHI).

Carol Chi Ngang

Dr. Carol Chi Ngang (LLD, LLM, IDHA, SUSTLAW, LLB) is a senior lecturer at the Department of Public Law, National University of Lesotho; research fellow at the Free State Centre for Human Rights, University of the Free State; and a guest lecturer at the Centre for Human Rights, University of Pretoria. He is the UNDP Human Rights research chair for Lesotho and a National Research Foundation of South Africa Category C2-rated researcher. He was a visiting researcher at the Van Vollenhoven Institute, Leiden University in 2022; Law and Development Research Group, University of Antwerp in 2016; and Cegla Centre for Interdisciplinary Research in Law, University of Tel-Aviv in 2015. His research interest combines human rights and development with a niche focus on the right to development and socio-economic and cultural rights wherein. He has published extensively, including books, book chapters, and journal articles. He is a member of the Law and Society Association (LSA), Law and Development Research Network (LDRN); associate editor of the *Lesotho Law Journal (LLJ)* and of *Turf Law Journal (TLJ);* and an advisory board member of the *International Journal of Ethiopia Legal Studies* (*IJELS*). He has also previously worked within the NGO sector in Cameroon and South Africa.

Joëlle Nwabueze

Joëlle Nwabueze is a lecturer and deputy dean at the Faculty of Law, Enugu State University of Science and Technology, Nigeria. She is fluent in French and English, and is passionate about the study of comparative intellectual property law between these two systems. Her academic background includes undergraduate and postgraduate studies at the University of Yaoundé in Cameroon (Licence, Maitrise, and DEA); secondary studies at the University of Nantes in France, where she obtained her university diploma in fundamental rights; and Handong International Law School in South Korea, where she obtained a master's degree in International Law. She studied with the WIPO Academy, University of Turin, as part of the master's course in intellectual property law at the University of Douala as part of her doctoral studies in intellectual property, which led to a first doctorate in law on the protection of traditional knowledge, then a second PhD at the University of Bern on digital cultural heritage and database technologies, including an analysis of protection in the fields of intellectual property and unfair competition, with a study of comparative law between the OAPI States, the European Union, and Nigeria. Joëlle is a member of the International Association for the Advancement of Teaching and Research in Intellectual Property Law (ATRIP).

Wycliffe Nyachoti Otiso

Dr. Wycliffe Nyachoti Otiso is a holder of a Bachelor of Laws degree from University of Warwick, Master of Laws degree from University of Nairobi, and a PhD in law and political science at the Universite de Pau et des Pays de L'Adour (UPPA). He is a qualified advocate of the High Court of Kenya and a certified professional mediator. Dr. Otiso is the chair of Public Law and a lecturer at Kisii University. He has taught constitutional and human rights law for over 11 years. Other teaching interests include disability law, law reform, social justice, and legal research. He has published papers on human rights protection, participatory governance, security sector reform and policing, and has presented papers on governance, access to justice, legal research, digital rights, and ethics. He is an editor of the Law Society of Kenya (LSK) Journal *Advocates Magazine* and peer reviews several journals. Dr. Otiso is also a *pro-bono* legal advisor to TEFL and IRDO, non-profit non-governmental organizations involved in advocacy on issues related to human rights, barriers to access to health, sexual violence, and access to justice.

Furaha-Joy Sekai Saungweme

Furaha-Joy Sekai Saungweme is a lawyer and the founder of Africa End Sexual Harassment Initiative (AESHI). She is a Georgetown Law LAWA fellow specialising in women's rights in Africa. Furaha sits on the Editorial Board of the Berkeley University Center on Comparative Equality and Anti-Discrimination Law (BCCE). In addition, she also serves as an Advisory Board member of the Decolonising Sexual and Gender Based Violence (SGBV) in Higher Education (HE): Innovations in Theory, Policy, and Practice, a project which is funded by the UK Research and Innovation (UKRI) Future Leaders Fellowship at the University of Westminster. She is a fellow of Women Leaders for the World, a project of How Women Lead based in California, USA, which is a champion for promoting women in leadership; a former company secretary; and trainer and advocate in GBV issues. Furaha has written widely on democracy, gender, and socio-economic rights in Africa, presenting research papers and discussions at academic institutions in Africa, Europe, and the USA.

Juliana Taiwo-Obalonye

Juliana is an assistant news editor with the *Sun Newspapers*, one of Nigeria's major national newspapers with a wide reach. She is a senior journalist with deep interest in women rights, gender inclusion, disability rights, civil society, and the impact of donor investment in the Global South, politics, and public policy spaces. Julianna's career in journalism spans over 27 years, where she has worked as a page planner, participated in field news coverage, and has been a State House correspondent covering presidential races in Nigeria for two leading national newspapers, the *Sun Newspapers* and *THISDAY Newspapers*. Juliana is currently pursuing a postgraduate MA in development communication at the Institute of Strategic and Development, Nasarawa State University, Keffi, Nasarawa State, Nigeria. She holds B.Sc. in mass communications from Nnamdi Azikiwe University, Awka, Anambra State, Nigeria, and a diploma in public relations from the Nigerian Institute of Journalism, Ikeja, Lagos, Nigeria.

Graham Towl

Graham Towl is a professor of forensic psychology at Durham University, UK. He is co-author of two books on addressing sexual violence at universities in the UK (2019 and 2020) and co-editor of *Stopping Gender-based Violence in Higher Education* (2023). He was the pro vice chancellor chair of the influential Durham University Sexual Violence Task Force in 2015/2016. Formerly, he was the chief psychologist at the Ministry of Justice, London, UK. As a practitioner psychologist, he has worked with sex offenders and victim survivors of sexual violence. He has published various blogs and articles on tackling sexual violence at universities and is committed to learning from and contributing to the work of others to more effectively tackle the problem of sexual violence.

Foreword

I have dedicated my life to advocating for the advancement of women's rights, equality, and justice in my country, Ethiopia, and beyond. Hence, the insidious impact of sexual harassment on the economic, social, and overall well-being of women deeply concerns me. I believe that sexual harassment obstinately persists and affects survivors on a regular basis and affects survivors in Africa and around the world. So we must act now.

Numerous reports documented that sexual harassment is ever-present in the workplace, in educational institutions, and elsewhere. It is a permanent constraint on the mobility of women and limits their access to resources and basic services. Sexual harassment, according to international human rights instruments,[1] includes 'unwelcome sexually determined behavior such as physical contact and advances, sexually colored remarks, showing pornography, and sexual demand, whether by words or actions'. The act, like other forms of violence, is deeply rooted in harmful social norms, gender inequality, and power relations. Even though the prevalence of unwanted sexual advances is high, it remains underreported because of power relations, lack of evidence, fear of retaliation, and a lack of trust in the justice system. These gaps can be narrowed through advocacy and the introduction of strong legislation. Legal frameworks that curb sexual harassment, particularly in the workplace and public domain, would be significant in making positive strides. These laws tend to reduce barriers to victims coming forward to report cases, provide dissuasive penalties on perpetrators, and may also deter potential offenders. Parallel to the criminal justice system, civil justice is pivotal in providing safety and protection mechanisms for women.

In the past few decades, the Ethiopian social structure was dominated by a strongly patriarchal culture and hegemonic gender discourses. To challenge these manifold and serious legal and social problems, our advocacy was based on the international human rights frameworks. We also used these instruments to promote the economic, political, and social rights of women and raise awareness of discriminatory acts, including violence against women. Along with our advocacy work, we realised the importance of institutionalising our struggle. Hence, in 1996 we established the Ethiopian Women Lawyers Association (EWLA). Since then, EWLA has been working on promoting the economic, social, and political rights of Ethiopian women through legal reform, legal aid, public education, capacity building, and research. The association has also made successful advocacy work that brought legal reforms under the family law, pension law, and the criminal code. Furthermore, EWLA has been a pioneer in introducing legal terminologies and concepts that were neither recognised as offenses nor had an equivalent terminology in the national language. As a result of EWLA's work, Ethiopia's Criminal Code recognised domestic violence as a crime and sexual harassment now has a defining terminology in the Ethiopian official language. Moreover, the extensive public education works have helped to increase awareness of the rights of women, in addition to early response and support mechanisms for victims of gender-based violence. Albeit quite moderate, we transformed women's engagement in the public sphere and introduced major gender discourse on our legal system. This shows the impact of the women's rights movement on the change of hegemonic power and cultural stagnation.

Fast-forward from my experience at EWLA, since I assumed office as the president of the Federal Supreme Court in November 2018, we have devoted resources to enhance access to justice, and promote gender equality and gender mainstreaming within the judiciary. During the past three years, 36 women judges were appointed at the Federal Courts, and we are developing a system to regulate workplace sexual harassment by initiating policies and introducing legislation. However, experience shows that organisational practice is often misaligned with formal policies or grievance procedures. To mitigate this, we need to create a strategy and strengthen our resources and management systems.

Advocacy is central in preventing, identifying, and managing violence. Therefore, we need social momentum, such as the 'Me Too' movement. Such movements are useful to shift the norms that surround sexual harassment and to publicly address systematic issues. Particularly in Africa, these kinds of movements can bring forward various scenarios of sexual harassment, reveal the prevalence and magnitude of the problem, challenge the status quo through research, dialogues, empowering survivors, lobbying legal reforms, and implementing policy and legal initiatives. While doing that, it is important to address multi-dimensional and intersectional axes of oppression surrounding every survivor such as ethnicity, disability, and class division. To address this, multifaceted works such as the contributions in this book are vital.

This compendium is a collection of concise but detailed comparative discussions and findings on sexual harassment and is a credit to the editors and contributors. The book is a culmination of countless hours of research writings, a collection studies and commentaries which offer specialized, rich, in-depth information on the necessity of sexual harassment laws in Africa. This brings in a comparative context of the development of sexual harassment laws in their countries through which Africa can use to develop best-practice benchmarks. I believe this kind of research will help us better understand where we are and what needs to be done.

Chief Justice Meaza Ashenafi
Judge of the Federal Courts of Ethiopia
Founder of the Ethiopia Women Lawyers Association

Note

1 CEDAW General Recommendations Nos 19 and 20, adopted at the Eleventh Session, 1992, Arts 2(f), 5 and 10(c); Beijing Platform for Action (Beijing, China–September 1995), para 16; Protocol to the African Charter on Human and Peoples' Rights on the Rights of Women in Africa, (Maputo, 11 July 2003), Arts 12–13.

1 The Menace of Sexual Harassment in the Workplace

A Legal and Human Rights Concern

Furaha-Joy Sekai Saungweme, Carol Chi Ngang and Graham Towl

Overview

Among the many wicked problems that women in Africa are confronted with daily is sexual harassment; a generic societal phenomenon promoted and sustained by structural systems and socio-cultural perceptions. It is a problem which existed before it became legally defined as such in the USA in 1970s.[1]

It is worth stating that sexual harassment is a generic societal phenomenon promoted and sustained by structural systems and socio-cultural perceptions which existed before it became legally defined as such in the USA in the 1970s. Furthermore, in light of what is a predominantly patriarchal global society, the fact cannot be denied that women are generally more at risk of being sexually harassed than men.[2] The corpus of research from across the African continent demonstrates that sexual harassment knows no boundaries. By this we mean that sexual harassment happens in all sectors of society, including in private and public spaces as well as in formal and informal work environments. Because the contributions in this book are specifically focused on sexual harassment within the workplace, in this introductory chapter, we highlight some key institutional workplace settings in Africa with the aim to show how and to what extent sexual harassment occurs in those settings and the menace it poses to victims and broader society.

The findings of a survey conducted in 2021 by the Inter-Parliamentary Union (IPU) and the African Parliamentary Union (APU) revealed that while a growing number of women are slowly gaining access to higher political offices as legislators in parliaments across Africa, the positions they hold do not prevent the perpetuation of sexual harassment against them.[3] The study found that 40% of women parliamentarians in Africa have been sexually harassed at work by their male colleagues, and that 83% of the acts of sexual harassment actually take place within the premises of parliament.[4] Such practices of course affect the job performance of female legislators and, thus, portray parliaments, which are supposed to be institutions of policy and law making against such offences, as not being any safer for women. In a case study illustration within the parliamentary space in Uganda, Sylvia Tamale draws attention to the fact that sexual harassment was an issue that

DOI: 10.4324/9781003373308-1

most women legislators reported having to deal with on a day-to-day basis.[5] Tamale cites one of the informant victims attesting that she thought her personality and status as a legislator would protect her but, on the contrary, the harassment by male legislators has become a commonplace behaviour which the women often just ignore.[6]

Another institutional workplace setting of interest is the higher education sector where studies reveal startling numbers of women – citing, for example, 99% of women in Egypt and three quarters of women in South Africa – have experienced sexual harassment.[7] While the findings of a cross-sectional study conducted over the period from 1996–2006 to determine whether sexual harassment actually happens in institutions of higher education in sub-Saharan Africa revealed an overwhelming positive response, many of the student participants lacked an understanding of what constitutes sexual harassment.[8] The demonstration of lack of knowledge on the nature of sexual harassment in the study by Menon *et al*, tells that contrary to available statistics, there are certainly many more victims of sexual harassment whose experiences are confused for normality and, accordingly, remain susceptible to the perils of the act and the likelihood of being sexually harassed repeatedly. According to Leila Wood *et al*, being female at higher education institutions 'increases the odds of experiencing both faculty/staff and peer sexual harassment by 86% and 147%, respectively'.[9] On account of the asymmetries that define teacher/student relationships at these institutions, Gouws and Kritzinger note that reporting sexual harassment could have serious repercussions and, thus, the vice gets covered up most of the time.[10]

The findings are even more surprising in the media sector, where the 'latest Women in News survey on sexual harassment in African media organisations highlights that 1 in every 2 women working in the media sector, experiences some form of sexual harassment'.[11] In another survey of media personnel in eight countries in eastern and southern Africa that looked at the rate of sexual harassment, the sources of harassment, how often victims report, and how organisations react to it, the findings showed that 'women are the prime targets of sexual harassment' with an average of 56% reporting to have experienced verbal harassment and 38% experiencing physical harassment, against 24% of men who reported experiencing verbal harassment and 15% who reported experiencing physical harassment.[12] As to why sexual harassment thrives within the media sector, it is noted that there are no robust policies in place aimed at preventing sexual harassment and, consequently, the number of victims that ever get to report the ordeal they experience remains quite minimal.[13]

Avenues for redress are not only lacking in the media sector but also in almost all other sectors across Africa. This creates a breathing space for the perpetuation of sexual harassment with impunity. Anti-sexual harassment advocates and other active voices have not been silent about unearthing and exposing the social injustices that result from sexual harassment. Their activism has led to global calls for action, notable among which is the #metoomovement, which has grown exponentially. The movement has leveraged a multiplication of inquiries into sexual harassment allegations in high places like the African Union, academic institutions like Makerere University in Uganda, and in big media houses like the South African Broadcasting Corporation (SABC), among others. A major bombshell was the release of the BBC Africa viral documentary *Sex for Grades*, which exposed sexual harassment by lecturers at institutions of higher learning in Africa, such as at the University of Lagos and the University of Ghana. A landmark judgment on sexual harassment was delivered in Zimbabwe in the *R M v Zizhou and Another* case,[14] where the plaintiff claimed compensation that was awarded after a 20-year litigation battle. Despite these exposures, the fact cannot be denied that knowledge and open conversations on sexual harassment are still largely stifled.

The selected examples discussed here are not exhaustive but intended to illustrate, as noted earlier, that sexual harassment is a societal ill and social injustice that knows no boundaries and is currently not regulated by a comprehensive regional legal or policy framework. This makes it a human rights concern necessitating closer attention. It is a human rights concern in the sense that it demeans and robs victims of their entitlement to life with dignity. Although not yet comprehensively regulated by any regional legal instrument, sexual harassment could, with respect to existing human rights instruments relating to provisions on the right to equality and non-discrimination, the right to human dignity, the right to privacy, and the right to personal security among others, correctly be considered a violation of the human rights. In the world of work, the International Labour Organisation (ILO) affirms in terms of its Discrimination (Employment and Occupation) Convention No 111 of 1958 that 'Sexual harassment is a serious manifestation of sex discrimination and a violation of human rights'.[15] Alluding to Convention No. 190 and Recommendation No 206, the ILO enjoins states to undertake to define and, most importantly, prohibit sexual harassment in their domestic legislation.[16]

Clearly, sexual harassment remains a topical issue across Africa, which makes this publication timely and relevant. More elaborate discussions on the multi-dimensional issues of sexual harassment are taken up in the various chapters. It is worth noting, however, that while it is germane with respect to the ILO recommendation, to legislate on sexual harassment at the domestic level – and besides the comprehensible suggestions and recommendations articulated in each of the chapters on how best to deal with the problem in each particular circumstance – the concluding chapter proffers the need for the adoption of an African Model Law on Sexual Harassment under the auspices of the African Union, which, we posit, would serve as a legally binding instrument applicable across the African continent and thus also enable the putting in place of relevant remedy and enforcement mechanisms to ensure adequate redress.

About the Book

This book is an edited volume comprised of a compilation of 13 chapter contributions, including this introductory chapter, 11 substantive chapters, and a concluding chapter. The chapters are authored principally by scholars from different parts of Africa who, in articulating different perspectives, have endeavoured to explore the question of sexual harassment and put together their findings, analysis, and argumentations in the most comprehensive manner that is envisaged to inform and create greater awareness on the matter. The book is the first of what we anticipate to eventually become the Africa End Sexual Harassment Initiative (AESHI) publication series on sexual harassment in Africa. The various chapter contributions portray how sexual harassment manifests in different work settings and the implication of that for women who are most affected. The book provides a balanced critique and useful materials for reflection and enabling critical and comparative analyses on the complexities, manifestations, and consequences of sexual harassment in Africa.

Beginning with this initial output, subsequent publications in the series are envisaged to explore other angles of the multifaceted problem, including, for instance, the intersectional dimensions of sexual harassment and its prevalence in other sectors of society, with the intention to disseminate both theoretical and empirical findings and robust analysis on the subject matter. Subsequent publications will certainly follow the same edited volume format without eliminating the possibility of regularly inviting African scholars and other experts to publish single-authored books or monographs on related aspects of sexual harassment as part of the publication series to maintain a regional and national focus on the sexual harassment. The foreword is written by Chief Justice Meaza Ashenafi of the Federal Courts of Ethiopia, who is also the founder of the Ethiopia Women Lawyers Association. As an authority on the subject, she highlights the importance of laws around sexual harassment, the intersectional challenges it poses to women in the workplace, as well as the role of the feminist movement in Africa to hold perpetrators accountable and give voice to survivors.

With the depth of research that resulted in the outputs contained in this book, the quality of the analysis and argumentations, and the overall substance of each of the chapters, we envisage that the book will become a useful source of knowledge as well as reference material for further research on sexual harassment. Three of the chapters have a continental and comparative focus while the rest are more country focused. The one chapter from the Southern Africa region articulates the perspective from South Africa; the four chapters from the Eastern Africa region articulate perspectives from Tanzania, Uganda, Ethiopia, and Kenya; and the three other chapters from the West Africa region articulate perspectives from Liberia and Nigeria. A synopsis of the chapters is provided in the following.

Synopsis of the Chapters

Chapter 2: Critical Reflections on Equality, Sexual Harassment, and the Right to Sustainable Development for Women in Africa

In chapter two, Carol Chi Ngang presents a critical analysis of the interwoven principle of equality in law, the right to a workplace free of sexual harassment, and the right to sustainable development for women in Africa. His analysis illustrates that genuine equality is not attainable under conventional legal frameworks. He argues that providing protection and entitlement to women in Africa instead requires a model law that prioritises the quest for justice above seeking to achieve equality under pre-existing instruments of law, many of which he says are overtly biased. He posits that abstract guarantees of equality in law largely only contain vestiges of hope and, at times, endless expectations. For him, this amounts to justice delayed and, thus, justice denied for women in their aspirations to live free from all forms of discriminatory practices that impact on their right to sustainable development as guaranteed in the Protocol on the Rights of Women in Africa. He concludes with the thesis that if Africa is to attain balanced sustainable development and that living standards are equalised for all, much thought needs to be given to the opportunities accessible to women and how they are perceived and treated in society, particularly with respect to gender discrimination and sexual harassment.

Chapter 3: Ending Sexual Harassment in Africa Through Human Rights Mechanisms: A Critical Appraisal of the Application of the Maputo Protocol by the African Human Rights System and the ECOWAS Court of Justice

Joëlle Nwabueze makes the argument in Chapter 3 that the use of African human rights mechanisms for the promotion of female human rights is a reliable path with the potential to end sexual harassment on the continent. She engages with the fundamental question of the scope of human rights in sexual harassment claims and examines the laws and mechanisms that regulate the way human rights claims are developed and applied to sexual harassment cases within the African human rights system. Her analysis focuses on the tripartite human rights judicial system of the African Union represented by the African Court and Commission on Human and Peoples' Rights and the Committee of Experts on the Rights and Welfare of the Child (ACERWC) on one side and the Community Court of Justice of the Economic Community of West African States (The ECOWAS Court of Justice) on the other side. The chapter specifically highlights how the interwoven judicial and quasi-judicial human rights mechanisms enforce the dispositions of the Protocol to the African Charter on Human and Peoples' Rights on the Rights of Women in Africa (Maputo Protocol) on the continent. The unavoidable issue of state obligation under international human rights mechanisms and the encumbrance to justice in sexual harassment claims is discussed. She concludes the discussion in the chapter with recommendations aimed at genuine enforcement of the dispositions of the Maputo Protocol by African human rights judicial institutions to eradicate the gangrene of sexual harassment on the continent.

Chapter 4: Single Incident, Big Impact: Exposing the Precarious Relationship Between Sexual Harassment and the Persistent Behaviour Standard

In Chapter 4, Furaha-Joy Sekai Saungweme and Megan E. Cistulli submit that the trivialisation of a single incident of sexual harassment contributes to a misapplication of the law specifically requiring persistent conduct before the offence of sexual harassment can be alleged. Comparing four major legal systems, they challenge such a characterisation as not only a legal lacuna but also as a dangerous premise that exacerbates gender inequality, access to justice, and fairness in the workplace. Their analysis delves first into South African law, wherein they examine the *Shoprite Checkers (Pty) Ltd v JL* case that dealt with a single incident of sexual harassment. They then proceed to explore the United Kingdom's (UK) approach to sexual harassment by looking at the Equality Act of 2010 and decisions of UK courts. They proceed further to assess United States (US) federal laws and its severe or pervasive standard by looking at two pivotal sexual harassment cases: *Meritor Savings Bank v Vinson* (1986) and *Harris v Forklift Systems, Inc* (1993). They conclude with an analysis of Kenya's legal system and its standard of persistent behaviour by examining some key cases and the Employment Act, the Sexual Offences Act, as well as the position under Ugandan law. They advance a concluding argument in the form of recommendations that requiring a persistent pattern of sexually harassing behaviour undermines the seriousness of sexual harassment, weakens potential credible claims, and deepens discrimination and unequal gender relations in the workplace.

Chapter 5: A Critical Analysis of Vicarious Liability for Sexual Harassment in South Africa

With focus on South Africa, in Chapter 5, Yondela Ndema provides a critical analysis of the vicarious liability of an employer with regard to sexual harassment in the workplace. She posits that like in many other countries, the workplace in South Africa has the potential to be two different environments. In her view, the workplace should be a place where there is dignity, self-esteem, self-worth, respect, ubuntu, individual autonomy, and equality. She notes that the workplace is rather frequently an environment characterised by insults, degrading treatment, disrespect, abuse of trust, and unfair discrimination. The human rights to dignity and equality, as she further notes, are important aspects of the Bill of Rights in the Constitution of the

Republic of South Africa 1996. Dignity and equality, as she explains, are critical founding values enshrined in Section 7(1) of the Constitution in terms of which sexual harassment is considered an unacceptable violation of human rights in an open and democratic South Africa. The harm resulting from sexual harassment gives rise to various remedies, which are not mutually exclusive. She submits that the plaintiff can have recourse to one or more of the available remedies, including a protection order from the Magistrate's Court. For her, because sexual harassment is potentially a labour issue, it can also be treated as a constitutional rights matter – a delict or unfair discrimination – and can even manifest itself as a specific offence in criminal law. In summary, the focal point of the chapter is a critique of the current law on sexual harassment in South Africa examined in light of the common-law principles of vicarious liability and statutory vicarious liability as has been applied by the courts in case law.

Chapter 6: Legal Protection of Women with Disabilities Against Sexual Harassment in Tanzania

Victoria Melkisedeck Lihiru's analysis in Chapter 6 presents the legal framework for addressing sexual harassment against women with disabilities in Tanzania. She illustrates that sexual harassment under Tanzania law is covered rather inadequately in different pieces of legislations. The chapter makes an account of the level of protection offered by selected Tanzania national legislation in comparison to the basic standards for the protection of women with disabilities against sexual harassment deduced from international instruments, including the International Labour Organization Convention 190. Lihiru's findings point to key gaps in the legal framework on sexual harassment and provides suggestions on how Tanzanian national laws could be brought to par with international standards. Although a robust and disability-sensitive specific law on sexual harassment is paramount, she contends that the legal system alone is not an adequate mechanism for curbing sexual harassment. For her, strengthening women and girls with disabilities' agency, training, awareness raising, and access to an effective justice system will add sufficient drive to the protection of women with disabilities against sexual harassment.

Chapter 7: Silent but Pervasive: Sexual Harassment Against Women Lawyers in Uganda

Workplace sexual harassment – according to Labila Sumayah Musoke and explained in Chapter 7 – is a multi-sectoral phenomenon affecting thousands of workers across Uganda, including the legal sector. She finds that while lawyers are the guardrails of democracy and justice, sexual harassment, which is a human rights and women's rights concern, is prevalent and pervasive within the legal profession. She highlights the story of Samantha

Mwesigye, a female Ugandan lawyer who shared her sexual harassment ordeal at the hands of her supervisor whilst working at the Ministry of Justice and Constitutional Affairs in 2019 and points out that Mwesigye's alleged sexual harasser (also a lawyer) now sits as a judge in the Uganda Court of Appeal – a promotion which came amidst widespread media scrutiny and an ongoing court process instigated by Samantha. Her story remains a reflection of the alarming levels of sexual harassment in the workplace which ignited the flames of a national movement to eradicate sexual harassment in the workplace. In the first part of the chapter, Ndema deconstructs sexual harassment as a form of gender-based violence, and then provides a contextual analysis of the problem with respect to the existing legal and policy framework. With a focus on the 'sheroe', Samantha, Musoke articulates the challenges of women lawyers in Uganda, which as she draws attention to, stemming from the patriarchal nature of the society and exacerbated by inadequate laws. In conclusion, she emphasises and recommends the need to shift the burden of proof from the survivor to the perpetrator while dealing with sexual harassment cases.

Chapter 8: The Cost of Workplace Sexual Harassment: A Critique of the Ethiopia Labour Law

In Chapter 8, Wubrest F. Adamu looks at the cost of sexual harassment and makes the argument that the achievement of workplace equality for women in Ethiopia is hindered by a myriad of factors that are rooted in cultural conceptions of gender, socio-economic conditions, as well as an inadequate legislative and policy framework. She notes that Ethiopia, being a deeply patriarchal society with strong traditional perceptions of the societal roles of men and women, has as a result lagged in comprehensively addressing some of the core triggers of workplace inequality, including sexual harassment. While Prime Minister Abiy Ahmed's cabinet is constituted of 50% women, and he appointed a woman as president and another woman as head of the Supreme Court for the first time in Ethiopia's history, Adamu admits that these measures have not necessarily eradicated sexual harassment in the workplace, but they are, indeed, steps of progress. Against this background, she underscores Ethiopia's inadequate sexual harassment laws as part of the problem and, therefore, highlights the need to employ the sexual harassment definition provided by the ILO as a standard definition. She further notes that in 2019, Ethiopia adopted a new proclamation which replaced the Labour Proclamation that has been in existence for the past 16 years. Her analysis explores the change in legislation and the approach to workplace sexual harassment, and questions whether the new law provides the anticipated answers given the cultural and socio-economic challenges beguiling Ethiopian women's enjoyment of equality in the workplace.

Chapter 9: Sexual Harassment and the Law in Kenya: Broadening Employee Rights in the World of Work

In Chapter 9, Wycliffe Nyachoti Otiso explores the issue of sexual harassment in relation to the law in Kenya. He observes that the enactment of the Sexual Offences Act in 2006, the comprehensive reform of labour laws in 2007, and the promulgation of the Constitution of Kenya in 2010 have had little deterrent effect on sexual harassment in the world of work in Kenya. He examines the adequacy of the law in sanctioning cases of sexual harassment in Kenya and analyses the courts' interpretation of pertinent terms including the term 'workers', 'employment', and 'violence', which are important in determining which acts constitute sexual harassment. His findings reveal that the courts are gradually adopting a broader interpretation of the meaning of sexual harassment. He notes, however, that there is little progress on the recognition of sexual harassment as an infringement of constitutional rights, including freedom from violence. He brings to the spotlight the fact that the adoption of the International Labour Organisation Convention on Violence and Harassment (ILO C190) has exposed the limited protective mechanisms in the existing provisions in Kenyan labour laws on the issue of sexual harassment and violence. In conclusion, he recommends the ratification of the ILO Convention on Violence and Harassment (C-190) by the government of Kenya to ensure better protection of employees from sexual harassment.

Chapter 10: Sexual Harassment and the Law in Liberia

Chapter 10 is focused on sexual harassment in Liberia, which Veronica Fynn Bruey describes as having a historical track record of failing to address sexual harassment, whether in the workplace, at school, or in the marketplace. Bruey notes that in its 176 years of being Africa's first republic, the daily occurrences in which girls and women are predisposed to sexual harassment in Liberia are innumerable. She explains, for instance, that going to the farm, fetching water, hawking/selling on the streets, during female student-male-teacher interaction, outings and clubbing at night, searching for employment, and even while at home looking after younger siblings, Liberia girls and women are exposed to sexual harassment. She points out that with an estimated population of 5.4 million people, post-war Liberia has a low human development index of 0.48, ranked as the 14th poorest country in the world. She adds that according to the World Bank (2017), the literacy rate for adult female ages 15 and above in Liberia is barely half (34%) that of males (63%) of the same age. These socio-economic ills, she notes, exacerbate the disproportional prevalence of sexual harassment against girls and women in Liberia. She draws attention to the establishment of the First Judicial Circuit, Criminal Court Assizes 'E' (2008) and the Sexual and Gender-based Violence Crimes Unit (2009) with a goal to fast-track and prosecute rape and other gender violence cases and posits this as an avenue of justice for sexual harassment complainants. Notwithstanding this modest progress, Bruey contends that Liberia still has no sexual harassment law and, as a consequence, rape has become so rampant that it was declared a national emergency in 2016. Drawing on theories of intersectionality and feminist-jurisprudence that are embodied in major regional and national laws and social policy frameworks, Bruey's analysis in this chapter broadly explores the history, state, and impact of sexual harassment in Liberia, which provides a comprehensive analysis on how sexual harassment manifests in public and private spaces.

Chapter 11: Sexual Harassment in the Nigerian Media Environment

Juliana Taiwo-Obalonye's study on sexual harassment in Chapter 11 illustrates that the media industry in Nigeria has been significantly impacted by sexual harassment, which has had negative effects on the women working in the industry. One major issue she articulates in the chapter is the absence of any policy framework addressing sexual harassment in the media by which perpetrators could be held accountable and punished. She defines sexual harassment as an offence primarily perpetrated by men who hold senior positions in the media industry. She discusses the importance of a media regulatory framework, using the Nigerian Bar Association sexual harassment policy as an example of what the media industry should emulate. She points out the mandate allocated to the media sector in terms of Section 22 of the 1999 Constitution of the Federal Republic of Nigeria, which provides that the media is constitutionally empowered to hold all institutions, including the government, to account. On the basis of that mandate, she argues that the Nigerian media sector ought to lead by example in holding its members to account against sexual harassment and, therefore, set a high standard rule of ethical conduct for them. Her study involved a survey and key informant interviews (KIIs) conducted to provide evidence of the prevalence of sexual harassment in the media sector through the lens of survivors, which then informed her conclusions and recommendations.

Chapter 12: Sexual Harassment and the Law in Nigeria: Exploring the Existing Legal Landscape and Highlighting the Gaps in Legal and Institutional Frameworks

In Chapter 12, Oluwatoyin Adejonwo also explores the question of sexual harassment in relation to the law in Nigeria. She emphasises that besides rape, which is common in Nigeria, Nigerian criminal law recognises other forms of sexual violence, including indecent assault. However, she underscores the fact that recent development in state laws and workplace policies now recognise sexual harassment and seek to punish such acts and that some state legislation, including the Criminal Law of Lagos State and the Criminal Law of Edo State, have enacted specific legislation on sexual harassment.

She also alludes to a bill pending before the National Assembly that seeks to criminalise and punish sexual harassment in universities and other tertiary institutions in Nigeria, such as the Tertiary Institutions Prohibition Bill and workplace policies against sexual harassment. She further submits that the Criminal Code and the Penal Code, being relics from the colonial era, do not provide for a separate offence of sexual harassment apart from the traditional offences of rape, indecent assault, and other sexual offences. She argues that women and girls are, accordingly, susceptible to sexual harassment at the hands of male perpetrators who take advantage of relational dynamics of trust and power to prey on the women's social, cultural, and economic vulnerabilities. She takes cognisance of the fact that while the laws and policies are emerging, implementation and enforcement may vary, and, thus, may pose challenges in reporting and prosecution. Her analysis in this chapter particularly focuses on mapping the existing legal landscape and gaps in the legal framework in relation to sexual harassment in Nigeria.

Chapter 13: Mapping Future Directions in Addressing Sexual Harassment in Africa

In this concluding chapter, we provide some brief antecedence on how sexual harassment came to be known as a global problem of enormous adverse proportions especially against women, including those in Africa. The developments both at the international and at the African continental levels motivated the research that resulted in the production of this book. In terms of future directions in redressing the scourge of sexual harassment, we recommend for the African Union to adopt a Model Law on Sexual Harassment, which, we estimate, would gain widespread acceptance and eventual incorporation into the domestic laws of every country on the African continent.

Notes

1 Carrie N. Baker *Race, Class, and Sexual Harassment in the 1970s* (Study of Women and Gender: Faculty Publications, Smith College, 2004).
2 L Fitzgerald, S Swan and V Magley 'But was it really sexual harassment? Legal, behavioural and psychological definitions of the workplace victimization of women' in W O'Donohue (ed) *Sexual Harassment: Theory, Research and Treatment* (Allyn & Bacon, 1997) 15.
3 Inter-Parliamentary Union 'Widespread sexism and violence against women in African parliaments according to new IPU report' *Press Release*, 23 November 2023, www.ipu.org/news/press-releases/2021-11/widespread-sexism-and-violence-against-women-in-african-parliaments-according-new-ipu-report (accessed on 18 August 2023); T Sanusi '5 stunning facts about abuse of women in African parliaments' *Global Citizen*, 11 March 2022, www.globalcitizen.org/en/content/women-africa-parliaments-gender-based-violence/ (accessed on 18 August 2023).
4 *Ibid.*
5 S Tamale '"Point of order, Mr. Speaker": African women claiming their space in parliament' (2000) 8/3 *Gender and Development* 12–13.
6 *Ibid,* 13.

7 C Dranzoa 'Sexual harassment at African higher education institutions' (2018) 94 *International Higher Education* 4.
8 JA Menon et al 'Knowledge and perception of sexual harassment in an institution of higher education in Sub-Saharan Africa' (2014) 41/3 *Medical Journal of Zambia* 137–143.
9 L Wood 'Sexual harassment at institutions of higher learning: Prevalence, risk and extent' (2021) 36/9–10 *Journal of Interpersonal Violence* 4522.
10 A Gouws and A Kritzinger 'Dealing with sexual harassment at institutions of higher learning: Policy implementation at a South African university learning: Policy implementation at a South African university' (2007) 21/1 *South African Journal of Higher Education* 69.
11 Women in News 'Sexual harassment in the media: Africa Report' *World Association of News Publishers (WAN-IFRA)* (2021), https://cdn.womeninnews.org/wp-content/uploads/2021/07/20210712-Low-Res-Sexual-Harassment-Report.pdf (accessed on 20 August 2023) 5–6; World Association of Newspapers and News Publishers 'Shocking sexual harassment statistics in African media' *Ifex*, 21 July 2021, https://ifex.org/shocking-sexual-harassment-statistics-in-african-media/ (accessed on 20 August 2023).
12 A Soyinka 'Sexual harassment is rife in many African media workplaces' *The Conversation*, 19 July 2021, https://theconversation.com/sexual-harassment-is-rife-in-many-african-media-workplaces-163451 (accessed on 20 August 2023).
13 *Ibid.*
14 (HH 675 of 2021) [2021] ZWHHC 675 (01 December 2021).
15 International Labour Organisation 'Sexual harassment in the world of work' www.ilo.org/wcmsp5/groups/public/–dgreports/–gender/documents/briefingnote/wcms_738115.pdf (accessed on 20 August 2023).
16 *Ibid.*

References

C Dranzoa 'Sexual harassment at African higher education institutions' (2018) 94 *International Higher Education* 4–5.

E Durojaye, S Nabaneh and T Adebanjo *Sexual Harassment, Law and Human Rights in Africa* (Palgrave Macmillan, 2023).

L Fitzgerald, S Swan and V Magley 'But was it really sexual harassment? Legal, behavioral and psychological definitions of the workplace victimization of women' in W O'Donohue (ed) *Sexual Harassment: Theory, Research and Treatment* (Allyn & Bacon, 1997) 5–28.

A Gouws and A Kritzinger 'Dealing with sexual harassment at institutions of higher learning: Policy implementation at a South African university learning: Policy implementation at a South African university' (2007) 21/1 *South African Journal of Higher Education* 68–84.

Inter-Parliamentary Union 'Widespread sexism and violence against women in African parliaments according to new IPU report' *Press Release*, 23 November 2023, www.ipu.org/news/press-releases/2021-11/widespread-sexism-and-violence-against-women-in-african-parliaments-according-new-ipu-report (accessed on 18 August 2023).

International Labour Organisation 'Sexual harassment in the world of work' www.ilo.org/wcmsp5/groups/public/–dgreports/–gender/documents/briefingnote/wcms_738115.pdf (accessed on 20 August 2023).

A Menon et al 'Knowledge and perception of sexual harassment in an institution of higher education in sub-Saharan Africa' (2014) 41/3 *Medical Journal of Zambia* 137–143.

R M v Zizhou and Another (HH 675 of 2021) [2021] ZWHHC 675 (01 December 2021).

T Sanusi '5 Stunning facts about abuse of women in African parliaments' *Global Citizen*, 11 March 2022, www.globalcitizen.org/en/content/women-africa-parliaments-gender-based-violence/ (accessed on 18 August 2023).

A Soyinka 'Sexual harassment is rife in many African media workplaces' *The Conversation*, 19 July 2021, https://theconversation.com/sexual-harassment-is-rife-in-many-african-media-workplaces-163451 (accessed on 20 August 2023).

S Tamale ' "Point of order, Mr. Speaker": African women claiming their space in parliament' (2000) 8/3 *Gender and Development* 12–13.

Women in News 'Sexual harassment in the media: Africa Report' *World Association of News Publishers (WAN-IFRA)*, 2021, https://cdn.womeninnews.org/wp-content/uploads/2021/07/20210712-Low-Res-Sexual-Harassment-Report.pdf (accessed on 20 August 2023).

L Wood 'Sexual harassment at institutions of higher learning: Prevalence, risk and extent' (2021) 36/9–10 *Journal of Interpersonal Violence* 4520–4544.

World Association of Newspapers and News Publishers 'Shocking sexual harassment statistics in African media' *Ifex*, 21 July 2021, https://ifex.org/shocking-sexual-harassment-statistics-in-african-media/ (accessed on 20 August 2023).

2 Critical Reflections on Equality, Sexual Harassment, and the Right to Sustainable Development for Women in Africa

Carol Chi Ngang

Introduction

In this chapter, I critically analyse the interwoven principles of equality in law, the right to a workplace free of sexual harassment, and the right to sustainable development for women in Africa.[1] This analysis illustrates that genuine equality is not attainable under conventional legal frameworks. Providing protection and entitlement to women in Africa instead requires a model law that prioritises the quest for justice and equity above seeking to achieve equality under pre-existing instruments of law, many of which are overtly biased. The concepts of equality and equity have been distinguished as follows: 'Equality means each individual or group of people is given the same resources or opportunities. Equity recognizes that each person has different circumstances and allocates the exact resources and opportunities needed to reach an equal outcome'.[2]

Abstract guarantees of equality in law largely only contain vestiges of hope and, at times, endless unmet expectations. This amounts to justice delayed, and thus, justice denied, for women in their aspirations to live free from all forms of discriminatory practices that impact their right to sustainable development as guaranteed in the Protocol on the Rights of Women in Africa.[3] If Africa is to attain balanced, sustainable development with living standards equalised for all, much thought needs to be given to the opportunities accessible to women and how they are perceived and treated in society, particularly with respect to gender discrimination and sexual harassment.

The 2030 global framework for development, in highlighting the resolve to eradicate inequalities and to create conditions for sustainable development and shared prosperity for all, guarantees that 'no one will be left behind'.[4] Integral to the Sustainable Development Goals (SDGs) is the commitment to '[a]chieve gender equality and empower all women and girls'.[5] Ensuring that women in Africa are not left behind in the global campaign for sustainable development necessitates making conditions favourable for equitable access to the opportunities that increase their prospects for advancement and eradicating existing impediments, such as gender discrimination and sexual harassment. It is worth highlighting that equality of opportunity fundamentally

DOI: 10.4324/9781003373308-2

differs from the principle of equality.[6] Equality of opportunity states that based on the characteristic differences among peoples, they are entitled to equitable enjoyment of the benefits of development[7] and the liberty to choose between alternatives, which, in effect, embody the freedom to define development in terms of actual livelihood priorities and situational exigencies.[8]

In reality, sexual harassment creates barriers for access to opportunities for women in Africa. This social injustice adversely affects women's capability to contribute to and actively participate in the processes for sustainable development. The chapter highlights sexual harassment at the workplace principally because the workplace provides a context for bettering standards of living and promotes sustainable development, which is supposed to be satisfactorily enabling for all. In the first part of the chapter, I argue that the orthodox abstract guarantees of equality in law cannot provide women in Africa with satisfactory entitlement and protection. The second part delves into the discussion on the right to sustainable development and freedom from sexual harassment in the workplace. In conclusion, I posit that as part of the right to sustainable development, African state governments are enjoined to take adequate legislative and other measures to create favourable conditions for women; anticipating new measures to reform the distinct attributes and situational realities that render women particularly vulnerable.

Equality in Law

The universal construct of the law operates on the ideals of equality and posits that everyone deserves equal rights, freedoms and opportunities, and the same dignity and respect. The principle of equality forms the foundation on which law is built. As Diminitrina Petrova affirms, 'the right to equality applies "in all areas of activity regulated by law" across all jurisdictions'.[9] Yet, despite the formal guarantees of equality in law, sexual harassment against women persists – an indication that substantive equality remains elusive, utopian, and largely unattainable owing to reticence in genuinely committing to exploring alternative approaches in redressing the issues that affect women.

Sexual Harassment

Despite equality guarantees, women experience various forms of harassment, including sexual harassment, daily. Whilst there is no universal definition of sexual harassment, the term fundamentally describes unacceptable conduct of a sexual dimension, which Louise Fitzgerald *et al* define as 'unwanted sex-related behaviour at work that is appraised by the recipient as offensive, exceeding her resources, or threatening her well-being'.[10] Sexual harassment is conceptually not gender-specific; it describes any form of unwelcome sexual behaviour by a man or woman that robs the target of honour and dignity and subjugates that person to the self-seeking wishes and desires of the other person who often exercises a degree of dominance.[11] That said, overwhelmingly, women are more likely to be the victim-survivors of sexual violence.

Paula McDonald defines sexual harassment as 'one of a range of abusive or counterproductive workplace behaviors which have hierarchical power relations at their core . . . [with] an explicitly sexual dimension'.[12] The definition alludes to the question of hierarchy and dominance (manifestations of inequality) that occur, as previously indicated, more frequently by the man over the woman. Stephanie Coontz and Peta Henderson point out sexual harassment as one of the earliest known and most widespread forms of inequality in human history with concrete repercussions for women all over the world; the material fact of male dominance, which is tested and explained by a combination of different theories.[13] Heather McLaughlin *et al* allude to feminist scholarship, which 'situates sexual harassment within broader patterns of discrimination, power, and privilege, linking harassment to sex-based inequality'.[14] Feminism movements seek the attainment of 'full gender equality in law', which would 'put an end to sexism, sexist exploitation, and oppression'.[15]

It is common knowledge that human societies all over the world have, from time immemorial, perpetuated inequalities. Consequently, the law as a body of rules, norms, and standards becomes relevant as an instrument for recourse in regulating societal functions and operations. Given existing inequalities that shape society, the law seeks, as much as is reasonably possible, to balance the asymmetries. Yet, although sexual harassment has been rightly criminalised and codified as a legal offence in many jurisdictions around the world, with an increasing number of related punitive workplace policies being put in place, the practice persists and is, more often than not, perpetrated with impunity.[16] Sound reasoning demands a critical reflection on equality to determine whether, how, and to what extent it provides real redress against sexual harassment.

Abstractions of Equality

The Equal Rights Trust's Declaration of Principles on Equality noted that while the entitlement to equality before the law and the protection of all persons against discrimination are fundamental norms of international human rights law, equality remains an illusion to many several decades after the adoption of the Universal Declaration of Human Rights.[17] According to Susan Sturm, it is uncontroversial that inequalities persist but that the 'explanations and solutions for this continuing inequality have become more complex and elusive'.[18]

Various international, regional, and domestic law instruments seek to achieve equality in terms of protection, access to opportunities, and guarantees of fairness and justice to all peoples without distinction or discrimination of any form. In its abstract generic nature, the principle of equality in law is broadly constructed on the theoretical understanding that no human person is superior to others in terms of innate worth, dignity, and entitlement to respect. The human rights framework commonly enshrines the *erga omnes* principle (applicable to everyone) that all men and women are born free and endowed with inalienable rights. The Universal Declaration of Human Rights provides that: 'All are equal before the law and are entitled without any discrimination to equal protection of the law'.[19] Article 3 of the International Covenant on Civil and Political Rights assures that: 'The States Parties to the present Covenant undertake to ensure the equal right of men and women to the enjoyment of all civil and political rights set forth in the present Covenant'. The International Covenant on Economic, Social and Cultural Rights equally guarantees in article 3 that: 'The States Parties to the present Covenant undertake to ensure the equal right of men and women to the enjoyment of all economic, social and cultural rights set forth in the present Covenant'.

Despite these formal equality guarantees, the gendered wording in the same instruments tends to favour men over women. For example, article 10 of the Universal Declaration stipulates that '[e]veryone is entitled in full equality to a fair and public hearing by an independent and impartial tribunal, in the determination of *his* rights and obligations and of any criminal charge against *him*' (emphasis added). Subsequent provisions of the covenants cited here also repeatedly use 'he' and 'his' and at no instance 'she' or 'her', reflecting the foundational bias embedded in the law. The same is true of the African Charter on Human and Peoples' Rights, which despite guaranteeing that '[e]very individual shall be entitled to equal protection of the law', proceeds in the remaining provisions to use 'he', 'his', and 'him' to represent every individual, which is literally understood to mean virtually everyone without any form of distinction as stated in article 2.[20] By way of rhetorical questions we may ask, does the law actually guarantee equality by such overtly gender-biased formulations? Can gender equality be achieved under these prevailing concepts of the law? These are critical questions that should preoccupy discourses on equality and advocacy for women's rights.

Prescriptions on equality conceptually set men and women at parity in the exercise and enjoyment of the full range of human rights, which, as previously indicated, are framed on the assumption of fairness in the way humanity should be perceived and treated in every society. Accordingly, legal processes and procedures should produce normatively just and equitable outcomes.[21] By implication, the law ought to show evidence of fairness and be succinctly explicit and unambiguous in its ordinary meaning. Unfortunately, this appears to be different with the equality provisions in legal instruments, which irrationally lean in favour of men much more than they assure that equality for women is attainable. Ronald Dworkin says: 'People who praise it or disparage it disagree about what they are praising or disparaging.'[22] By this, Dworkin means that the concept of equality does not provide any unit of universal acceptance of what it represents or aims to achieve.

The law makes provision for, but in practice does not guarantee, equality and has been seen in this regard as an instrument that rather breeds confrontation and antagonism and perpetuates violence among adversaries.[23] The prescriptive conception of equality and the presumption of it[24] convey optimism that its application would eventually remedy prejudices and deprivations. As a foundational principle of law, equality shapes the expectation, albeit controversially, that justice can be obtained where inequity and inordinate biases prevail. In reality, normative promises and the legitimate expectations they create often do not practically deal with the obvious power differentials to which most women are subjected and exposed to in various forms of sexual harassment. Arnold Rose says that applying the law to redress one set of societal problems often creates another set of societal problems.[25] It is the case, for instance, regarding land ownership, a crucial aspect of development. While the law guarantees equal access, the legal processes for obtaining land entitlement basically excludes most women from effective ownership.

Karen Celis *et al* argue that all over the world, in spite of the guarantees of equality in law, gender predominantly determines who gets what and how, who controls and governs and by what means, as well as who influences ways of knowing, thinking, and organising.[26] Women are 'particularly hard hit and affected in different ways' more than men who virtually dominate in actual spaces and positions of authority.[27] Various theories, ethical standards, and approaches postulating how the abstractions of equality could be made concrete and translated into reality[28] reveal deeper shortcomings. In Nwabufo Uzodike and Hakeem Onapajo's assessment of gender equality and female empowerment, the findings reveal that not much has been accomplished in practical terms in addressing the plight of African women.[29] While some progress has been made, it is uncertain if the gains in gender equality could ultimately add up to absolute parity. I contend that such parity remains elusive and illusionary. Whereas, if advocacy for gender equality were directed more towards achieving substantive equality, it is envisaged that the outcomes would be more beneficial to women.

As defined by the Supreme Court of Canada in the *Andrews v Law Society of British Columbia* case, substantive equality is based on the idea that 'the promotion of equality entails the promotion of a society in which all are secure in the knowledge that they are recognised at law as human beings equally deserving of concern, respect and consideration'.[30] Substantive equality, as Anne Smith also explains, is concerned with ensuring that laws and policies do not impose subordinating treatment on persons that are already socially, politically, or economically disadvantaged.[31] It requires that laws are applied to treat individuals as substantive equals, recognising and accommodating differences among people rather than emphasising sameness. For Morsen Mosses, the 'conception of substantive equality favours a treatment that goes beyond "being treated equally" and aims to correct all kinds of discrimination'.[32] It is concerned with eliminating the barriers that exclude women from freely participating in the workplace and society as a whole.[33] The substantive equality approach envisages positive discrimination (affirmative action and preferential treatment) based on the recognition that all persons are not on the same playing field.[34]

Permissible Differentiation

While the promise of equality in law creates legitimate expectations which women have leaned on in emphasising gender mainstreaming in development programming,[35] it is, however, only built on anticipation while its definitive manifestation remains uncertain. A fundamental attribute of human rights law is that 'equality is an entitlement and not a benefit, and must be legally enforceable, like every other human right'.[36] However, the equality provisions discussed here do not guarantee substantive outcomes in any human relationship. On the contrary, those provisions not only legitimise inequalities but provide justification to look beyond the equality principle with the acknowledgement that society is patterned along identity attributes and situational differences. One reason is that the law allows for 'permissible differentiation' – the 'recognition that different rules have priority over the principle of equality and justify the unequal distribution of duties or rights'.[37] Daniel Lach outlines the following criteria in conceptualising differentiation:

(i) the criterion for the classification of subjects leading to the differentiation of their legal situation should be objective, real, and noticeable;
(ii) the objectively existing differences between the parties should be legally relevant, have a direct, rational relation to the aim and the main content of the norms in which the controlled standard is contained, and achieving that aim;
(iii) the adopted criterion must be proportionate, which means that the weight of interest, which is designed to differentiate the situation of the addressees of the norm, must be in proportion to the seriousness of the interests that will be affected as a result of the unequal treatment of similar subjects;
(iv) the statutory classification of subjects resulting in the differentiation of their legal status must be fair, which means that the choice of a specific criterion of differentiation should result from the adopted system of values, principles or constitutional norms justifying different treatment of similar subjects.[38]

Peter Westen asserts that equality needs to be distinguished from 'identity', understood to imply sameness and distinguished from 'similarity', which barely describes proximity in features.[39] A comprehensive reading of equality presupposes a fundamental recognition of the difference between what is being considered based on equality with another. Equality need not mean that there can scarcely be any absolute sameness between variables, but only similarities in comparable value traits.[40] Human relations are naturally delineated by dissimilarities which need to be recognised and reflected in the law rather than overlooking such dissimilarities in favour of promoting gender equality, which, some have argued, is largely unattainable. Gender equality, as it would apply under positive law, would entail men and women competing for equal opportunities. However, they both manifest indisputably different traits, necessitating that they should, indeed, be treated differently. This is sometimes referred to as equity.[41]

The Declaration of Principles on Equality recognised that '[t]o realise full and effective equality it is necessary to treat people differently according to their different circumstances, to assert their equal worth and to enhance their capabilities to participate in society as equals'.[42] And this is how equality may be distinguished from equity. Paula Dressel notes that 'The route to achieving equity will not be accomplished through treating everyone equally. It will be achieved by treating everyone justly according to their circumstances'.[43] The Declaration of Principles on Equality is, however, not legally binding, but it provides a framework of reasoning in conceptualising differentiation in law and practice. Recognition of difference allows distinct categories of people to be perceived as deserving of preferential treatment. For example, women-specific instruments include the 1979 Convention on the Elimination of All Forms of Discrimination against Women and the 2003 Protocol to the African Charter on the Rights of Women (Maputo Protocol) at the global and African continental levels, respectively.[44] Instead of highlighting the issues necessitating preferential treatment for women, these instruments repeatedly emphasise gender equality as a means of combating discrimination against women.[45]

Thinking of protection and entitlement for women in terms of abstract gender equality provisions is not, by any means, unreasonable. The question is whether such emphasis in an all-exclusive, women-specific instrument of law adds any much value. Shifting the focus to the distinctive attributes regarding gender roles that qualify women for special protection could be more helpful. Differentiation allows the law to be applied differently in favour of vulnerable groups that otherwise may remain susceptible to further disadvantage owing to the deficits in generic law or societal realities. For instance, compared to the Maputo Protocol which alludes to gender equality, the United Nation's Declaration on the Rights of Indigenous Peoples highlights the affirmation that although equal to all other peoples, indigenous peoples consider themselves different and desire to be respected as such while equally recognising the right of other peoples to be different.[46]

Indigenous peoples have, in asserting such distinctiveness, achieved major substantive gains in claiming entitlement to ancestral lands and natural resources, among other benefits.[47] However, indigenous women continue to face disproportionate levels of discrimination and violence despite the positive gains for indigenous peoples as a whole and despite the Declaration, which draws special attention to the needs and rights of indigenous women.

Indigenous women have, in this regard, called on the Committee on the Elimination of Discrimination against Women to adopt a general recommendation on indigenous women, taking into consideration

> issues related to the[ir] individual and collective rights to equality, non-discrimination and self-determination; social and economic rights, including the rights to decent work and to land, territory and resources; the right to water and food; cultural rights; civil and political rights; and the right to live free of any form of violence.[48]

The issues that generally affect women in Africa are complex and multidimensional. One focus of basic statements on gender equality is political representation.[49] Yet, the challenges confronting most women across the continent are about more than just the lack of power but about day-to-day livelihood realities. Poverty and underdevelopment have commonly been recognised as having a feminine face globally and more particularly in Africa where women experience some of the worst living conditions.[50] The principle of differentiation provides a framework for redressing a broad range of concerns for women, achievable through asserting the composite right to sustainable development, which emphasises the eradication of poverty wherein gender inequalities have been more pronounced.

Right to Sustainable Development for Women in Africa

The Maputo Protocol enshrines the guarantee that the women of Africa are entitled to assert and fully enjoy the right to sustainable development.[51] This is supported by the African Charter, which provides the umbrella guarantee that all peoples have a right to economic, social, and cultural development.[52] Sustainable development within the context of the Maputo Protocol is a process that should culminate in 'a higher quality of life' free from poverty for the women of Africa.[53]

Equality of Opportunity for Development

The right to development imposes an obligation for immediate realisation requiring states, as stipulated in the Declaration on the Right to Development, to adopt appropriate national development policies to ensure constant improvement in living standards.[54] The African Charter and the Maputo Protocol enjoin state governments to take necessary measures and create an enabling environment for achieving the right to sustainable development.[55] States are enjoined to ensure, *inter alia*, equality of access to basic entitlements to livelihood sustainability, requiring effective measures in activating women's participation in the development process.[56] To guarantee equality of opportunity for development, the state must take requisite measures that equalise options for attaining a higher quality of life, free from the burdens of poverty and other constraints for all women on the continent.[57] This can most comprehensibly be understood within the context of redistributive justice,[58] requiring equitable (re)distribution of the resources for development. The African Charter states that the right to development is to be achieved with due regard to 'the equal enjoyment of the common heritage'.[59] It implies that Africa's wealth of natural resources ought to be explored in a manner that affords broad-based equitable benefits.

In the context of the right to sustainable development, equality of opportunity entitles present generations of African women to enjoy a higher quality of life without jeopardising prospects for successive generations to the same high standards of life.[60] This is an absolute entitlement that the women of Africa have; that is, they are entitled to assert a claim not necessarily on the basis of gender equality, but simply because they are women. This is justified by real-life circumstances where natural personality traits are defined by incontrovertible differences in terms of unique attributes; where, for example, it is explained that men tend to be more bossy, domineering, and assertive and exhibit higher levels of these traits than women, while, on average, women are to a greater extent found to be more nurturing, tender-minded, and altruistic than men,[61] and also by the fact that priorities are not always the same for all peoples. Equality of opportunity for indigenous peoples, for example, might entail restitution of entitlement to natural resources from which they were dispossessed. For women, equality of opportunities might entail eliminating existing obstacles to the realisation of the right to development, including those identified in the Declaration of the Right to Development,[62] as well as other 'informal barriers and overlapping disadvantages' to development, such as those encountered at the workplace.[63]

Right to a Conducive Work Environment

The value of a human right is best appreciated when it is threatened or violated. To appreciate the right to a conducive work environment, defined as a workplace that promotes employee safety, performance, productivity, and the attainment of set goals,[64] it is essential to look at the impediment of sexual harassment to the enjoyment of that right.

The Impediment of Workplace Sexual Harassment

For decades, sexual harassment has limited women's prospects for advancement and has left them prone to underdevelopment and impoverishment.[65] The focus on women in this analysis does not overlook that men are also sometimes victims of sexual harassment. The purpose here is to reiterate that over one-half of working women have been subjected to sexual harassment[66] compared to a much lower proportion of men who have been subjected to workplace sexual harassment.[67] Thus, sexual harassment, specifically against women, deserves closer attention, particularly because '[d]espite being illegal, costly, and an affront to dignity, sexual harassment is pervasive and challenging to eliminate'.[68] Sexual harassment includes a wide range of unacceptable conduct of a sexual nature that infringes on the rights of another. It thus makes the workplace hostile or offensive and a barrier to fair work practices.[69]

The International Labour Organisation defines 'sexual harassment as a sex-based behaviour that is unwelcome and offensive to its recipient' and a major pervasive concern at both domestic and international levels.[70] The primary challenge to eliminating the behaviour seems to be the failure to concretely situate the problem within the parameters of the inherent inequalities characterised by power asymmetries between men and women that persist in the workplace. Even though states are enjoined to take effective measures to ensure that women have an active role in the development process,[71] the gap between the law and actual experience of sustainable development for the women of Africa is still quite disproportionately broad.

The right to sustainable development is conceived within the framing of the capabilities theory, which supports the need for expanded opportunities and choices and the capacity to set development priorities freely.[72] It entails, as stated in both the African Charter and the Maputo Protocol, sufficient legislative and other policy measures to ensure that claimants can effectively exercise and enjoy the right by productively participating in and contributing meaningfully to the processes for socio-economic and cultural development.[73] The Declaration on the Right to Development enjoins states to 'take steps to eliminate obstacles to development' resulting from failure to observe guaranteed rights.[74] Sexual harassment violates the right to a conducive work environment and, thus, an obstacle to development that must be eliminated.

Normative Framework to Secure an Enabling Work Environment

Equality of opportunities for development entails exploring options and possibilities, including the right to work and a conducive workplace. Because sexual harassment hinders women's productivity at the workplace, the question is how we can eliminate such practices so that the women of Africa can productively explore work as a means to achieve sustainable development as promised to them in the Maputo Protocol.[75] Recourse to the law, albeit an appropriate remedy, is problematic as the existing frameworks of law, including those that provide the right to an enabling work environment, do not provide women sufficient protection and entitlement.

The Convention on the Elimination of All Forms of Discrimination against Women provides that 'States Parties shall take all appropriate measures to eliminate discrimination against women in the field of employment in order to ensure, on a basis of equality of men and women, the same rights'.[76] The presumption of equality and of equal rights, even though persuasive, is basically *lex ferenda* (what the law is envisaged to be), which pulls women from a position of disadvantage into a disproportionate competition that renders them susceptible to be preyed upon by men. Disproportionate competition means the situation where opportunities for women are compounded by high rates of unemployment which practically limit their prospects for advancement; the ability to compete based on equality with men rather exposes them to rivalries for ascendancy than the protection of their substantive rights and freedoms. Unlike other instruments, the Maputo Protocol provides that:

> States parties shall adopt and enforce legislative and other measures to guarantee women equal opportunities in work career advancement and other economic opportunities. In this respect, they shall:
>
> a) promote equality of access to employment; . . .
> c) ensure transparency in recruitment, promotion and dismissal of women and combat and punish sexual harassment in the workplace;
> d) guarantee women the freedom to choose their occupation, and protect them from exploitation by their employers violating and exploiting their fundamental rights as recognised and guaranteed by conventions, laws and regulations in force.[77]

Regarding domestic law, most countries in Africa have domesticated legislation against sexual harassment in the workplace.[78]

Justice and Equity Considerations

The recognition of difference is based on the doctrine of equity, which Camelia Ignătescu says, 'represents the field, from which the relationships between people start to be interpreted from the prospect of what is just, fair or good'.[79] According to Margaret White, equity embodies justice attainable through fairness and not necessarily through the stringent application of the law.[80] Differentiation on its part is defined by considerations of equity.[81] Even though equity is portrayed as seemingly contrasting to the rigid rules of positive law,[82] it is a set of rules that are more inclined to natural law and fairness and affirmed as a general principle, which in itself is directly applicable as law[83] with the corrective capacity to moderate the general law.[84] To say that considerations of equity define differentiation means that it forms an integral part of the law of equity.

Equity as law that embodies the principle of differentiation then becomes applicable law relevant for regulating conflicts of interest, imbalances in power relations, and the inequalities that disfavour women. In essence, considerations for a model law for women in Africa should emphasise differentiation (rather than equality) as the foundational principle of the law of equity applicable to women. The idea of applicable law becomes central to litigation in the sense that 'a judge's job is to adjudicate fairly so that justice is done', which puts the judge in the position of having to choose between 'which law to apply and what facts to apply it to'.[85]

Agreeing with Anthony D'Amato that justice cannot replace law because the law is a fact,[86] the important consideration, therefore, becomes how to infuse facts into principles of law so that applicable law can produce justice. If the applicable law emphasises equality as a fact, the law will have to apply to that fact. Likewise, if the applicable law accentuates differentiation as a fact, the law will equally have to apply to that fact. Following the maxim that 'equity will not suffer a wrong to be without a remedy', to create sustainable development justice for the women of Africa, exception can and indeed should be taken to the general rule of law because the facts of the law should only be used as a tool to render justice[87] (remedy) where there is a right (*ubi jus, ibi remedium*). This would constitute the framework of normativity to which the women of Africa could have recourse with the conviction that appropriate corrective and redistributive remedies in terms of revised laws and allocated job opportunity quotas could be obtained.

In applying the provisions of existing instruments of law, justice may only occasionally be achieved, but not at all times, essentially because the law 'in itself cannot solve human problems'.[88] Hans Kelsen sees justice, on the one hand, as a possible but not necessarily absolute quality of a social order that regulates mutual human relations and, on the other hand, as a virtue of just conduct that conforms to the norms of a social order that is acceptable and satisfactory for the common good.[89] Acknowledging that what may be considered acceptable and satisfactory for the common good is controversial, it is not complicated to understand that a norm (virtue of just conduct) that guarantees protection against injustices, such as those perpetrated on women, safeguards their legitimate entitlements to life with dignity and, therefore, can be construed to form the basis of justice. Justice is portrayed in these terms as a 'correction of the principle of equality in favour of the citizens [like women] who are in the most difficult economic situation'.[90]

In contrast to the common perception about the law being a guarantor of equity and justice, it generally does not automatically guarantee that equity and justice would be achieved in its application. Equity and justice are usually only attainable to the extent that relevant enforcement mechanisms uphold those values with impartiality and neutrality.[91] In the absence of a defined framework on differentiation based on which deviation from the general rule of law is directly permissible, I concur with d'Amato on having to infuse justice into a reading of the law. It entails, as Camelia Ignătescu reasons, that in the 'process of the creative application of the positive law . . . 'the judge must be equitable'.[92]

> For promoting the principles of equity, the diversity and the multiple problems which exist in different environments and spheres of life must be taken into consideration [citation omitted]. Those convoked to make and carry out the law, must know and take into account the needs and expectations of the people. Some have special needs, . . . others have a very difficult financial situation, or they such do not have means of

subsistence, or the mechanical application of the dispositions of some norms to all the categories of the society can generate severe illegal inequities in a rule of law.[93]

The right to development requires that development be determined by considerations of equity and justice,[94] necessitating, according to Katrina Tomasevski, redress of some sort in terms of restorative or redistributive justice.[95] For White, equity embodies justice attainable through fairness and not necessarily through the stringent application of the law.[96] In thinking about redistributive or restorative justice, Lach says that 'fair distribution can be either equal . . . or unequal – differentiated'.[97] For example, because women have largely been deprived of entitlement to land, which is a crucial factor for development, the right to development, which is guaranteed to all the peoples of Africa, necessitates the affirmative application of restorative and redistributive justice in allocating land to women in a positively discriminatory manner. In the *Ogiek Community* case, the African Court on Human and Peoples' Rights used applicable laws in determining the special differentiated status that indigenous peoples enjoy under international law.[98] The law is, however, yet to be read in like manner in recognising the differentiated status of indigenous women in Africa who, as noted earlier, are still subjected to disproportionate levels of discrimination and violence.

As is the case with indigenous peoples, recognition of the distinctiveness of the sort would provide avenues for redress to women who assert the right to sustainable development and seek workplaces free from sexual harassment, much more than can be envisaged under the principle of equality. The African Commission noted in the *Endorois* case that even as it arouses debates in recognising 'peoples' and 'indigenous communities' as essentially different, it is inevitable to do so because 'some marginalised and vulnerable groups in Africa are suffering from particular problems' and, therefore, cognisance needs to be taken that 'many of these groups have not been accommodated by dominating development paradigms and in many cases, they are being victimised by mainstream development policies and thinking' that infringe on their human rights.[99] The marginalised and vulnerable groups that the Commission refers to do not exclude women who bear the brunt of development challenges despite being more than half of Africa's population.[100]

Conclusion

As part of the obligation imposed by the right to sustainable development to which the women of Africa are entitled, state governments are enjoined to take adequate legislative and other measures intended to create favourable conditions and an enabling environment for asserting that right, including workplaces free from sexual harassment. The obligation to take adequate measures entails admitting that existing frameworks of law, including the Maputo Protocol, which are constructed on the foundation of formal equality, do not sufficiently guarantee protection. I have advanced the argument that generic law, in its orthodox formulation, makes generous offerings of equality, which largely only convey hope and sometimes endless unmet expectations.

Equality is not likely to become a reality until gender dynamics have effectively changed. Overlooking the promises of formal equality and exploring instead, practical ways based on substantive equality in dealing with the gender prejudices that affect women is not only rational, but, arguably, also crucial. Doing so might provide the starting point for altering the meta-narrative on equality, which seems to omit seeing the innate attributes, including the gender roles that distinguish women from men, as defining parameters for crafting genuine protection and effective guarantees of substantive rights and freedoms.

Notes

1 Protocol to the African Charter on Human and Peoples' Rights on the Rights of Women in Africa adopted in Maputo, Mozambique on 11 July 2003 (Maputo Protocol).
2 Milken Institute School of Public Health *Equity vs Equality: What's the Difference* (The George Washington University 2020), https://onlinepublichealth.gwu.edu/resources/equity-vs-equality/ (accessed on 1 February 2023).
3 Maputo Protocol (n 1) art 19.
4 Transforming Our World: The 2030 Agenda for Sustainable Development UN General Assembly Resolution A/RES/70/1 adopted on 25 September 2015 paras 3–4.
5 *Ibid* goal 5.
6 P Westen *Speaking of Equality: An Analysis of the Rhetorical Force of 'Equality' in Moral and Legal Discourse* (Princeton University Press, 1990) 171–172.
7 A Sengupta 'Realising the right to development' (2000) 31/2 *Development and Change* 575; Declaration on the Right to Development Resolution A/RES/41/128 adopted by the UN Gen Ass on 4 December 1986 arts 1(1) and 6(2) (DRTD); Vienna Declaration and Programme of Action adopted at the UN World Conference on Human Rights UN Doc.A/CONF.157/24, 25 June 1993 para I(10).
8 Sengupta (n 7) 578.
9 D Petrova 'The declaration of principles on equality: A contribution to international human rights' (2008) *The Equal Rights Review* 64.
10 L Fitzgerald, S Swan and V Magley 'But was it really sexual harassment? Legal, behavioral and psychological definitions of the workplace victimization of women' in W O'Donohue (ed) *Sexual Harassment: Theory, Research and Treatment* (Allyn & Bacon, 1997) 15.
11 *Ibid.*
12 P McDonald 'Workplace sexual harassment 30 years on: A review of the literature' (2012) 14/1 *International Journal of Management Reviews* 2.
13 S Coontz and P Henderson 'Explanations of male dominance' in S Coontz and P Henderson (eds) *Women's Work, Men's Property: The Origins of Gender and Class* (Verso Books, 1986).
14 H McLaughlin et al 'Sexual harassment, workplace authority, and the paradox of power' (2012) 77/4 *American Sociological Review* 626.
15 Council of Europe 'Feminism and women's rights movements' www.coe.int/en/web/gender-matters/feminism-and-women-s-rights-movements (accessed on 17 September 2021).

16 J Hersch 'Sexual harassment in the workplace' (2015) *IZA World of Labour 188* 1–4.
17 Declaration of Principles on Equality adopted in 2008 under the auspices of Equal Rights Trust, London 1.
18 S Sturm 'Equality and inequality: Legal aspects' (2001) *International Encyclopaedia of the Social and Behavioural Sciences* 4717; see also MA Kilgour et al 'The UN global compact and substantive equality for women: Revealing a "well hidden" mandate' (2007) 28/4 *Third World Quarterly* 751–773; M Rosenfeld 'Substantive equality and equal opportunity: A jurisprudential appraisal' (1986) 75/5 *California Law Review* 1687.
19 Universal Declaration of Human Rights adopted by the UN General Assembly, Resolution 217 A(III) of 10 December 1948, art 7.
20 African Charter on Human and Peoples' Rights, adopted in Nairobi, Kenya on 27 June 1981.OAU Doc CAB/LEG/67/3 Rev.5 (1981), art 3.
21 AM Hernandez 'A principle of equitable access to sustainable development: Internalizing externalities in the global climate talks' (2014) 2/1 *Review of Business and Economics Studies* 76.
22 R Dworkin *Sovereign Virtue: The Theory and Practice of Equality* (Harvard University Press, 2000).
23 C Menke 'Law and violence' (2010) 22/1 *Law and Literature* 1–17; DC Hay 'Time, inequality, and law's violence' in A Sarat and TR Kearns (eds) *Laws Violence* (The University of Michigan's Press, 1993) 1646.
24 Westen (n 6) 230–236.
25 AM Rose 'Law and the causation of social problems' (1968) 6/1 *Social Problems* 33.
26 K Celis et al 'Introduction: Gender and politics – A gendered world, a gendered discipline' in G Waylen et al (eds) *The Oxford Handbook of Gender and Politics* (Oxford University Press, 2013) 1–2.
27 Celis et al (n 26) 2–4.
28 Sturm (n 18) 4717–4722; S Gosepath 'Equality' *Stanford Encyclopedia of Philosophy*, https://plato.stanford.edu/entries/equality/ (accessed on 31 August 2020).
29 UO Uzodike and H Onapajo 'Women and development in Africa: Competing approaches and contested achievements' (2013) 20/2 *Alternations* 27.
30 [1989] 1 SCR 143.
31 A Smith 'Equality constitutional adjudication in South Africa' (2014) 14/2 *African Human Rights Law Journal* 613.
32 M Morsen 'A note on Vanuatu's cases on the right to equality' (2017) 23 *Comparative Law Journal of the Pacific* 84.
33 Smith (n 31) 613.
34 *ibid.*
35 UN Women 'Gender mainstreaming in development programming: Guidance note' (2014) *UN Women* 7.
36 Declaration of Principles on Equality (n 17) 59.
37 DE Lach 'Equality vs differentiation: On solidarity and justice in social law' (2016) 20/205 *Adam Mickiewicz University Law Review* 118.
38 *ibid* 117–118.
39 Westen (n 6) 39 & 120; Gosepath (n 28).
40 Gosepath (n 28).
41 Westen (n 6) 204.
42 Petrova (n 9) principle 2.
43 P Dressel 'Racial equality or racial equity? The difference it makes' *Race Matters Institute*, 2014, http://viablefuturescenter.org/racemattersinstitute/2014/04/02/racial-equality-or-racial-equity-the-difference-it-makes/ (accessed on 1 February 2023).

44 Apart from these instruments that protect the rights of women, there are other specific treaty instruments that provide protection for children's rights, indigenous peoples' rights, sexual minority rights and the rights of persons with disabilities among others.

45 See the provisions of the Maputo Protocol and of the Convention on the Elimination of All Forms of Discrimination against Women, adopted and by General Assembly Resolution 34/180 of 18 December 1979.

46 Maputo Protocol (n 1) preamble paras 7, 9 and 10; Declaration on the Rights of Indigenous Peoples Resolution 61/295 adopted by the UN General Assembly on 13 September 2007, preamble para 2.

47 *Centre for Minority Rights Development (Kenya) and Minority Rights Group International on behalf of Endorois Welfare Council v Kenya* Comm 276/2003 (2009) AHRLR 75 (ACHPR 2009) para 227; *African Commission on Human and Peoples' Rights (Ogiek Community) v Republic of Kenya* (2017) Appl No 006/2017 (*Ogiek* case) paras 105–112; L Claridge 'Litigation as a tool for community empowerment: The case of Kenya's Ogiek' (2018) 11/1 *Erasmus Law Review* 57–58.

48 UN Permanent Forum on Indigenous Issues Report on the eighteenth session (22 April–3 May 2019) to the Economic and Social Council, E/2019/43-E/C.19/2019/10 para 53.

49 TB Kellow 'Women, elections and violence in West Africa: Assessing women's political participation in Liberia and Sierra Leone' (2010) International Alert 10; Inter-Parliamentary Union (IPU) 'Women in politics' January 2012, www.ipu.org/pdf/publications/wmnmap12_en.pdf (accessed on 24 September 2020); UN Department of Economic and Social Affairs *The World's Women 2010: Trends and Statistics* (New York: United Nations, 2010) 116; Uzodike and Onapajo (n 29) 44–45.

50 HM McFerson 'Poverty among women in sub-Saharan Africa: A review of selected issues' (2010) 11/4 *Journal of International Women's Studies* 50–52; Uzodike and Onapajo (n 29) 27.

51 Maputo Protocol (n 1) art 19.

52 African Charter (n 20) art 22.

53 Maputo Protocol (n 1) art 19(d).

54 DRTD (note 7) art 2(3).

55 African Charter (n 20) art 22(2); Maputo Protocol (n 1) art 19.

56 DRTD (n 7) art 8(1).

57 Maputo Protocol (n 1) art 19(d).

58 LB Joseph 'Some ways of thinking about equality of opportunity' (1980) 33/3 *The Western Political Quarterly* 393–400.

59 African Charter (n 20) art 22(1).

60 Maputo Protocol (n 1) art 19.

61 YJ Weisberg et al 'Gender differences in personality across the ten aspects of the big five' (2011) 2/178 *Frontiers in Psychology* 1–3.

62 DRTD (n 7) art 5.

63 J Klugman and M Morton 'Enabling equal opportunities for women in the world of work: The intersections of formal and informal constraints' in H Cissé et al (eds) *The World Bank Legal Review, Volume 5: Fostering Development through Opportunity, Inclusion, and Equity* (World Bank Group, 2013) 505–522.

64 S Oktafiena et al 'Creating conducive work environments that affects employee performance improvement' (2019) 6/7 *International Journal of Innovation, Creativity and Change* 271–277.

65 T Mogapaesi 'Sexual harassment in the workplace and women's access to justice: Lessons for Botswana from a South African perspective' (2019) 45/3 *Commonwealth Law Bulletin* 431–432; A Raj et al 'Effects of sexual harassment on

advancement of women in academic medicine: A multi-institutional longitudinal study' (2020) 20/100298 *eClinical Medicine* 1.

66 CN Nana 'Sexual harassment in the workplace in South Africa: The unlimited vicarious liability of employers?' (2008) 52/2 *Journal of African Law* 345; D Zalesne 'Sexual harassment in the United States and South Africa: Facilitating the transition from legal standards to social norms' (2002) 25 *Harvard Women's Law Journal* 152–155.

67 C Muller et al 'Sexual harassment in the workplace: Unanticipated consequences of modern social control in organizations' (2001) 28/4 *Work and Occupations* 411–412.

68 Hersch (n 16) 1–4.

69 The World Bank *Women, Business and the Law 2014: Removing Restrictions to Enhance Gender Equality* (Bloomsbury Publishing, 2013); Nana (n 66) 246; Hersch (n 16) 2.

70 International Labour Organisation 'Sexual harassment at work – Fact sheet' (d.n.a) Declaration on Fundamental Principles and Rights at Work 1–3.

71 DRTD (n 7) art 8(1).

72 M Nussbaum *Creating Capabilities: The Human Development Approach* (Harvard University Press, 2011) 17–18; A Sen *Development as Freedom* (Oxford University of Press, 1999) 3–11 & 87–95; A Sen 'Development as capability expansion' in S Fudaka-Parr and AK Shiva Kumar (eds) *Readings in Human Development: Concepts, Measures and Policies for a Development Paradigm* (Oxford University Press, 2003) 6–11.

73 DRTD (n 7) art 2(2–3).

74 DRTD (n 7) art 6(3).

75 Maputo Protocol (n 1) art 19.

76 CEDAW (n 45) art 11(1).

77 Maputo Protocol (n 1) art 13.

78 The World Bank *Women, Business and the Law 2014: Removing Restrictions to Enhance Gender Equality* (Bloomsbury Publishing, 2013) 2; Hersch (n 16) 7.

79 C Ignătescu 'Equity: The essential value of law' (2013) 4/4 *Postmodern Openings Journal* 28.

80 JM White 'Equity: General principle of law recognised by civilised nations' (2004) 4/1 *QUTLJJ* 103.

81 CC Ngang 'Differentiated responsibilities under international law and the right to development paradigm for developing countries' (2017) 11/2 *Human Rights & International Legal Discourse* 272.

82 White (n 80) 115.

83 *Continental Shelf (Tunisia v Libya)* ICJ [1982] ICJ Rep 18, para 71; White (n 80) 115.

84 White (n 80) 105.

85 A D'Amato 'On the connection between law and justice' (1992–93) 26 *U.C. Davis L. Rev.* 542.

86 *Ibid* 539.

87 *Ibid* 529.

88 *Ibid* 528.

89 H Kelsen *What is Justice?: Justice, Law and Politics in the Mirror of Science – Collected Essays* (The Law Book Exchange Ltd, 2000) 1–3.

90 Lach (n 37) 120.

91 Ignătescu (n 79) 30.

92 *Ibid* 79, 26.

93 *Ibid* 79, 30.

94 A Sengupta 'Conceptualising the right to development for the twenty-first century' in UN Human Rights *Realizing the Right to Development: Essays in Commemorating 25 Years of the United Nations Declaration on the Right to Development* (United Nations Publication, 2013) 69; OO Oduwole 'International law and the right to development: A pragmatic approach for Africa' (2014) *International Institute of Social Studies* 19.
95 K Tomasevski *Development Aid and Human Rights: A Study for the Danish Centre for Human Rights* (Pinter, 1989) 48.
96 White (n 80) 103.
97 Lach (n 37) 123.
98 *Ogiek Community* (n 47) paras 103–112.
99 *Endorois* (n 47) para 148.
100 C Klaa 'Role of African women in development and economic life: Reality and challenges' (2020) 4/1 *International Journal of Inspiration & Resilience Economy* 1–9.

References

African Charter on Human and Peoples' Rights, adopted in Nairobi, Kenya on 27 June 1981.OAU Doc CAB/LEG/67/3 Rev. 5 (1981).

African Commission on Human and Peoples' Rights (Ogiek Community) v Republic of Kenya (2017) Appl No 006/2017 (*Ogiek* case) paras 105–112.

Andrews v Law Society of British Columbia [1989] 1 SCR 143.

K Celis et al 'Introduction: Gender and politics – A gendered world, a gendered discipline' in W Georgina et al (eds) *The Oxford Handbook of Gender and Politics* (Oxford University Press, 2013).

Centre for Minority Rights Development (Kenya) & Minority Rights Group International on behalf of Endorois Welfare Council v Kenya Comm 276/2003 (2009) AHRLR 75 (ACHPR 2009).

L Claridge 'Litigation as a tool for community empowerment: The case of Kenya's Ogiek' (2018) 11/1 *Erasmus Law Review* 57–58.

Continental Shelf (Tunisia v Libya) ICJ [1982] ICJ Rep 18.

S Coontz and P Henderson 'Explanations of male dominance' in S Coontz and P Henderson (eds) *Women's Work, Men's Property: The Origins of Gender and Class* (Verso Books, 1986).

Council of Europe 'Feminism and women's rights movements' www.coe.int/en/web/gender-matters/feminism-and-women-s-rights-movements (accessed on 17 September 2021).

A D'Amato 'On the connection between law and justice' (1992–93) 26 *The UC Davis Law Review* 527–582.

Declaration of Principles on Equality adopted in 2008 under the auspices of Equal Rights Trust, London.

Declaration on the Right to Development Resolution A/RES/41/128 adopted by the UN Gen Ass on 4 December 1986.

Declaration on the Rights of Indigenous Peoples Resolution 61/295 adopted by the UN General Assembly on 13 September 2007.

P Dressel 'Racial equality or racial equity? The difference it makes' *Race Matters Institute*, 2014, http://viablefuturescenter.org/racemattersinstitute/2014/04/02/racial-equality-or-racial-equity-the-difference-it-makes/ (accessed on 1 February 2023).

R Dworkin *Sovereign Virtue: The Theory and Practice of Equality* (Harvard University Press, 2000).

L Fitzgerald, S Swan and V Magley 'But was it really sexual harassment? Legal, behavioral and psychological definitions of the workplace victimization of women' (5–28) in W O'Donohue (ed) *Sexual Harassment: Theory, Research and Treatment* (Allyn & Bacon, 1997).

S Gosepath 'Equality' *Stanford Encyclopedia of Philosophy*, https://plato.stanford.edu/entries/equality/ (accessed on 31 August 2020).

D Hay 'Time, inequality, and law's violence' in A Sarat and T Kearns (eds) *Law's Violence* (The University of Michigan's Press, 1993).

A Hernandez 'A principle of equitable access to sustainable development: Internalizing externalities in the global climate talks' (2014) 2/1 *Review of Business and Economics Studies* 74–87.

J Hersch 'Sexual harassment in the workplace' (2015) *IZA World of Labour 188* 1–10.

C Ignătescu 'Equity: The essential value of law' (2013) 4/4 *Postmodern Openings Journal* 25–33.

International Labour Organisation 'Sexual harassment at work – Fact sheet' (d.n.a) Declaration on Fundamental Principles and Rights at Work.

L Joseph 'Some ways of thinking about equality of opportunity' (1980) 33/3 *The Western Political Quarterly* 393–400.

T Kellow 'Women, elections and violence in West Africa: Assessing women's political participation in Liberia and Sierra Leone' (2010) International Alert 10; Inter-Parliamentary Union (IPU) 'Women in Politics' January 2012, www.ipu.org/pdf/publications/wmnmap12_en.pdf (accessed on 24 September 2020).

H Kelsen *What is Justice?: Justice, Law and Politics in the Mirror of Science – Collected Essays* (The Law Book Exchange Ltd, 2000).

M Kilgour et al. 'The UN global compact and substantive equality for women: Revealing a "well hidden" mandate' (2007) 28/4 *Third World Quarterly* 751–773.

C Klaa 'Role of African women in development and economic life: Reality and challenges' (2020) 4/1 *International Journal of Inspiration and Resilience Economy* 1–9.

J Klugman and M Morton 'Enabling equal opportunities for women in the world of work: The intersections of formal and informal constraints' in H Cissé et al (eds) *The World Bank Legal Review, Volume 5: Fostering Development through Opportunity, Inclusion, and Equity* (World Bank Group, 2013) 505–522.

D Lach 'Equality vs differentiation: On solidarity and justice in social law' (2016) 20/205 *Adam Mickiewicz University Law Review* 111–133.

P McDonald 'Workplace sexual harassment 30 years on: A review of the literature' (2012) 14/1 *International Journal of Management Reviews* 1–17.

H McFerson 'Poverty among women in sub-Saharan Africa: A review of selected issues' (2010) 11/4 *Journal of International Women's Studies* 50–72.

H McLaughlin et al 'Sexual harassment, workplace authority, and the paradox of power' (2012) 77/4 *American Sociological Review* 625–647.

C Menke 'Law and violence' (2010) 22/1 *Law and Literature* 1–17.

Milken Institute School of Public Health 'Equity vs equality: What's the difference' *The George Washington University*, 2020, https://onlinepublichealth.gwu.edu/resources/equity-vs-equality/ (accessed on 1 February 2023).

T Mogapaesi 'Sexual harassment in the workplace and women's access to justice: lessons for Botswana from a South African perspective' (2019) 45/3 *Commonwealth Law Bulletin* 431–432.

M Morsen 'A note on Vanuatu's cases on the right to equality' (2017) 23 *Comparative Law Journal of the Pacific* 81–95.

C Muller et al 'Sexual harassment in the workplace: Unanticipated consequences of modern social control in organizations' (2001) 28/4 *Work and Occupations* 411–446.

C Nana 'Sexual harassment in the workplace in South Africa: The unlimited vicarious liability of employers?' (2008) 52/2 *Journal of African Law* 345–267.

CC Ngang 'Differentiated responsibilities under international law and the right to development paradigm for developing countries' (2017) 11/2 *Human Rights and International Legal Discourse* 265–288.

M Nussbaum *Creating Capabilities: The Human Development Approach* (Harvard University Press, 2011).

OO Oduwole 'International law and the right to development: A pragmatic approach for Africa' (2014) *International Institute of Social Studies* 1–31.

S Oktafiena et al 'Creating conducive work environments that affects employee performance improvement' (2019) 6/7 *International Journal of Innovation, Creativity and Change* 271–277.

D Petrova 'The declaration of principles on equality: A contribution to international human rights' (2008) *The Equal Rights Review* 58–70.

Protocol to the African Charter on Human and Peoples' Rights on the Rights of Women in Africa adopted in Maputo, Mozambique on 11 July 2003 (Maputo Protocol).

A Raj et al 'Effects of sexual harassment on advancement of women in academic medicine: A multi-institutional longitudinal study' (2020) 20/100298 *eClinical Medicine* 1–8.

A Rose 'Law and the causation of social problems' (1968) 6/1 *Social Problems* 33–43.

M Rosenfeld 'Substantive equality and equal opportunity: A jurisprudential appraisal' (1986) 75/5 *California Law Review* 1687–1712.

A Sen 'Development as capability expansion' in S Fudaka-Parr and AK Shiva Kumar (eds) *Readings in Human Development: Concepts, Measures and Policies for a Development Paradigm* (Oxford University Press, 2003).

A Sen *Development as Freedom* (Oxford University of Press, 1999).

A Sengupta 'Conceptualizing the right to development for the twenty-first century' in UN Human Rights *Realizing the Right to Development: Essays in Commemorating 25 Years of the United Nations Declaration on the Right to Development* (United Nations Publication, 2013).

A Sengupta 'Realising the right to development' (2000) 31 *Development and Change* 553–578.

A Smith 'Equality constitutional adjudication in South Africa' (2014) 14/2 *African Human Rights Law Journal* 609–632.

S Sturm 'Equality and inequality: Legal aspects' (2001) *International Encyclopaedia of the Social and Behavioural Sciences* 894–902.

The World Bank *Women, Business and the Law 2014: Removing Restrictions to Enhance Gender Equality* (Bloomsbury Publishing, 2013).

K Tomasevski *Development Aid and Human Rights: A Study for the Danish Centre for Human Rights* (Pinter, 1989).

Transforming Our World: The 2030 Agenda for Sustainable Development UN General Assembly Resolution A/RES/70/1 adopted on 25 September 2015.
UN Department of Economic and Social Affairs *The World's Women 2010: Trends and Statistics* (New York: United Nations, 2010).
UN Permanent Forum on Indigenous Issues Report on the eighteenth session (22 April–3 May 2019) to the Economic and Social Council, E/2019/43-E/C.19/2019/10.
UN Women *Gender Mainstreaming in Development Programming: Guidance Note* (UN Women, 2014).
Universal Declaration of Human Rights adopted by the UN General Assembly, Resolution 217 A(III) of 10 December 1948.
U Uzodike and H Onapajo 'Women and development in Africa: Competing approaches and contested achievements' (2013) 20/2 *Alternations* 27–51.
Vienna Declaration and Programme of Action adopted at the UN World Conference on Human Rights UN Doc.A/CONF.157/24, 25 June 1993.
Y Weisberg et al 'Gender differences in personality across the ten aspects of the big five' (2011) 2/178 *Frontiers in Psychology* 1–11.
P Westen *Speaking of Equality: An Analysis of the Rhetorical Force of 'Equality' in Moral and Legal Discourse* (Princeton University Press, 1990).
M White 'Equity: General principle of law recognised by civilised nations' (2004) 4/1 *QUTLJJ* 103–116.
D Zalesne 'Sexual harassment in the United States and South Africa: Facilitating the transition from legal standards to social norms' (2002) 25 *Harvard Women's Law Journal* 152–155.

3 Ending Sexual Harassment in Africa Through Human Rights Mechanisms

A Critical Appraisal of the Application of the Maputo Protocol by the African Human Rights System and the ECOWAS Court of Justice

Joëlle Nwabueze

Introduction

Sexual harassment occurs when a person is a victim of any form of unwanted verbal, non-verbal, or physical conduct of a sexual nature with the purpose or effect of violating his/her dignity as a person.[1] The Istanbul Convention of the Council of Europe and the related directive on the implementation of the principle of equal treatment for men and women[2] emphasise that sexual harassment occurs in particular when creating an intimidating, hostile, degrading, humiliating, or offensive environment.

In societies where patriarchy and all forms of discrimination and violence against women and girls is structurally embedded in socio-political and cultural systems, sexual harassment seems rampant at all corners. The potential of non-discrimination rules, criminalisation of non-consensual sexual conduct, efficient systems of accountability, and sustainable protection of basic human rights, etc., human rights law seems to offer many possibilities for the answerability of the offenders and restoration of aggrieved female falling under the sword of harassment based on sex. It therefore becomes relevant to question the actionability of sexual harassment as a human rights claim. Henceforth, the question of determination of the legal guarantees against sexual harassment in regional human rights mechanisms, such as the African ones with widespread sex-based harassment. Are human rights mechanisms in Africa capable of guaranteeing the availability, accessibility, and acceptability of remedies to all aggrieved female parties?

To answer the question, this chapter first examines the interrelation between sexual harassment and human rights. This presupposes an analysis of the female rights violated in the act of sexual harassment and their justifiability under human rights law. In part two, the human rights standards regulating the protection of females are discussed. This chapter more precisely reviews the Protocol to the African Charter on the Rights of Women in Africa

DOI: 10.4324/9781003373308-3

(Maputo Protocol) which specifically complements the equality section enshrined in the African Charter on Human and Peoples' Rights to enhance women's protection against sexual abuses. It therefore speaks life into the vow of substantive gender equality for the attainment of roles and rewards in Africa. It becomes relevant, at this point, to question the contribution of the regional human rights mechanisms in the fulfilment of these promises of equality and sexual security birthed from the Maputo Protocol.

To what extent can an aggrieved girl or woman in a case of sexual harassment rely on the dispositions of the Maputo Protocol to seek justice in the African Union Human Rights system or the ECOWAS Community Court of Human Rights? Discussing this question, the present chapter examines in a third part the tripartite human rights system of the African Union represented by the African Court and Commission on Human and Peoples' Rights and the Committee of Experts on the Rights and Welfare of the Child (ACERWC) on one side and, on the other, the Community Court of Justice of the Economic Community of West African States (The ECOWAS Court of Justice). The jurisprudence of the African human rights judicial institutions is subsequently reviewed prior to discussing their capacity to adjudicate on any dispute relating to the interpretation and application of the Maputo Protocol in sexual harassment cases.

In the last part of the chapter, I discuss states' obligation to bring their laws in line with international human rights standards. The chapter notes that as in all regions of the world, some laws in Africa still exist which jeopardise sexual freedom[3] and fail to sustain female rights in cases of sexual harassment. The chapter ends with recommendations to ensure accountability of sexual harassers and repealing of unfriendly female laws to foster the end of sexual harassment on the continent.

Scope of Women and Girls' Human Rights in the Context of Sexual Harassment

Today it has become an almost universally recognised and accepted concept that individuals possess certain definite political, civil, economic, and social rights which governments have the duty and responsibility of protecting and enforcing. The concept of 'human rights' cannot be taken away from human being because these are rights to which each and everyone is entitled as natural right. As such, every individual is entitled to such rights and cannot be eroded by another. This prompted Thomas Jefferson to assert, after John Locke and Montesquieu, that men are 'free people claiming their rights as derived from the laws of nature and not as the gift of their government'.[4] This is echoed in the Universal Declaration of Human Rights:[5] 'All human beings are born free and equal in dignity and rights', and that 'Recognition of the inherent dignity and of the equal and inalienable rights of all members of the human family is the foundation of freedom, justice and peace in the world'.

Women and girls, as with men and boys, have a right to have their substantive legal and basic human rights: right to dignity, right to equality, and right to non-discrimination. Those rights are inherent and inalienable by virtue of humanism. A woman's rights and obligations as a legal person cannot be defiled in the affairs of life by virtue of her sexual identity. The benefits of legal protection can neither be challenged nor withdrawn on the ground of feminist sexual identity. Once a woman suffers harassment on the ground of her sexual identity as female,[6] it is a case of human right violation, affecting several basic rights.

Females' Rights to Dignity and Privacy

Every female, as every human being, is clothed with dignity and honour. A woman's sexual independence is an essential feature of physical and mental integrity,[7] which are the basic human rights values protected by the criminalisation of the forcefulness at the core of the act of sexual harassment. The act of sexual harassment is unwanted and undesirable. Its effect is to intimidate and offend, especially when assessed against power imbalances which escalate a hostile work environment in which the perpetrator thrives and the victim usually becomes more fearful.[8] Human rights law protects from inhumane and degrading treatment, and the intrusion into one's working and private life. Because the woman's privacy is invaded without her consent during the act of sexual harassment, the perpetrator is liable for human rights violations.

Women's Rights to Equality and Non-Discrimination

In addition, any act of sexual harassment is an arbitrary distinction based on sex between women and men. The woman in this context is approached on the ground of inequality compared to men. This contradicts international standards ascertaining that human rights are held equally by men, women, and children. Well-renowned feminist scholar Catharine Mac Kinnon[9] highlights that sexual harassment connotes an illegal sex discrimination.

Overview of Sexual Abuse and Domestic Violence as Human Rights Violations

Sexual harassment equally corroborates domestic violence and sexual abuse, which have been acknowledged in international human rights law[10] as human rights violations. The WordWeb dictionary defines the harassment as 'The act of tormenting by continued persistent attacks and criticism' and 'A feeling of intense annoyance caused by being tormented'. Torment refers to an 'unbearable physical pain' or 'Intense feelings of suffering; acute mental or physical pain'.[11] It becomes indisputable that any act of sexual harassment carries the ingredient of violence manifested by the torment, pain, and anguish endured by the aggrieved female. Relating violence to human rights violations, the Convention on the Elimination of All Forms of Discrimination against Women (CEDAW)[12] specifically emphasises that 'Violence against women is an obstacle to the achievement of the objectives of equality.'

A similar recognition is found in Article 1 of the 1993 UN Declaration on the Elimination of Violence against Women, which purposely emphasises:

> Violence against women shall be understood to encompass physical, sexual and psychological violence occurring in the family, including battering, sexual abuse of female children in the household, dowry-related violence, marital rape, female genital mutilation and other traditional practices harmful to women, non-spousal violence and violence related to exploitation.

Sexual harassment henceforth impairs the women's ability to participate in life matters on a basis of equality, dignity, and non-discrimination.[13] Therefore, it is relevant to review the applicable legal regulatory framework in regional African human rights legal instruments prior to analysing the enforcement mechanisms.

Regional Mechanisms for the Protection against Sexual Harassment under the Human Rights Framework in Africa

In the first part of this section, I discuss the rights of women encapsulated in regional human rights legal instruments in Africa, most specifically the Maputo Protocol and the Niamey Guidelines on sexual harassment. The second part is dedicated to the review of the African human rights enforcement mechanisms.

The Maputo Protocol and Sexual Harassment

The Protocol to the African Charter on the Rights of Women in Africa (Maputo Protocol) was adopted to precisely balance the equality section enshrined in the African Charter on Human and Peoples' Rights. The previously mentioned section was found to be restrictive in respect of the discrimination suffered by women because of stereotyped cultures and traditions in Africa.

The Maputo Protocol arose as a shining star in the dark realm of sexual harassment in Africa. Most precisely, it ascertains the state's duty to protect the African woman and girl-child from all forms of abuse, including sexual harassment, and provide for sanctions against the perpetrators of such practices.[14] It is a potentially ground-breaking instrument in the elimination of sexual harassment in Africa. The Maputo Protocol outstands by its essential legislative dispositions addressing violence against women. It defines sexual violence, including sexual harassment,[15] and obliges states in the same vein to appropriately address all forms of violence against women, including unwanted sex.[16] It is a substantial reinforcement of the dispositions of Article 18(3) of the African Charter which provides for the non-discrimination of women. The Protocol obliges member states to guarantee the elimination of all forms of discriminations against women. It goes further to provide women with adequate rights recognition to enable the punishment of acts of violence. It explicitly recognises every woman's right to dignity.[17] According to the Protocol, every woman should have the right to dignity which is inherent in a human being, and the recognition and protection of her human and legal rights. As such, no violence should be perpetrated against women, which implies that all acts perpetrated against women which cause or could cause them physical, sexual, psychological, and economic harm, including the threat to take such acts, or to undertake the imposition of arbitrary restrictions on or deprivation of fundamental freedoms in private or public life in peace time and during situations of armed conflicts or of war.[18]

The Niamey Guidelines on Sexual Harassment

The Guidelines on Combating Sexual Violence and its Consequences in Africa (The Niamey Guidelines) is ground-breaking in the legislative process of the field of sexual harassment at the regional level in Africa.[19] The guidelines were adopted by the African Commission on Human and Peoples' Rights during its 60th Ordinary Session held in Niamey, Niger, from 8 to 22 May 2017, and operate as a guiding tool, supporting states in their willingness to effectively combat the plague of sexual violence and sexual harassment on the continent.

The Niamey guidelines provides a deep understanding of the key terms related to sexual harassment. They precisely define, among others, the term 'victim', and also highlight the interrelation between the terms 'sexual violence' and 'sexual harassment'. According to the guidelines, sexual violence is not limited to physical violence and does not necessarily involve physical contact – like sexual harassment, it takes many forms.[20] The Niamey guidelines provide certain general principles and obligations of states which fit the narrative of promoting women's human rights against sexual harassment:

- ensure the respect of the rights of the victims of sexual harassment irrespective of their sex, age or tribe as part of the non-discrimination principle;
- protect the victims and witnesses from negative consequences in the course of investigations;
- prevent sexual violence and its consequences;
- adopt the necessary measures to guarantee that victims are protected;
- guarantee access to justice and investigate and prosecute the perpetrators of sexual violence; and
- provide remedies and reparation for victims.

In this second part, I focus on the prevention of sexual violence and its consequences, while the other parts are dedicated to protecting and supporting the victims, investigating and prosecuting those responsible, the right to reparation, and the implementation of regional and international obligations.

The Niamey guidelines are a relevant echo to the Maputo Protocol which enjoins states parties to the African Union to prevent sexual violence, prosecute perpetrators of sexual violence, and rehabilitate victims of sexual violence.[21] Though the guidelines as soft laws do not have the binding character of a legal norm, they nevertheless assist lawyers, prosecutors, officials, and victims in the steps to undertake while filing a complaint for sexual harassment. Beyond all, it sets the stage for anti-sexual harassment laws by providing the straightforward architecture of a bill.

Human Rights Enforcement Mechanisms

Women's basic rights are recognised in the constitutions of several African nations and transformed into actual judicial remedies at national, regional, and international levels. Without judicial remedies, citizens' theoretical constitutional human rights would be seriously diminished. The availability of judicial remedies for human rights' violations is significant in two aspects. First, it is the duty of the state and regional human rights institutions to restore justice when human rights violations occur within a state or a region principally. Second, it is essential and obvious that states and regional human rights systems remain primarily responsible in international law for enforcing the protection of human rights within their jurisdictions.

In this section, I respond to the question of to what extent the regional African human rights system contributes to the elimination of sexual harassment in the continent.

The architecture of the African regional human rights system includes the African Court, the African Commission on Human and Peoples' Rights, the African Children's Rights Committee, and the ECOWAS Court of Justice. By its nature, judicial power includes: (i) the power to assume compulsory jurisdiction, (ii) the power to render authoritative and binding decisions, and (iii) the power to enforce compliance. Aggrieved females who are litigants in sexual harassment cases are permitted to claim two or more remedies cutting across damages, punitive, and compensatory remedies in one suit at the same time. The scope of judicial power is clearly captured by Nwabueze as follows:

- the power to assume compulsory jurisdiction at the instance of a party and to inquire into the dispute;
- the power to determine authoritatively or conclusively the facts of the dispute;
- the power to determine authoritatively the law relevant to the dispute;

- the competence to arrive at a decision on the application of the relevant law to the facts and therefore finally dispose of the whole dispute;
- the decision arrived at is binding on the parties to the dispute; and
- the power to enforce compliance with the decision.[22]

In this section, I examine the scope of the powers of the institutions within the African human rights system in the adjudication of sexual harassment claims. I first review the architecture of the African human rights system before delving into the review of the jurisprudence of African human rights judicial institutions as it relates to the Maputo Protocol and to the adjudication of sexual harassment claims. I review the structures of the African Court, the African Commission on Human and Peoples' Rights, and the African Children's Rights Committee.

After the transition from the Organisation of the African Union (OAU) to the African Union (AU) in 2000, the overseeing institution of African states adopted promotion and protection of human rights in the continent as a primary objective. The African human rights system was consequently established with a set of norms and institutions accepted by states as binding. The norms in the African human rights system include the African Charter on Human and Peoples' Rights (Banjul Charter), the African Charter on the Rights and Welfare of the Child, the Protocol to the African Charter on the Rights of Women in Africa, the OAU Convention Governing the Specific Aspects of Refugee Problems in Africa, and the African Charter on Democracy, Elections and Governance.

The human rights institutions are the African Commission on Human and Peoples' Rights (ACHPR),[23] and the African Court on Human and Peoples' Rights, including various committees and working groups. The architecture of the African Union's human rights system denotes a stand-alone committee functioning as a quasi-judicial human rights institution, which is the Committee of Experts on the Rights and Welfare of the Child (ACERWC).

The African Court on Human and Peoples' Rights

The African Court adjudges cases related to the violations of articles of the African Charter on Peoples' and Human Rights. Violations may concern concrete acts of harm, but also legal or policy frameworks that deny or deprive rights, failure to take necessary positive steps, or inadequate remedial systems. Communications must be sent after exhausting local remedies, if any, unless it is obvious that the procedure is unduly prolonged. This case is an exception to the rule of exhaustion.[24] The African Court applies the provisions of the African Charter, or any human rights instruments ratified by the states concerned.[25] The African Court has a dual jurisdiction: firstly, the court gives advisory opinions; and, secondly, decides complaints against the states that have accepted its jurisdiction.

Complaints may be referred to the court by the commission at any stage of the proceedings, following a failure to comply with provisional measures or following a failure to respect the commission's final judgment where the state in question has ratified the Protocol of the Court. Complaints may be submitted directly to the court where a state has accepted its jurisdiction.[26] Unfortunately, out of 55 member states, only 30 have ratified the Protocol to the African Charter on Human and Peoples' Rights on the Establishment of the African Court on Human and Peoples' Rights.[27] Non-governmental organisations (NGOs) may submit cases to the court.[28] Cases may be submitted by members of those NGOs in their individual capacity on behalf of the victims in question[29] if they have had their observer status recognised by the African Commission. As of December 2022, only eight states had accepted the ability of individuals and NGOs to petition the court directly with observer status before the African Commission.[30] The African Court's judgments are binding as a matter of international law. The African Court is a supranational human rights adjudication mechanism, based on the exhaustion requirement of national remedies. The court decides on individual complaints of human rights violations. Nevertheless, it does not operate as a superior court over the sub-regional courts.

The African Commission on Human and Peoples' Rights

Cases can be brought to the commission directly by victims on behalf of themselves and others, or by lawyers or NGOs on behalf of an individual or on behalf of multiple victims. The African Commission operates in a three-stage procedural mechanism:[31] first, seizure of the commission with a submission of a written complaint narrating the alleged human rights violation and related sections of the African Charter violated; second, submission of admissibility briefs within 30 days of submission of the complaint. Afterwards, the state will be given the right to response to the submission. A new deadline of 60 days applies. Third, and within a period of 30 days, a second and last submission by the claimant in response to the points presented by the state. The African Protocol grants power to the commission to create subsidiary mechanisms[32] such as special rapporteurs, committees, and working groups.[33]

The African Commission's human rights system is quasi-judicial by nature. The claimant and the state do not appear in person before the commission. The arguments are exclusively written pleadings.[34] The commission's decisions are recommendations which constitute authoritative interpretations of the charter, which is binding on state parties.

The African Committee of Experts on the Rights and Welfare of the Child

There are several working groups, human rights bodies, special rapporteurships, and committees established to advance specific human rights under the African Human Rights System.[35] Those mechanisms play an important role in the advancement of specific rights and guide their protection and enforcement. Their responsibilities include collecting and distributing information on respect for the human rights of vulnerable groups such as women and children. However, the African Committee of Experts on the Rights and Welfare of the Child (ACERWC) plays a particular role. Compared to other committees and working groups within the African Union human rights system, it operates a unique quasi-judicial human rights mechanism. It assesses states' compliance with child human rights standards (to include girls and boys) enshrined within the African Union System. In this vein, it contributes greatly to the protection of children from sexual harassment under the African Human Rights System. The ACERWC is a Committee of the African Union mandated to monitor implementation of the African Charter on the Rights and Welfare of the Child.[36] The African Child Charter is a regional human rights instrument addressing issues of particular interest and importance to children in Africa, including the sensitive issue of protection of children from sexual harassment. The committee decisions are General Comments, with guiding and interpreting authoritative force regarding the dispositions of the African Charter on the Rights and Welfare of the Child.

The ECOWAS Court of Justice

The Economic Community of West African States (ECOWAS) aims to adapt better to the international environment, bringing about more equity, transparency, and greater functionality in accordance with global best practices. ECOWAS as a community is taking ownership of the grand objectives designed to improve the living conditions of the citizenry, ensure economic growth, and create an environment conducive to development and meaningful integration.[37] The ECOWAS Court of Justice (ECJ) comprises 15 West African countries.[38] Only ECOWAS member states may be sued before it, and the community institutions, not individual defendants.[39] The court's regulating instruments include the revised ECOWAS Treaty, ECOWAS Court Protocol, and the treaties and protocols made by the Authority of Heads of State and Government pursuant to the Revised Treaty. ECJ operates as subregional court in the exercise of its human rights jurisdiction. The court is the final arbiter for settling disputes under the treaty,[40] and deals with matters referred to it by member states or the Authority of Heads of State and Government in ECOWAS concerning disputes between member states or by one or more member states and an ECOWAS institution on the interpretation and application of the ECOWAS treaty.[41] The ECJ's decisions on human rights matters interpret the African Charter on Human and Peoples' Rights. The Charter's dispositions are considered as constitutional principles shared by all member states, and as legally binding on ECOWAS member states.[42]

With the amendments brought in 2005[43] in the West African Community Court of Justice, individuals have been granted access to bring cases, including on human rights matters, before the West African Court. Corporations and individuals can submit complaints alleging human rights violations by the community or member state. The ECJ judgment is immediately binding on member states. The judgment automatically becomes part of the national law of the highest precedential value. The rules made by ECOWAS supersede rules made by individual member states if they are inconsistent.[44] Article 7(1) of the Revised Treaty provides that the authority may impose sanctions against states which do not fulfil their obligations regarding ECOWAS; this would certainly include a refusal to comply with the decisions of the ECOWAS Court. The court is not constrained by the fact that the ECOWAS protocols have not been domesticated by any given member states. For example, on 1 July 1994, Nigeria ratified the Revised Treaty. By virtue of the principle *pacta sunt servanda*,[45] Nigeria is bound by the judgment of the court.

Adjudicating Sexual Harassment Claims in the African Human Rights System: Place and Role of the Maputo Protocol

The Protocol to the African Charter on Human and Peoples' Rights on the Rights of Women in Africa (the Maputo Protocol) was adopted in 2003 to fill the gap left in the African Charter on Peoples' and Human Rights and related to the specific violations of women's rights resulting from discrimination, harmful practices, and sexual health. It recognises that 'every woman should have the right to dignity inherent in a human being and to the recognition and protection of her human and legal rights.' The use of the Maputo Protocol as an efficient advocacy tool in sexual harassment claims is evidenced in its article defining violence as 'all acts perpetuated against women which cause or could cause them physical, sexual, psychological, and economic harm, including the threat to take such acts.' In this section, I review the jurisprudence of African human rights regional systems as they relate to the Maputo Protocol and the adjudication of sexual harassment claims.

Adjudicating Women's Rights Before the African Court

The percentage of cases litigated before the African Court on Human and Peoples' Rights and related to sexual harassment is extremely low. If the tendency to bring general human rights complaints before the court is very high, it does not seem to be the same for sexual harassment and gender-based discriminations generally. The research findings indicated that only one case relating to the sexual abuse of women in Mali has been adjudicated before the African Court: *APDF and IHRDA v Republic of Mali*.[46] Mali drafted a Persons and Family Code in 2011[47] intended to protect the rights of individuals and the family units. After strong opposition by Muslims leaders, the act was amended and adopted on 2 December 2011. Two NGOs, the APDF and the IHRDA, opposed the new act on the ground that it violated provisions of the African Children's Charter, the Maputo Protocol, and the CEDAW related to the minimum (18 years) age to marry, consent to marriage, right to inheritance, and elimination of practices harmful and discriminatory to the rights of women and children,

The African Court affirmed that in relation to the Maputo Protocol, the country of Mali had violated the right to non-discrimination of women and children as guaranteed by Article 2 of the Maputo Protocol, Articles 3 and 4 of the ACERWC, and Article 16(1) of the CEDAW. Other violations were established. This was based on the difference of treatment noticed by the court between boys and girls. While the amended Family Act set the minimum age of marriage for boys at 18 years old, the minimum for girls was 16 years old. The court added that, among others, the right to consent to marriage was equally violated,[48] which contravened the dispositions of the Maputo Protocol.[49] The court concluded by asking the state of Mali in the final judgment to amend its Family Code to comply with international human rights laws.

Sexual Harassment Claims and the African Commission

In this section, I begin by reviewing the claims of sexual harassment birthed from the African Union Commission as a political institution, and, secondly, the claims of sexual harassment brought before the African Commission as a quasi-judicial institution.

Cases of Sexual Harassment within the African Union Commission

Sanitising Africa by removing the gangrene of sexual harassment starts with the African Union as an institution. Many female employees of the African Union Commission reportedly suffered sexual harassment during the last decade, with 'female employees, on internships, volunteer programmes or short-term contracts, sexually harassed by senior staff'[50] to exploit employees without job security. The 'sexual trap' set by well-positioned line officers within the African Union Commission was in exchange of employment contracts. Commenting on the event, BBC Afrique reported that '44 cases of alleged sexual harassment and that young women were being "exploited for sex in exchange for jobs"'.[51] Proceedings at the African Commission for sexual harassment were exclusively administrative, without judicial processes. The African Union organised a three-stage procedure involving first, reception of a complaint; second, establishment of a high-level committee by the chairperson upon report of the abuse; and third, launch of the inquiry for confidential interviews of all staff who had a complaint. In its report published on the website[52] of the African Union Commission, the committee confirmed cases of sexual harassment and sexual exploitation of young women in exchange of jobs.

As part of the limitations noticed during the facts-finding procedure was the fact that the African Union Commission did not have an internal process and sexual harassment policy. This lack inevitably fuelled the harassment of subordinates by their superiors within the institution.[53] In order to fill the gap in the regulation within the African Union, the committee recommended 'a comprehensive sexual harassment policy[54] that protects the victims and takes the strongest punitive measures against any perpetrator'.[55]

Quasi-Inexistence of Cases of Sexual Harassment Before the African Union Commission

Unlike the African Court and according to harassment, apart from the aforementioned administrative proceedings related to sexual harassment, the African Commission did not register cases on sexual harassment. Meanwhile, the commission has received and finalized numerous complaints on human rights violations. Gender-based discrimination complaints brought before the commission nevertheless demonstrate that human rights mechanisms in Africa are capable of guaranteeing the availability, accessibility, and acceptability of remedies for sexual harassment complainants. The *Equality Now and Ethiopian Women Lawyers Association (EWLA) v Federal Republic of Ethiopia*[56] case is an illustrative example. In this case, a young girl named Zebene and aged 13 was sexually assaulted in Ethiopia, abducted, and forced to enter a contract of marriage against her will and in violation of Ethiopian laws.

Although the offender and his accomplices were condemned by a lower court, the decision was quashed by the High Court. The offender appealed and was found not guilty of the offence. Later, the Cassation Bench of the Supreme Court and the Federal Cassation Court of Ethiopia rejected the subsequent appeal by the complainants, maintaining that there had been no fundamental error of the law in the case. Having exhausted all domestic remedies, the complainants appealed to the African Commission, maintaining that the Ethiopian government had failed in its obligation under the African Charter to provide the girl with equal protection of the law and respect for her rights to security of person, dignity, and freedom from cruel, inhuman, or degrading treatment.[57]

Even though the commission acknowledged the failure of the state in its duty to diligently examine the case, most specifically the dispositions of Articles 3, 4, 5, and 6 of the charter, related to the violation of the minor's right to be free from torture or inhuman or degrading treatment, it refused to recognise a violation of the girl's right to non-discrimination based on sex which is guaranteed under Article 2 of the African Charter. It is this chapter's position that the decision of the African Commission in this case dated 2007 was ambivalent and did not accommodate all the developments brought by the Maputo Protocol since 2005.

Sexual Harassment Claims and the African Children's Rights Committee

The African Children's Charter protects children from sexual exploitation and other forms of abuse.[58] The Maputo Protocol defines women as 'persons of female gender, including girls'.[59] Its provisions henceforth apply to adult women as well as female children. ACERWC as a committee receives communications on alleged violations of children's rights and conducts investigations.[60] Henceforth, in the case of any child victim of sexual harassment, the litigant may ground the complaint on the dispositions of the Maputo Protocol and address it to the African Children's Committee.

Although the research did not reveal sexual harassment claims in the history of the African Children's Rights Committee, cases studied by the committee exemplify the possibility for complainants in sexual harassment claims to use the provisions of the Maputo Protocol to form the basis of human rights complaints before the committee. The following case reflects a better representation of the transformative features of the Maputo Protocol in the African human rights adjudication system on the sexual abuse of minor girls: the Institute for Human Rights and Development in Africa and Finders Group Initiative on behalf of *TBA (a Minor) v Cameroon*.[61]

This case is an historical hallmark from ACERW, as it is the first decision of the Child Rights Committee relating to sexual abuse against minors. The case relates to sexual abuse of a young girl, aged 10, in the country of Cameroon in Central Africa. The perpetrator is an important businessman. Two non-governmental organisations representing the minor, the Institute for Human Rights and Development in Africa and Finders Group Initiative, filed a complaint against the local police for failure to arrest the perpetrator according to the laws of the state in spite of the medical report and identification of the perpetrator's residence as place of abuse, both evidencing the harm suffered by the young girl.

The report filed by the police three months later was dismissed by the examining magistrate who refused to acknowledge the existing evidence and snubbed the request to produce a copy of the decision to enable its appeal. As a reaction to the respondents' disclosures of the miscarriages of justice entailing the case proceedings, the perpetrator filed a defamation complaint, a backlash to frustrate the legal steps of the complainant! Determined to see justice done in this case, the complainants submitted a grievance to the African Committee of Experts on the Rights and Welfare of the Child alleging violation of Article 24(3) of the Convention on the Rights of a Child, the dispositions of the African Charter and the Maputo Protocol, as well as other international human rights standards. After investigations and contrary to the African Commission's decision against Ethiopia in the previous case, the African Children Committee found that that Cameroon's lack of due diligence violated the non-discrimination provision of the Children's Charter since the sexual assault against the minor was gender-based violence, which is a form of gender-based discrimination in the international human rights law system.

The African Children Committee equally established that the response of Cameroon to the claims of rape of a minor violated Article 1 of the Children's Charter. The article requires states to legislate and adopt other measures to protect children from sexual abuse. The committee affirmed that the due diligence to prevent, investigate, prosecute, and punish sexual violence and other human rights violations is a corollary of the obligation to protect under human rights law. The African Children Committee also declared that sexual violence is a type of gender discrimination according to the dispositions of Article 3 of the African Children's Charter. The country of Cameroon was consequently recommended to implement the Children Charter's dispositions, to prosecute and punish the offender, and compensate the minor.

I have demonstrated in this section that human rights mechanisms in Africa can guarantee the availability, accessibility, and acceptability of remedies for sexual harassment complainants in light of the innovative principles brought by the Maputo Protocol in this field, taking Ethiopia and Cameroon as case studies. Ethiopia and Cameroon took note of the commission's remarks and, accordingly, adopted anti-sexual harassment legislation. In Cameroon, the amended Penal Code entitled 'Sexual Harassment' stipulates the following:

1) whoever takes advantage of the authority conferred on him by his position to harass another using order threats, constraints or pressure in order to obtain sexual favours, shall be punished with imprisonment for from 6 (six) months to 1 (one) year and with fine of from CFAF 100.000 (one hundred) to CFAF 1.000.000 (one million).
2) The penalty shall be imprisonment for from 3 (three) Years where the victim is a minor.
3) The penalty shall be imprisonment for from 3 (three)-5 (five) years where the offender is in charge of the education of the victim.[62]

In Ethiopia, the revised Penal law takes into account gender-based violence and revised the penalties applicable in cases of violation.[63] In the next section, I explore how and to what extent the ECOWAS Court of Justice has adopted the standard of the Maputo Protocol in the court's jurisprudence in relation to sexual harassment cases.

Adjudicating Sexual Harassment Claims Before ECOWAS Court of Justice

In the Community Court of Justice of the Economic Community of West African States, holden in Abuja, Nigeria, in the case of *Dorothy Njemanze and 3 Others v Nigeria*,[64] the Court of Justice of the West African Community of States adjudicated a well-renowned claim on sexual abuses and gender-based discriminations. In this case, the plaintiffs, Dorothy Njemanze and three others, alleged abductions against women on the street of Abuja, sexual assaults, violence, beatings by the Society against Prostitution and Child Labour in the company of the Abuja Environmental Protection Board and Nigerian Security agents. Some of the women were harassed, abused, sexually assaulted, and humiliated. These sad events were followed with unlawful detention in inhumane conditions without access to their counsels, families, food, or water during a minimum of 24 hours. They were not charged for any offence or given a reason for the said abduction. The next day, the claimants were released with no reason(s) for their arrests and detention, nor were they charged for any offence whatsoever. The lawyer of one of the complainants sent a complaint on her behalf to the Minister of the Federal Capital Territory, who responded by sending her a written apology. No further step/action/investigation was taken by the state authorities.

The plaintiffs approached the ECOWAS Court of Justice for, among others, the failure and/or refusal of the State of Nigeria to investigate, discipline, and prosecute the persons responsible for the violations of the plaintiffs' rights, the agents of the AEPB, the Nigerian Police, and the Nigeria Military, which constitute a violation of article 1 of the African Charter on Human and Peoples' Rights and Articles 5, 8, and 25 of the Maputo Protocol. The case was filed on 17 September 2014, and was a joint action between Institute for Human Rights and Development in Africa, IHRDA, Alliances for Africa, Nigerian Women Trust Fund, and the law firm of SPA Ajibade, with support from Open Society Initiative for West Africa (OSIWA).[65]

After hearing the defendant and concluding the investigations, the court, in its final judgment, declared that the failure on the part of the country of Nigeria to recognise, promote, and protect the rights of the plaintiffs and the failure to take measures to give effect to the rights of the plaintiffs constituted multiple violations of Articles 1, 2, 3, 5, and 18(3) of African Charter on Human and Peoples' Rights; articles 2, 3, 4(1) and (2), 5, 8, and 25 of the Maputo Protocol; Articles 2, 3, 5(a), and 15(1) of the Convention on the Elimination of All Forms of Discrimination Against Women; Articles 2(1) and (3), 3, 7, and 26 of the International Covenant on Civil and Political Rights; Articles 10, 11, 12, 13, and 16(1) of the Covenant Against Torture and other Cruel, Inhuman or Degrading Treatment or Punishment; and Articles 1, 2, 5, 7, and 8 of the Universal Declaration of Human Rights. Nigeria was ordered to pay 6 million to Naira and compensatory damages to each of the complainants, except the second one. The jurisprudential analysis of the decisions of the African human rights system has unveiled the legal capacity of females, whether girls or women, and victims of sexual harassment, to seek justice within the African Human Rights judicial institutions while relying on the dispositions of the Maputo Protocol.

States' Obligations

Human rights-based legal guarantees are certainly not alone sufficient to eradicate the gangrene of sexual harassment. Nevertheless, they are efficient and reliable. A human rights approach to ending sexual harassment is valuable, as it affords the opportunity to implement women's rights at both national and regional levels in Africa.[66] Nevertheless, the prior harmonisation of human rights standards at the state level is essential to foster the eradication of sexual harassment. A right enforcement necessitates an amendment of the existing laws in line with human rights standards. State parties under the Maputo Protocol have the legal obligation to combat all forms of discrimination against women through appropriate legislative, institutional, and other measures, most specifically those harmful practices which endanger the health and general well-being of women. In this regard, it is important for states to emphasise the principles of equality and non-discrimination between women and men and ensure their effective application.[67]

However, the architecture of the legal systems of many African countries is dualistic. As such, as in any dualist legal order, a treaty can have domestic legal effect only where steps prescribed by national law are taken to deliberately infuse the treaty into domestic law.[68] For an international legal norm to be applicable in the national legal order, it must be received through domestic legislative measures. The non-domestication of the Maputo Protocol by several African nations has hindered the implementation of the plethora of women's human rights in national legal systems. As an example, since the adoption of the Protocol on 11 July 2023, Nigeria is one of the signatories to the protocol but has failed to domesticate and fully implement its provisions. Section 12(1) of the Nigerian Constitution[69] requires a legislative enactment by the National Assembly before implementation of a treaty: 'No treaty between the Federation and any other country shall have the force of law to the extent to which any such treaty has been enacted into law by the National Assembly'.

In dualist systems of which many African countries are related, without the signature, ratification2, and domestication of the Maputo Protocol, states are not obligated to abide by and hold to the standards set by the protocol for female human rights. Domesticating the Maputo Protocol therefore stands as a legal obstacle to the accountability of perpetrators of sexual harassment in Nigeria and in many countries. This certainly poses devastating consequences on the human rights of women and girls in the country,[70] as well as the spread of sexual harassment. To remedy this legislative deadlock, the judiciary plays an important role in Africa to eliminate unfriendly female laws that impede female rights development.

Conclusion and Recommendations

At the end of this review, it is worth recalling the statistics prompting the quest for ending sexual harassment in Africa. In sub-Saharan Africa, almost 39% of girls are married before the age of 18; more than 70% of women report having been victims of domestic violence, including sexual violence; and more than 90% report having been the victims of sexual harassment and not feeling safe in public places.[71] Providing adequate, effective responses to cases of sexual harassment and gender-based violence filed within the African Human Rights system seems to be a fruitful enterprise. The review of the jurisprudence of the African Human Rights system in this chapter revealed an effective response in most cases through the lens of the dispositions of the Maputo Protocol. But still, a lot needs to be done for human rights mechanisms to become a perfected tool in the battle for the elimination of sexual harassment in Africa.

Ill-suited laws are still part of African legal frameworks, portraying stereotyped cultural and patriarchal traditions all vehicles of sexual harassment in family and social circles. Those retrograded behaviours are manifest in schools, offices, university lecture halls, and such. Those laws should be repealed and the perpetrators of sexual harassment duly prosecuted. The requirement of exhaustion of national remedies still prevents many victims from approaching the gate of the African Union human rights system. It is recommended that those rules of prosecution be flexible, as in the case of the ECOWAS Court of Justice, to accommodate this quest for justice. Finally, many states are yet to ratify the dispositions of the Maputo Protocol. Without the encapsulation of human rights treaties in the national corpus of African states' legislations, a state cannot be held accountable under human rights legal instruments for sexual harassment. It is expected that the domestication process will be completed.

Notes

1 The Istanbul Convention of the Council of Europe.
2 See Art 2 Directive 2002/73/EC of the European Parliament and of the Council of 23 September 2002 amending Council Directive 76/207/EEC on the implementation of the principle of equal treatment for men and women as regards access to employment, vocational training and promotion, and working conditions.
3 E Kismödi et al 'Advancing sexual health through human rights: The role of the law' (2015) 10/2 *Glob Public Health* 252–267.
4 T Jefferson 'Declaration of independence, 1776' US Department of State – Office of the Historian, https://history.state.gov/milestones/1776-1783/declaration.
5 Universal Declaration of Human Rights adopted by the United Nations General Assembly, Resolution 217 A(III) of 10 December 1948.
6 K Slote and C Cuthbert 'Domestic violence and sexual abuse: A women's human rights information sheet' (2000) *National Violence against Women Prevention Research Center Women's Rights Network Wellesley Centers for Women – Intimate Partner Sexual Abuse: A Human Rights Information Sheet*, https://mainweb-v.musc.edu/vawprevention/advocacy/humanrgts.shtml.
7 Rape and sexual violence: Human rights law and standards in the International Criminal Court, Amnesty International, 13.
8 See Sex Discrimination Act 1981 (Cth).
9 C MacKinnon *Sexual Harassment of Working Women* (Yale University Press, 1979) 1–55, 215–221, 239–255, 298–300.
10 See United Nations Declaration on the Elimination of Violence Against Women (1993); see also UN World Conference on Human Rights in Vienna (1993).
11 WordWeb Dictionary.
12 General Recommendation No 19(1) (1992) CEDAW.
13 Beijing Platform for Action, Para 112 (1995).
14 Art 12(c) of the Maputo Protocol.
15 Art 1 of the Maputo Protocol.
16 *Ibid* Art 4.

17 Art 3(1) of the Maputo protocol 'Every woman shall have the right to dignity inherent in a human being and to the recognition and protection of her human and legal rights'; see also Art 3(4), which provides that 'States Parties shall adopt and implement appropriate measures to ensure the protection of every woman's right to respect for her dignity and protection of women from all forms of violence, particularly sexual and verbal violence'.
18 *Ibid* Art 1.
19 The Guidelines on Combating Sexual Violence and its Consequences in Africa.
20 Sect 3(3.1) of the Niamey Guidelines.
21 E Durojaye 'The Niamey Guidelines to Combat Sexual Violence and its consequences in Africa and Sexual Harassment: A case study of Nigeria' (2022) 33/1 *Stellenbosch Law Review* 78–99.
22 B Nwabueze 'Constitutional law'.
23 Art 30 Organisation of African Unity, 1986.
24 Art 56(5) of the African Charter on Human and Peoples' Rights.
25 Art 7 of the Protocol to the African Court.
26 Art 2 of the Protocol to the African Court.
27 Algeria, Benin, Burkina Faso, Burundi, Cameroon, Chad, Cote d'Ivoire, Comoros, Congo, Gabon, Gambia, Ghana, Kenya, Libya, Lesotho, Mali, Malawi, Mozambique, Mauritania, Mauritius, Nigeria, Niger, Rwanda, Sahrawi Arab Democratic Republic, South Africa, Senegal, Tanzania, Togo, Tunisia, and Uganda.
28 Art 5(3) and 34(6) of the Protocol.
29 Art 5(3) of the Protocol.
30 Those eight States are: Benin, Burkina Faso, Cote d'Ivoire, Ghana, Malawi, Mali, Tanzania, and Tunisia.
31 Art 56 of the African Charter.
32 Special Mechanisms, African Commission on Human and Peoples' Rights (au.int)
33 Examples include: Advisory Committee on Budgetary and Staff Matters, Committee on the Protection of the Rights of People Living with HIV (PLHIV) and Those at Risk, Vulnerable to and Affected by HIV, Committee for the Prevention of Torture in Africa, Committee on Resolutions, Special Rapporteur on Freedom of Expression and Access to Information, Special Rapporteur on Human Rights Defenders, Special Rapporteur on Prisons and Conditions of Detention, Special Rapporteur on Refugees, Asylum Seekers, Migrants and Internally Displaced Persons, Special Rapporteur on Rights of Women, Working Group on Communications, Working Group on Death Penalty and Extra-Judicial, Summary or Arbitrary Killings in Africa, Working Group on Economic, Social and Cultural Rights, Working Group on Extractive Industries, Environment and Human Rights Violations, Working Group on Indigenous Populations/Communities in Africa, Working Group on Rights of Older Persons and People with Disabilities, etc.
34 Rule 99 of the Commission's 2010 Rules of Procedure.
35 https://achpr.au.int/en/mechanisms.
36 Adopted on 11 July 1990 and came into force on 29 November 1999.
37 www.ecowas.org.
38 Benin, Burkina Faso, Cape Verde, Côte d'Ivoire, Gambia, Ghana, Guinea, Guinea-Bissau, Liberia, Mali, Niger, Nigeria, Senegal, Sierra Leone, and Togo.
39 *SERAP v The President of the Federal Republic of Nigeria* ECW/CCJ/APP/07/10.
40 Art 11 and 15 ECOWAS Revised Treaty.
41 *Ibid* Art 9(2).
42 Art 1(h) of Protocol A/SP1/12/01; see also Art 9 of the 1991 Protocol which expands the jurisdiction and competence of the court to accommodate human rights claims.
43 Supplementary Protocol A/SP.1/01/05.

44 *Musa Saidykhan v The Republic of Gambia*, Suit No: ECW/CCJ/APP/11/07.
45 Agreements are binding.
46 (046/2016) [2018] AfCHPR 15; (African Court on Human and Peoples' Rights) Decision of 11 May 2018.
47 No 2011–087.
48 Art 16(a) and (b) of the Convention on the Elimination of All Forms of Discrimination Against Women CEDAW)
49 Art 2 Maputo Protocol and Art 16(a) and (b) Convention on the Elimination of All Forms of Discrimination Against Women CEDAW
50 Outcome of the Investigation of allegations of harassment against women and other institutional malpractices in the African Union Commission at https://au.int/en/pressreleases/20181122/outcome-investigation-allegations-harassment-against-women-and-other.
51 www.bbc.com/news/world-africa-46319227.
52 https://au.int/en/pressreleases/20181122/outcome-investigation-allegations-harassment-against-women-and-other
53 *Ibid.*
54 Point No 4, African Union Sexual Harassment Committee Report reads: 'iv) Sexual harassment policy: under active consideration by the Commission.
55 *Ibid.*
56 Communication 341/2007 adopted by the African Commission on Human and Peoples' Rights during the 19 Extra-Ordinary Session, from 16 to 25 February 2016.
57 equality_now_ethiopian_w_omen_lawyers_association_decision_2007_0.pdf (escr-net.org).
58 Art 16, 27 and 29 of the African Children's Charter.
59 Art I (k) of the Maputo Protocol.
60 Art 44 and 45 of the Treaty.
61 Communication No 006/Com/002/2015, Merits Decision, 31st Ordinary Session (2018).
62 Sect 302 Cameroon Penal Code Cameroonian Penal Code.
63 A Marew and B Alemtseyahe 'The ethiopian legal frameworks for the protection of women and girls from gender-based violence, Pan-African' (2021) 2/1 *Journal of Governance and Development*.
64 Suit No ECW/CCJ/APP/17 Judgment N° ECW/CCJ/JUD/08/17.
65 ECOWAS court orders Nigerian govt to pay N18 million to women maltreated for allegedly being prostitutes Premium Times Nigeria (premiumtimesng.com).
66 K Slote and C Cuthbert 'Domestic violence and sexual abuse: A women's human rights information sheet' *National Violence Against Women Prevention Research Center, Women's Rights Network Wellesley Centers for Women – Intimate Partner Sexual Abuse: A Human Rights Information Sheet*, musc.edu.
67 F Benya, S Widnall and P Johnson 'Legal and policy mechanisms for addressing sexual harassment' in F Benya, S Widnall and P Johnson (eds) *Sexual Harassment of Women: Climate, Culture, and Consequences in Academic Sciences, Engineering, and Medicine* (National Academies Press, 2018).
68 MN Shaw *International Law*, 8th ed (Cambridge University Press, 2017) 97–100.
69 1999 Constitution of the Federal Republic of Nigeria as amended.
70 J Nwabueze 'Women and law: Place and role of international human rights standards in combating unfriendly female laws in 'Strengthening the rule of law to promote women's right to equality and non-discrimination in Africa' Equality and Anti-Discrimination Research Group Africa, 2022.
71 https://achpr.au.int/en/node/848.

References

M Abebe and B Alemtseyahe 'The Ethiopian legal frameworks for the protection of women and girls from gender-based violence, Pan-African' (2021) 2/1 *PanAfrican Journal of Governance and Development* 1–21.

Advisory Committee on Budgetary and Staff Matters, Committee on the Protection of the Rights of People Living with HIV (PLHIV) and those at Risk, Vulnerable to and Affected by HIV.

F Benya, S Widnall and P Johnson 'Legal and policy mechanisms for addressing sexual harassment' in F Benya, S Widnall and P Johnson (eds) *Sexual Harassment of Women: Climate, Culture, and Consequences in Academic Sciences, Engineering, and Medicine* (National Academies Press, 2018).

Cameroon Penal Code Cameroonian Penal Code as Amended,

Communication 341/2007 adopted by the African Commission on Human and Peoples' Rights during the 19 Extra-Ordinary Session, from 16 to 25 February 2016.

Convention on the Elimination of All Forms of Discrimination against Women, 1979.

Directive 2002/73/EC of the European Parliament and of the Council of 23 September 2002 amending Council Directive 76/207/EEC on the Implementation of the Principle of Equal Treatment for Men and Women as Regards Access to Employment, Vocational Training and Promotion, and Working Conditions.

Dorothy Njemanze and 3 Others v Nigeria, Judgment N° ECW/CCJ/JUD/08/17.

E Durojaye 'The Niamey guidelines to combat sexual violence and its consequences in Africa and sexual harassment: A case study of Nigeria' (2022) 33/1 *Stellenbosch Law Review* 78–99.

General Recommendation No 19(1) (1992) CEDAW.

Institute for Human Rights and Development in Africa and Finders Group Initiative on behalf of TBA (a Minor) v Cameroon, Communication No 006/Com/002/2015, Merits Decision, 31st Ordinary Session (2018).

T Jefferson 'Declaration of independence, 1776' US Department of State – Office of the Historian, https://history.state.gov/milestones/1776-1783/declaration.

E Kismödi et al 'Advancing sexual health through human rights: The role of the law' (2015) 10/2 *Glob Public Health* 252–267.

C MacKinnon *Sexual Harassment of Working Women* (Yale University Press, 1979).

Musa Saidykhan v The Republic of Gambia, Suit No ECW/CCJ/APP/11/07.

J Nwabueze 'Curbing sexual harassment of students by educators in tertiary institutions in Nigeria: Place and role of legal polices' in AM Noel and DB Oppenheimer (eds) *The Global Me-Too Movement* (Full Court Press, 2020).

J Nwabueze 'Women and law: Place and role of international human rights standards in combating unfriendly female laws' in *Strengthening the Rule of Law to promote Women's Right to Equality and Non-discrimination in Africa* (Equality and Anti-Discrimination Research Group Africa, 2022).

Protocol to the African Charter on Human and People's Rights on the Rights of Women in Africa, 2003.

Rape and sexual violence: Human rights law and standards in the International Criminal Court, Amnesty International, 13.

Revised Treaty of the Economic Community of West African States (ECOWAS).

SERAP v The President of the Federal Republic of Nigeria ECW/CCJ/APP/07/10.

Sex Discrimination Act 1981 (Cth).

MN Shaw *International Law*, 8th ed (Cambridge University Press, 2017).

K Slote and C Cuthbert 'Domestic violence and sexual abuse: A women's human rights information sheet' (2000) *National Violence against Women Prevention Research Centre Women's Rights Network Wellesley Centres for Women – Intimate Partner Sexual Abuse: A Human Rights Information Sheet*, https://mainweb-v.musc.edu/vawprevention/advocacy/humanrgts.shtml.

Special Mechanisms, African Commission on Human and Peoples' Rights (au.int)

Suit No ECW/CCJ/APP/17 Judgment N° ECW/CCJ/JUD/08/17.

The Guidelines on Combating Sexual Violence and Its Consequences, 2017.

The Istanbul Convention on Preventing and Combating Violence Against Women and Domestic Violence, adopted by the Council of Europe on 11 May 2011. Entered into force on 1 August 2014.

Treaty establishing the Economic Community of West African States (ECOWAS) signed in Lagos on 28 May 1975.

United Nations Declaration on the Elimination of Violence against Women, adopted by General Assembly Resolution 48/104 of 20 December1993.

United Nations World Conference on Human Rights in Vienna, Austria from 14 to 25 June 1993.

Universal Declaration of Human Rights adopted by the United Nations General Assembly, Resolution 217 A(III) of 10 December 1948.

4 Single Incident, Big Impact

Exposing the Precarious Relationship Between Sexual Harassment and the Persistent Behaviour Standard

Furaha-Joy Sekai Saungweme and Megan E. Cistulli

Introduction

A major South African retail company found itself embroiled in a sexual harassment lawsuit involving one of its managers against an employee working under his direct chain of command. In this case, the complainant found herself at the receiving end of unwelcome conduct of a sexual nature when her immediate boss, the general manager, decided it would be humorous to slap her 'playfully' on her buttocks and then giggle. This assault, which could have been resolved within a period of 24 hours, escalated from a disciplinary process to an arbitration hearing, and then finally to the Labour Court of South Africa, leading to a judgment seven years after the incident in favour of the complainant.

In this chapter, we draw a thorough line between what constitutes sexual harassment as characterised under various laws which contextualise sexual harassment as 'persistent conduct' or a 'single incident'. We question the use of the word 'persistent' as a determinant factor in assessing the validity or viability of a sexual harassment claim and as an element which defines the prohibited act. We note that requiring the element of persistent conduct is to also be dismissive of a single incident of sexual harassment. Having said that, our analysis of court cases involving a single incident of sexual harassment suggests such a standard involves additional hurdles which a complainant must overcome, often framed around the test of seriousness. As we probe into what the courts take into account in determining the seriousness of a single-incident case before it can rise to the level of sexual harassment there is clearly a subjective and objective test employed by the courts that sets a higher bar to prove such an allegation as opposed to what must be established when the facts point towards a persistent pattern of sexually harassing behaviour. In the case of the single incident, a complainant must not only prove that the single incident of sexual harassment occurred but also that it was sufficiently serious. In contrast, in a claim of persistent sexually harassing behaviour the ordinary elements of sexual harassment would likely

DOI: 10.4324/9781003373308-4

suffice when established. We argue that the requirement of persistent conduct to define sexual harassment is an artificial and unnecessary standard and contributes to a perception that sexual harassment is a milder form of other kinds of gender-based violence. It is a moot point that when addressing the crime of rape, the criteria of 'persistent conduct' does not arise. In fact, it is sufficient on the allegation of rape for the relevant authorities to undertake investigations and prosecute if there is sufficient evidence. Indeed, it is a moot point that the offence of indecent exposure, for instance, is not dependent on whether or not the behaviour was persistent. On the same rationale, intimate partner violence (IPV) is not less severe on the simple assertion or evidence that 'it only happened once'. A legal absurdity would most certainly be created if in any of the previous scenarios a legal threshold of persistent behaviour was required to establish that the alleged conduct amounted to any form of violation or offence.

In juxtaposing the requirement of persistent conduct against the single incident, there are pertinent questions on what is a fair and reasonable balance involving the extent of application accorded to a subjective or objective test. The single-incident criteria, we argue, potentially undermines the subjectivity test and the experiences of a complainant because what constitutes 'serious' may be more subjective that objective. We look at specific sexual harassment laws in selected African countries and how the courts interplay persistent conduct and the single incident. Approaches adopted within the United Kingdom (UK) and United States of America (USA) also form part of our analysis, allowing a stronger comparative context of the legal and socio-cultural interpretations of the conflicting yet intersecting approaches to sexual harassment. In addition, we bring to the forefront a depiction of the cultural perceptions of sexual harassment across the various jurisdictions and how that ultimately influences the formation of legal terminology around persistent and incident standards.

Once Is Enough under South African Law: ShopRite Checkers Case

In the case of *Shoprite Checkers (Pty) Ltd v JL*,[1] a teller salesclerk was assisting the general manager to assess the status of an order. Whilst she was accessing a computer, the general manager slapped her on her left buttock, and immediately thereafter giggled as he walked out of the office space. A grievance was laid by the teller salesclerk leading to an investigation by Shoprite, during which the alleged perpetrator, the complainant, and witnesses were interviewed. The outcome of this investigation eventually led to the complainant being charged with making a false accusation of sexual harassment against her manager. The complainant sought redress through arbitration to which the arbitrator concluded that Shoprite had committed an unfair labour practice when it suspended the complainant; she was in fact unfairly constructively dismissed. In addition, the arbitrator found that the employee was unfairly discriminated against in that she was sexually harassed by her manager and that the employer was therefore liable in terms of Section 60 of the Employment Equity Act (EEA).[2] The fact that there was no history of animosity between them[3] also worked in her favour, as it tended to show lack of ill motive.

Shoprite appealed against the finding and award of compensation for the unfair discrimination claim based on sexual harassment, in terms of Section 10(8)6 of the EEA.[4] Part of its appeal strategy was the reliance on the fact that the sexual harassment in this particular incident was a single incident and therefore not worthy of the amount of award made to the complainant by the arbitrator.[5] This was argued despite the fact that South African law specifically lays out that a single incident constitutes sexual harassment. In addition, the appeal contended that the amount of compensation awarded was excessive given that the offence was not 'serious'. In support of this, Shoprite compared the compensation awarded in the case of *Ntsabo v Real Security*[6] for what it referred to as a 'far more serious sexual harassment', a case which was reflective of not only a pattern of harassing conduct but also involved sexual assault.

The facts of the case are pertinent to the question we are interrogating in this chapter, namely, the use of the single-incident test and persistent conduct standard created to establish sexual harassment. Whilst the appeal court found that the complainant was subjected to sexual harassment based on the single incident of sexual harassment, it did agree to a reduction; the arbitrators award was reduced from R50,000 to R25,000.[7] It appears that the court did find the argument of the single incident and the less serious nature of the conduct persuasive enough to reduce the original compensation.

The single incident is addressed under South Africa's Code of Good Practice on the Prevention and Elimination of Harassment in the Workplace[8] (harassment code) which became effective on 18 March 2022. The code distinguishes between and defines harassment and sexual harassment. Sexual harassment is defined as a form of unfair discrimination; it must be unwanted conduct of a sexual nature.[9] Under the definition of harassment, the theme of repeated and serious conduct is required to prove the offence of harassment. Harassment may occur because of a pattern of persistent conduct or a single instance or event. In the case of a single instance, harassment will be present if the conduct is of a serious nature.[10]

In stark contrast to the harassment definition, the code provides that a single incident of unwelcome sexual conduct may constitute sexual harassment[11] without any caveat; in other words, there is no standard provided in respect of what is serious. However, it can be reasonably argued that what constitutes 'serious' is subjective. Such a subjective test can be ascertained from the text of the code which provides that the test for establishing whether sexual harassment occurred includes specific factors, such as the impact of the sexual conduct on the employee.[12] Further to that, it is not necessary that the perpetrator is aware that the behaviour is unwelcome.[13] This strongly suggests that what is deemed serious is to a large extent dependent on the risk and harm perceived and experienced by the victim; indeed, a subjective test narrated from the perspective of the victim and yet subjective to objective testing by the courts. The argument therefore submitted by Shoprite alleging that the sexual harassment was only a single incident and not as serious as that which occurred in the Ntsabo case should have not, on that basis alone, led to a reduction in compensation. This was a misapplication of the law by the courts and a misinterpretation as submitted by Shoprite.

Notably, the South African position is one replicated under international law instruments such as the International Labour Organisation's (ILO) Convention on the Elimination of Violence and Harassment in the World of Work (ILO C190),[14] which recognises that violence and harassment including sexual harassment can be a single or repeated occurrence.[15] The publication of the code follows South Africa's ratification of the ILO C190.

Depending on the Circumstances? The UK Approach

UK law addresses sexual harassment through the Equality Act of 2010,[16] which defines sexual harassment as unwanted conduct of a sexual nature. Whilst the act is silent as to categorising sexual harassment within the context of a single incident or repeated conduct, the issue has been litigated in the UK courts. The Employment Appeal Tribunal[17] is an Independent Tribunal which determines legal disputes relating to employment law throughout Great Britain and is a superior court of record. One of the first cases which the tribunal dealt with on whether a single incident of sexual conduct amounts to 'harassment' was in the case of *Bracebridge Engineering Ltd v Darby*.[18] The facts of this case are that two of Mrs. Darby's male supervisors, Mr. Daly and Mr. Smith, allegedly grabbed and sexually assaulted Mrs. Darby in the manager's office at Bracebridge by forcibly groping and touching her 'private parts'. The tribunal rejected the respondent's argument that only a 'course' of conduct could constitute harassment and found that this single incident of sexual harassment was sufficiently detrimental to Mrs. Darby and therefore no pattern of harassment was necessary to a finding that she had been sexually harassed.

> The first point taken by Mr de Mello for the appellant company before us is that this was a single act, a single incident and it cannot properly be described as sexual harassment. He referred us to the definition in the Shorter Oxford English Dictionary. It seems to us that 'sexual harassment' is a phrase which can embody a whole number of notions. It would seem that whether or not harassment is a continuing course of conduct, there was here an act which was an act of discrimination against a woman because she was a woman, and it was a most unpleasant one, and one which in our judgment clearly falls within the proper intention and meaning of the Act. We would deplore any argument that could be raised that merely because it was a single incident – provided

> it is sufficiently serious, I think one must say that – that it could not fall within the wording of the subsection.[19]

According to the tribunal, such an act was serious enough to constitute sexual harassment for the purposes of the Sex Discrimination Act 1975,[20] which has now been consolidated into the Equality Act 2010.

The Employment Appeal Tribunal (EAT) also grappled with the question of the single incident in 1994 in the case of *In situ Cleaning Co Ltd and Anor v Heads*.[21] The tribunal noted that whether a single act of verbal sexual harassment would be sufficient to found a complaint was a question of fact and degree. In applying *Bracebridge*, the EAT upheld the tribunal's ruling that the comment 'hiya, big tits' from a male director to a female employee was serious enough to constitute sexual harassment. Concluding also that not only was intention not relevant, but a complaint should also be dealt with 'from the perception of the person aggrieved'.

However, the *Dos Santos v Preview Services* case[22] demonstrates how there may be circumstances where a single sexual remark is not serious enough in nature to constitute sexual harassment according to the tribunal. In this case, it held that the comment 'as long as it's not a sexual favour' by a male manager in reply to a female employee asking for a favour (for, in fact, an envelope) did not objectively constitute sexual harassment. The tribunal took into account the context of the long-standing professional relationship between the manager and the female employee, the fact that the comment had been intended to be a joke (albeit a poor joke), and that there had been a reasonably long delay before the female employee complained about the remark. However, this judgment does not undermine the clear pattern followed by the tribunal establishing that in the right circumstances, a one-off act of unwanted sexual conduct can constitute sexual harassment.

The Single Incident and Pervasive Standard under United States' Law

In this section, we explore the 'severe or pervasive' standard as codified in Title VII of the Civil Rights Act of 1964[23] and later interpreted by the US Supreme Court's decisions in the *Meritor Savings Bank v Vinson* case[24] and *Harris v Forklift Systems, Inc* case.[25] In the enforcement mechanism of Title VII, the US Equal Employment Opportunity Commission (EEOC) is also discussed.[26] Against that backdrop we contrast the approaches of state laws towards the single-incident rule and the federal 'severe or pervasive' standard. Specifically, we explore the New York State Human Rights Law (NYSHRL)[27] and how this likely influenced legislative developments in other states such as California.[28] It is important to note that US law adopted a federal legal system[29] whose effect and purpose is the enforceability of federal law at the national level.[30] Importantly, each state within the US has its own constitution and laws, which can expand or limit protections for people within each state. Upholding and shaping the broader federal system, the US Constitution[31] ratified in 1788 and adopted in 1789, is the supreme law of the land.

Title VII of the Civil Rights Act of 1964 and the EEOC

Title VII protects all persons from sexual harassment in the workplace.[32] It categorises sexual harassment as a form of sex discrimination that violates the law in two specific ways, either *quid pro quo* harassment[33] or an act that creates a hostile work environment.[34] An individual who has been sexually harassed should file a complaint with the EEOC, as it is the federal agency which investigates sexual harassment complaints in the workplace.[35]

The US Supreme Court's Interpretation of Title VII

According to the EEOC, 'harassment becomes unlawful where enduring the offensive conduct becomes a condition of continued employment, or the conduct is severe or pervasive enough to create a work environment that a reasonable person would consider intimidating, hostile, or abusive'.[36] The US Supreme Court and lower courts have interpreted Title VII's 'severe or pervasive' standard in the following legal decisions.

The *Meritor Savings Bank v Vinson* case was the first sexual harassment case brought before the US Supreme Court.[37] In this case, Michelle Vinson, a female bank employee, alleged that her supervisor subjected her to repeated sexual harassment. The court held that sexual harassment was a form of sex discrimination prohibited by Title VII of the Civil Rights Act of 1964. Crucial for the focus of this chapter, the court outlined the relationship between creating a hostile work environment and actions which are 'severe or pervasive'. The court held that 'For sexual harassment to be actionable, it must be sufficiently severe or pervasive to alter the conditions of [the victim's] employment and create an abusive working environment'.[38]

In 1993, the court revisited the 'severe or pervasive' standard in *Harris v Forklift Systems, Inc.*[39] In this case, Teresa Harris, a female employee at a forklift manufacturing company, sued her employer on the grounds that her boss, Charles Hardy, subjected her to frequent sexist and degrading comments, leading to a hostile work environment. Although the trial court found in favour of Forklift Systems, stating Harris did not prove the harassment was severe or pervasive enough to create a hostile work environment, the US Supreme Court decided:

> Conduct need not be tangible to alter the terms or conditions of employment; a discriminatory work environment based on racial or sexual innuendo, ridicule, and insult can be as intimidating and offensive as the most severe forms of overt discrimination.[40]

At the same time, the court reaffirmed the decision in *Meritor Savings Bank* and stated that 'Conduct that is not severe or pervasive enough to create an objectively hostile or abusive work environment an environment that a reasonable person would find hostile or abusive is beyond Title VII's purview'.[41] Essentially, the court reaffirmed that sexual harassment must be sufficiently severe or pervasive enough to create a hostile work environment. This approach was maintained in *Oncale v Sundowner Offshore Services, Inc.*[42] In this case, the plaintiff alleged his male co-workers repeatedly subjected him to sexual assault on an oil platform in the Gulf of Mexico. The crucial part of the court's holding not only established that same-sex harassment was covered under Title VII, but for the purposes of this chapter, the decision established that the sexual harassment must be objectively severe to constitute harassment.[43] In other words, the court established the standard for analysing same-sex harassment claims under the law, which states that 'a discriminatory work environment is one that is "permeated with discriminatory intimidation, ridicule, and insult" ', that is 'sufficiently severe or pervasive to alter the conditions of the victim's employment and create an abusive working environment'.[44]

In *Faragher v City of Boca Raton*,[45] the court addressed this issue when it concluded that 'isolated incidents' of sexual harassment, unless 'extremely serious', do not amount to a hostile work environment.[46] Whilst the facts of the *Faragher* case deal with a pattern of sexual harassment, the court touched on the issue of the single incident:

> So, in *Harris*, we explained that in order to be actionable under the statute, a sexually objectionable environment must be both objectively and subjectively offensive, one that a reasonable person would find hostile or abusive, and one that the victim in fact did perceive to be so. We directed courts to determine whether an environment is sufficiently hostile or abusive by 'looking at all the circumstances', including the 'frequency of the discriminatory conduct; its severity; whether it is physically threatening or humiliating, or a mere offensive utterance; and whether it unreasonably interferes with an employee's work performance'. Most recently, we explained that Title VII does not prohibit 'genuine but innocuous differences in the ways men and women routinely interact with members of the same sex and of the opposite sex'. A recurring point in these opinions is that 'simple teasing', offhand comments, and isolated incidents (unless extremely serious) will not amount to discriminatory changes in the 'terms and conditions of employment [footnotes omitted].[47]

Whether a single incident or pervasive behaviour, the crucial element underlying the justification for a legitimate claim of sexual harassment is degree of seriousness, which is exemplified in the following paragraphs in three single-incident cases. After the precedent set in the *Meritor Savings Bank*,[48] *Harris*,[49]

Faragher,[50] and *Oncale*[51] cases, single incidents of sexual harassment needed to pass muster under the same high standard of 'severe or pervasive'.

In the case of *Clark County School District v Breeden*,[52] the plaintiff, Regina Breeden, a Clark County bus driver, alleged a fellow employee, Fred Shore, made a sexually charged comment. Namely, he mentioned that if she wanted to keep her job, she should 'suck his private part'.[53] The plaintiff immediately reported the comment to her superior, who conducted a swift investigation and disciplined Shore with a three-day suspension. The Clark County School District offered to transfer the plaintiff to a new bus route; however, she declined. The court found that this single incident, although offensive, did not rise to the level of creating a hostile work environment and, therefore, held as follows:

> We conclude that a reasonable person could not have found that the single comment at issue here constituted actionable sexual harassment. The comment, while unquestionably offensive, does not remotely approach the threshold necessary to sustain a hostile work environment claim.[54]

Another example of a single-incident case is *Baskerville v Culligan Int'l Co.*[55] In this case, the plaintiff, a female employee alleged that her male supervisor had sexually assaulted her by grabbing her breasts and buttocks. The court found that this conduct was severe enough to create a hostile work environment, despite being a single incident. The court also reinforced the standard for establishing a hostile work environment:

> The standard for establishing a hostile work environment is high, and typically requires a showing of a pattern of offensive conduct. Isolated acts or occasional episodes of harassment will not merit relief under Title VII; in order to be actionable, the incidents of harassment must occur in concert or with a regularity that can reasonably be termed pervasive.[56]

A third example of a single incident of sexual harassment is the case of *Pryor v Jaffe and Asher*.[57] The plaintiff met her supervisor at a bar after work, who rubbed her hand in a sexually suggestive fashion; when the plaintiff attempted to leave, her supervisor pulled her in for an unwelcomed embrace and kiss. The court concluded that the plaintiff's allegations about this single incident were sufficient to sustain a claim of sexual harassment.

New York State Human Rights Law (NYSHRL)

The New York State Human Rights Law (NYSHRL),[58] codified in Chapter 18 Article 15 of the New York Consolidated Laws,[59] provides a key example of a state civil rights law that contrasts in approach towards the severe or pervasive standard required to establish sexual harassment under federal law. Title VII's 'severe or pervasive' standard is not applicable under the NYSHRL as of 2019 following an amendment.[60] Specifically, the amendment eliminated the requirement that sexual harassment needs to be 'severe or pervasive' to be actionable. The NYSHRL is not to be confused with the New York City Human Rights Law (NYCHRL),[61] which is codified in Title 8 of the Administrative Code of the City of New York. The NYCHRL only applies to employers in New York City.

The NYSHRL defines sexual harassment as:

> unwelcome conduct of a sexual nature, such as unwelcome sexual advances, requests for sexual favours, and other verbal, nonverbal, or physical conduct of a sexual nature, when such conduct has the purpose or effect of unreasonably interfering with an individual's work performance or creating an intimidating, hostile, or offensive work environment.[62]

The NYSHRL standard is even broader than federal law in that a single incident is enough to raise a claim of sexual harassment. This means there is a broader protection for employees and increased access to justice when faced with a single incident of sexual harassment.

For example, in the same-sex sexual harassment case of *Perry v Slensby*,[63] the male plaintiff alleged his male supervisor massaged his shoulders inappropriately whilst making lewd sexual comments. The court found that the single incident was sufficient to state a plausible claim for sexual harassment.[64] Although the single incident is sufficient to bring a claim, the incident may not hold water in court. In the *Perry* case, the incident did not hold up in court:

> while a single episode may be sufficient to give rise to a hostile work environment claim, the booking-room incident falls short of the severity required to make out such a claim. Compare *Alfano v Costello*, 294 F.3d 365, 374 (2d Cir. 2002) (noting that generally 'episodic' events will generally not suffice to establish a hostile work environment), with *Mathirampuzha v Potter*, 548 F.3d 70, 79 (2d Cir. 2008) (noting that a single incident of 'rape, for example' could create a hostile work environment (internal quotations omitted)). We have emphasized that for a single incident to suffice for a hostile work environment claim, it must be 'extraordinarily severe'. [footnotes omitted][65]

This approach by New York of broadening sexual harassment to include a single incident has impacted other states across the US. An example being California, whereby in January of 2018, the California Legislature held a hearing to examine the 'severe or pervasive' standard and invited New York Human Rights Commissioner Carmelyn Malalis to speak on the issue.[66]

Following this hearing, the California Legislature passed Senate Bill 1300[67] in 2018 addressing sexual harassment.[68] SB 1300 amended § 12923 of the California Government Code, encouraging CA courts to apply a more lenient standard as compared to the demanding criterion outlined in the 'severe or pervasive'.[69] One of the most notable changes to § 12923 of the California Government Code aids the California Legislature and other California courts in rejecting the decision of *Brooks v City of San Mateo* (2000).[70] Specifically, Section b of the California Government Code § 12923 explicitly states:

> A single incident of harassing conduct is sufficient to create a triable issue regarding the existence of a hostile work environment if the harassing conduct has unreasonably interfered with the plaintiff's work performance or created an intimidating, hostile, or offensive working environment. In that regard, the **Legislature hereby declares its rejection of the United States Court of Appeals for the 9th Circuit's opinion in *Brooks v City of San Mateo* (2000) 229 F.3d 917 and states that the opinion shall not be used in determining what kind of conduct is sufficiently severe or pervasive to constitute a violation of the California Fair Employment and Housing Act.**
>
> (emphasis added)

In *Brooks*, the plaintiff and then-police officer Katherine Brooks filed suit after several male police officers made derogatory comments against women, displayed pornographic materials in the workplace, and touched her inappropriately over her breast. The issue was whether an employer could be held liable for their employee's single incident of sexual harassment. The US Supreme Court found in the *Brooks* case that

> [T]he one-time touching of Brooks's breast and stomach over her sweater does not rise to the level of a hostile work environment. Because the conduct complained of was not severe or pervasive, the city is not liable for the actions of [the co-worker].[71]

Consequently, SB 1300 gives the California lower courts the option to reject the court's rationale in the *Brooks* decision when deciding what kind of conduct is sufficiently severe or pervasive to constitute a violation of the California Fair Employment and Housing Act. SB 1300 expands the definition of unlawful harassment while simultaneously reducing the plaintiff's burden of proof, which opens the door for more single-incident claims to go to trial.

All in all, California and New York provide two examples of states with legislation combatting the federal 'severe or pervasive' standard. Namely, CA SB 1300 helps guide CA courts and legislators by encouraging a more lenient standard when adjudicating claims of sexual harassment, shifting away from the federal 'severe or pervasive' standard.

For example, SB 1300 offers courts the empowerment to reject the 'single incident' defence on summary judgement when the facts of a case reflect egregious sexually offensive conduct. Along a similar vein, the entire state of New York, under the NYSHRL, posits that the 'severe or pervasive' standard is too stringent a requirement to meet for a plaintiff when bringing a claim of unlawful harassment. In brief, when juxtaposing state and federal laws in the United States, the NYSHRL and the CA SB 1300 exemplify expanded protections for people faced with one-off incidents of sexual harassment. Of course, the federal 'severe or pervasive' standard codified in Title VII and US Supreme Court jurisprudence continues to permeate and influence the societal expectation that sexual harassment requires pervasive behaviour.

Once Is Not Enough? Kenya Laws Acquiescence to the Pervasive and Persistent Standard

Kenya law addresses sexual harassment through two principal laws, namely the Employment Act[72] as well as the Sexual Offences Act.[73] Whilst the Employment Act is silent as to the persistent or one-off nature of sexual harassment, the Sexual Offences Act is not. Section 23 provides that:

> Any person, who being in a position of authority, or holding a public office, who persistently makes any sexual advances or requests which he or she knows, or has reasonable grounds to know, are unwelcome, is guilty of the offence of sexual harassment and shall be liable to imprisonment for a term of not less than three years or to a fine of not less than one hundred thousand shillings or to both.

For conduct to rise to the level of sexual harassment under the act, it must be persistent; however, the veracity and efficacy of the persistent nature of the act has not been tested in Kenyan courts. This may largely be due to the fact that an allegation of sexual harassment as prescribed by the Sexual Offences Act has not been brought before the criminal courts. Instead, sexual harassment has been litigated primarily through the civil courts and on a reliance of the Employment Act, which defines sexual harassment broadly as of a *quid pro quo* nature or that which creates a hostile environment. Sexual harassment under the Employment Act must be of a sexual nature, unwelcome and can be written, visual, or physical, direct, indirect, and impacting negatively on the employee's employment, job performance, or job satisfaction.[74]

The Employment and Labour Relations Court (ELR)[75] is governed by the Employment and Labour Relations Act,[76] which grants the ELR Court the authority to adjudicate on 'disputes relating to or arising out of employment disputes between the employer and the employee' including matters relating to sexual harassment.[77] Under the Employment Act, there is no burden to prove a pattern of behaviour nor the seriousness of a single incident of sexual harassment. It is sufficient that the sexual harassment in question meets the requirements of the law.

In the matter between *JWN v Securex Agencies (K) Limited Civil*,[78] a claim for damages in respect of unfair termination was sought within the context of allegations of a sexual nature made against the claimant publicly and which were unfair, unreasonable, irrational, and disregarded the human dignity of the claimant. The facts were that the claimant was employed as a security guard. Allegations of a video surveillance of the claimant engaging in sexual acts whilst on duty arose and were investigated without the knowledge of the claimant. In fact, the claimant only became aware that she had been the subject of an investigation after its conclusion when the announcement was made to her and in front of her colleagues. This embarrassed and humiliated her, particularly because of the sexual nature of the alleged misconduct. This set of circumstances would not fall squarely within a legal description of a one-off sexual incident, nor could it be perceived as a pattern or persistent sexually harassing conduct. It is a unique set of circumstances which turns mainly on the sexual nature of the allegations. The court, in finding that the claimant had been sexually harassed within the meaning of section 6(1)(b) of the Employment Act did so on the basis that 'an employee is sexually harassed if the employer of that employee or a representative of that employer or a co-worker uses language *whether written or spoken* of a sexual nature'.

While we question whether the facts of this case truly meet the requirements of what constitutes sexual harassment,[79] the facts hang in between what could potentially be labelled a one-off sexual harassment incident and persistent conduct of a sexual nature. The case of *POV v Board of Trustees, AF and 2 Others*[80] represents another sexual harassment matter dealt with by the Employment and Labour Relations Court of Kenya which leans towards a potentially one-off incident of sexual harassment. The facts of this case are that the claimant was employed by the first respondent through the second respondent as a training and investigative consultant in Kenya for a period of two years commencing 5 January 2010. Her work was to travel nationally and regionally engaging with women farmers. The second respondent interviewed the claimant, leading the contract of employment being signed between the claimant and the second respondent. On a trip to Swaziland, the second respondent began to make sexual innuendos, telling the claimant that he found her attractive.

During this trip, he angrily claimed that he had spent money on her and questioned why she had rebuffed his proposal for a romantic lunch. The second respondent then proceeded to book a hotel room for the two to share on this work-related trip, thus forcing her to sleep on the floor. She reported the incident to her brother and a ticket for her return to Kenya was purchased. On her return, she immediately lodged a complaint with the company. However, on his return to Kenya, the second respondent proceeded to terminate her contract through an e-mail communication. The reason for termination was said to be the claimant's alleged misconduct in South Africa; her salary for that month was not paid. She wrote a letter of demand through her lawyers seeking damages, notice, and unpaid salary from the respondents. Any defence of a one-off incident would not stand because there had been prior incidences in Malaysia and Whistling Thorns where she had rebuffed his advances. It was the South Africa incident that led her to file a complaint. In addition, even if this had been a case of a single incident, we submit that the additional consideration of the seriousness of the conduct would have been impossible for the second respondent to rely on given the physical assault.

What can be deduced from the two discussed cases is that is that any consideration of sexual harassment within the context of persistent conduct or a single one-off incident has not yet been evaluated by the courts to determine the occurrence of sexual harassment. Furthermore, the inclusion of the persistent nature of sexually harassing behaviour contained under the Sexual Offences Act appears to have no rational connection to the developing jurisprudence of sexual harassment in Kenya's employment law; in fact, if left unaddressed, we argue that this indirectly allows for a single-incident defence under either of the two sexual harassment laws.

Generally, the requirement of establishing persistent conduct has not been emulated in other African jurisdictions with similar sexual harassment laws. Neither have we detected any provisions alluding to the recognition of a single incident meeting the standard of sexual harassment as in the case of South Africa. To underscore this, we will discuss in brief two of Kenya's neighbour's approaches; namely, Tanzania and Uganda and their interpretation of sexual harassment and the single incident.

Neither Here nor There? Tanzania, Uganda, and Zimbabwe

Under Tanzania's Sexual Offences Act,[81] 'any person who, with intention, assaults or by use of criminal force, sexually harasses another person, or by the use of words or actions, causes sexual annoyance or harassment to such other person, commits the offence of sexual harassment'.[82] The criminalisation of sexual harassment under Tanzania law does not raise the issue of persistent conduct or a single incident as a determinant factor.

The Employment and Labour Relations Act of Tanzania[83] requires every employer to promote equality and eliminate discrimination in any employment policy or practice.[84] The act, however, does not specifically refer to sexual harassment, neither is there any reference to 'persistent' conduct or the single incident. Uganda's Employment Law Act[85] has provisions specific to sexual harassment defined as a direct or implicit request to an employee for sexual intercourse, sexual contact, or any other form of sexual activity that contains:

- an implied or express promise of preferential treatment in employment;
- an implied or express threat of detrimental treatment in employment;
- an implied or express threat about the present or future employment status of the employee.[86]

Closer to the jurisdiction of South Africa is Zimbabwe, which defines sexual harassment under its labour law[87] as an unfair labour practice.[88] This occurs when an employer demands sexual favours from an employee in specific circumstances expounded on by the act. None of these acts require that there be a pattern of behaviour established or any consideration of whether the prohibited conduct is a one-off incident.

Conclusion

The requirement that sexual harassment must be persistent in nature to substantiate the offence of sexual harassment is clearly erroneous and allows for harmful judicial interpretations on matters brought before them. This was demonstrated in the US *Clark County School District* case where the conduct did not amount to creating a hostile environment primarily because it was deemed to be a one-off occurrence. Similarly, in the US case of *Brooks*, an allegation of sexual harassment was also rejected on the basis that it failed to pass the so-called severe or pervasive standard; in short, the court assessed that a single incident failed to meet the standards established under the US federal law.

We also found that whilst there are advantages to move away from the persistent or the severe or pervasive standard, a reliance on ensuring that the single incident becomes a viable element of sexual harassment is not necessarily a cure to the gap created by the persistent conduct requirement. This is especially so where the success of a single-incident claim is dependent on an embedded test of seriousness. In both the cases of *Baskerville* and *Pryor*, cited under the US section of our chapter, the court found in favour of the victims of sexual harassment because the single incident of sexual harassment in both cases was sufficiently serious in the eyes of the court.

As was highlighted in the first section of our chapter, under South African law, a single incident is specifically cited as being sufficient to support a claim of sexual harassment. In other words, it will not suffice to argue as a defence that the alleged sexual harassment in question was a one-off incident. Yet, despite this law, the defendant company on appeal in the Shoprite case relied on the single incident as a defence to not only have the arbitrators award overturned but to also seek a lower punitive amount which had been granted to the complainant on the basis that the single incident in question did not rise to degree of seriousness. Shoprite contended that the compensation awarded in the case of *Ntsabo v Real Security*[89] was in respect of a 'far more serious sexual harassment' with a clear pattern of harassing conduct and which also involved sexual assault. The court agreed and reduced the original award made to the complainant based on the seriousness of the sexual harassment.

The apparent implication is that even where sexual harassment laws expressly recognise the validity of a single incident in support of a sexual harassment claim, a further legal hurdle must be overcome in the form of the seriousness of the single incident. The question of the single incident arose in the 1994 UK case of *In Situ Cleaning Co Ltd and Anor v Head.*[90] The

Employment Appeal Tribunal essentially found for a single act to rise to the level of sexual harassment as a question of fact and degree. In addition to this, we would add that a finding of sexual harassment in a single-incident case should involve a subjective enquiry; one which considers the impact that the act had on the complainant. This would clearly entail assessing the facts as well as the psychological, emotional, and mental impact of the single incident.

Questions such as how the complainant felt after the alleged words or actions were made, what was the demeanour of the complainant before and after the alleged words or actions were made, and how was the complainant treated by co-workers and management after the sexual harassment. The potential probing questions are not exhaustive, but they are a critical approach to a holistic objective and subjective assessment of the seriousness of the sexual harassment. The risk of maintaining a purely objective standard is that it can lead to an injustice with regards to the outcome of the court case at hand. The injustice, put quite simply, lies in failing to acknowledge and consider the impact of a single incident of sexual harassment through the lens of the victim.

Notes

1 The Labour Court of South Africa, C 886/17and C627/2018.
2 Para 34 of the Shoprite case.
3 Para 24 of the Shoprite case
4 A person affected by an award made by a commissioner of the CCMA pursuant to a dispute contemplated in subsection (6)(aA) may appeal to the Labour Court against that award within 14 days of the date of the award, but the Labour Court, on good cause shown, may extend the period within which that person may appeal.
5 Para 78 of the Shoprite case.
6 *Ntsabo v Real Security* CC (2003) 24 ILJ 2341 (LC).
7 Para 80.
8 Government Gazette, 18 March 2022 No 46056. It replaced the Amended Code of Good Practice on the Handling of Sexual Harassment Cases in the Workplace, published in 2005 and provides guidance to employers and employees on the elimination and prevention of harassment as a form of unfair discrimination in the workplace.
9 Art 5 and 5.2.
10 Harassment Code, Art 4.5.1.
11 Art 5.2.7.
12 Art 5.3.2.4.
13 Art 5.3.1.
14 Eliminating Violence and Harassment in the World of Work Convention No 190, Recommendation No 206, and the accompanying Resolution. Convened at Geneva by the Governing Body of the International Labour Office and having met in its 108th (Centenary) Session on 10 June 2019.
15 C190 Art 1(a)(b).
16 UK Equality Act 2010, Chapter 15, Sect 26(2).
17 Employment Tribunals Act 1996, Sect 20.
18 *Bracebridge Engineering Ltd v Darby* [1990] IRLR 3.

19 Para 9.
20 Sex Discrimination Act 1975, Sect 1(1)(a), 6(2)(b), 41(1) and Employment Protection (Consolidation) Act 1978, Sect 55(2)(c).
21 [1994] UKEAT 576/92/0505/ 1995 IRLR 4. Appeal No EAT/576/92.
22 *Dos Santos v Preview Services LTD* ET/2700170/10.
23 Title VII of the Civil Rights Act of 1964, 42 USC §§ 2000e et seq (1964).
24 *Meritor Savings Bank v. Vinson*, 477 US 57 (1986).
25 *Harris v Forklift Systems Inc*, 510 US 17 (1993).
26 US Department of State 'Harassment' Equal Employment Opportunity Commission, https://www.eeoc.gov/harassment.
27 NY Exec Law § 290–301.
28 Senate Bill 1300 (enacted), 2018 Cal Stats ch 955 (West).
29 For further reading on federalism, please *see* KE Whittington 'The constitution and federalism' (2014) 13 *Geo J L and Pub Pol'y* 3; J Bulman-Pozen and HK Gerken 'Federalism and separation of powers in the United States' (2014) 127 *The Harvard Law Review* 2230; AF William 'The political economy of American federalism' (2015) 9 *Journal of Economic Surveys* 800.
30 Entities include organisations, businesses, and individuals within the United States.
31 US Constitution (1787).
32 Notably, Title VII applies to employers with 15 or more employees, including state and local governments.
33 Civil Rights Act 1964, s 2000e-2(a)(1). For further reading on quid pro quo harassment *see* CA MacKinnon 'Sexual harassment of working women: A case of sex discrimination' (1979) *Yale Law Journal*, 891–932.
34 Civil Rights Act 1964, s 2000e-2(a)(1).
35 For further reading on the EEOC, *see* AJ Colvin and DM Zorn 'The power of process: The role of the Equal Employment Opportunity Commission in employment discrimination litigation' (2019) 53/3 *Law and Society Review* 719–750.
36 Equal Employment Opportunity Commission 'Harassment' www.eeoc.gov/harassment (accessed on 24 April 2023).
37 *Meritor Savings Bank v Vinson*, 477 US 57 (1986).
38 *Meritor Savings Bank v Vinson*, 477 US 57, 67 (1986).
39 *Harris v Forklift Sys Inc*, 510 US 17 (1993).
40 *Harris v Forklift Systems Inc*, 510 US 17, 21–22 (1993).
41 *Harris v Forklift Systems Inc*, 510 US 17, 21 (1993).
42 *Oncale v Sundowner Offshore Services, Inc*, 523 US 75 (1998).
43 *Oncale v Sundowner Offshore Services, Inc*, 523 US 75, 78 (1998) (holding that 'nothing in Title VII necessarily bars a claim of discrimination 'because of . . . sex' merely because the plaintiff and defendant . . . are of the same sex'; at 78 (explaining that same-sex harassment 'cannot be ignored merely because the harasser and victim are of the same sex' and that 'the objective severity of harassment should be judged from the perspective of a reasonable person in the plaintiff's position') at 81 (stating that 'mere utterance of an . . . epithet which engenders offensive feelings in an employee does not sufficiently affect the conditions of employment to implicate Title VII) at 82 (holding that 'a discriminatory work environment is one that is 'permeated with discriminatory intimidation, ridicule, and insult', that is 'sufficiently severe or pervasive to alter the conditions of the victim's employment and create an abusive working environment' ")
44 *Oncale v Sundowner Offshore Services, Inc*, 523 US 75, 82 (1998).
45 *Faragher v City of Boca Raton*, 524 US 775 (1998).
46 *Faragher v City of Boca Raton*, 524 US 775, 787 (1998).
47 *Ibid.*

48 *Meritor Savings Bank v Vinson*, 477 US 57 (1986).
49 *Harris v Forklift Sys Inc*, 510 US 17 (1993).
50 *Faragher v City of Boca Raton*, 524 US 775 (1998).
51 *Oncale v Sundowner Offshore Services, Inc*, 523 US 75, 82 (1998).
52 *Clark County School District v Breeden*, 532 US 268 (2001).
53 *Clark County School District v Breeden*, 532 US 268, 271 (2001) (quoting plaintiff's allegations of sexual harassment).
54 *Clark County School District v Breeden*, 532 US 268, 271 (2001).
55 *Baskerville v Culligan Intern Co*, 50 F.3d 428 (7th Cir 1995).
56 *Baskerville v Culligan Intern Co*, 50 F.3d 428, 430 (7th Cir 1995).
57 *Pryor v Jaffe and Asher, LLP*, 992 F Supp 2d 252 (SDNY 2014).
58 NY Exec Law § 290–301.
59 New York State Senate, Assembly Bill A8421 (2019), https://legislation.nysenate.gov/pdf/bills/2019/A8421.
60 New York State Human Rights Law § 292 et seq (McKinney 2019), as amended by NYL 2019, ch 95.
61 Administrative Code of the City of New York, Title 8.
62 New York State Department of Labour 'Sexual harassment prevention' *New York*, www.ny.gov/programs/combating-sexual-harassment-workplace/sexual-harassment-prevention.
63 *Perry v Slensby* No 19–2706 (2d Cir Jun 3, 2020). Find the original case here: https://pospislaw.com/wp-content/uploads/2018/03/Perry-v.-Slensby-SDNY-16-cv-8947-Feb.-28–2018.pdf.
64 *Ibid* 3–4.
65 *Ibid*.
66 California Legislature, Senate Committee on Judiciary, Select Committee on Women, Work and Families, and California Legislative Women's Caucus 'Justice for victims: Re-examining California's legal standards for sexual harassment' (Informational Hearing, 11 January 2018, State Capitol, Hearing Room 4203).
67 California Omnibus Sexual Harassment Bill, SB 1300, 2017–2018 Leg, Reg Sess (Cal 2018).
68 Senate Bill 1300 (enacted), 2018 Cal Stats ch 955 (West).
69 CA Govt Code § 12923 (2022).
70 *Brooks v City of San Mateo* (2000) (9th Cir.) 229 F.3d 917.
71 *Brooks v City of San Mateo*, 229 F.3d 917 at 926 (9th Cir. 2000).
72 Employment Act No 11 of 2007. Date of assent; 22 October 2007 Date of commencement; 2 June 2008.
73 The Sexual Offences Act No 3 of 2006 date of Assent: 14 July 2006, date of Commencement; 21 July 2006.
74 Sect 6 of the Employment Act.
75 Art 162 of the Constitution of Kenya, 2010 establishes the Employment and Labour Relations Court
76 ELR Act No 20 of 2011. Date of assent, 27 August 2011. Date of commencement, 30 August 2011.
77 *Ibid* ELR Act.
78 *JWN v Securex Agencies (K) Limited Civil* Case No 359 of 2007.
79 A case of defamation might have been more legally accurate.
80 *POV v Board of Trustees, AF and 2 Others* [2014] EKLR.
81 Tanzania Sexual Offences Special Provisions Act, Act No 4 of [1998], 1 July 1998, www.refworld.org/docid/3ae6b5098.html.
82 *Ibid*, Part 12, Section 138D.
83 Tanzania, Employment and Labour Relations Act, of 2004 (No 6 of 2004) [CAP. 366 R.E. 2019].
84 Sect 7: Sub-Part C: Discrimination.

85 Uganda Employment Act, 2006 Employment (Sexual Harassment) Regulations, 2012 Statutory Instrument 15 of 2012, Published in Uganda Gazette No 21 on 20 April 2012, Assented to on 28 April 2011, Commenced on 20 April 2012.
86 *Ibid*, Part 2: Interpretation.
87 Zimbabwe, Labour Act [Chapter 28:01][short title amended by section 2 of Act 17 of 2002].
88 Part III – Unfair labour practices 8(g).
89 *Ntsabo v Real Security* CC (2003) 24 ILJ 2341 (LC).
90 [1994] UKEAT 576/92/0505/ 1995 IRLR 4. Appeal No EAT/576/92.

References

Administrative Code of the City of New York, Title 8.

Baskerville v Culligan Intern Co 50 F.3d 428 (7th Cir 1995).

Baskerville v Culligan Intern Co 50 F.3d 428, 430 (7th Cir 1995).

Bracebridge Engineering Ltd v Darby [1990] IRLR 3.

Brooks v City of San Mateo 229 F.3d 917 (9th Cir. 2000).

Brooks v City of San Mateo 229 F.3d 917 at 926 (9th Cir. 2000).

J Bulman-Pozen and H Gerken 'Federalism and separation of powers in the United States' (2014) 127 *Harvard Law Review* 2230.

CA Govt Code § 12923 (2022).

California Legislature, Senate Committee on Judiciary, Select Committee on Women, Work & Families, and California Legislative Women's Caucus 'Justice for victims: Re-examining California's legal standards for sexual harassment' (Informational Hearing, 11 January 2018, State Capitol, Hearing Room 4203).

California Omnibus Sexual Harassment Bill, SB 1300, 2017–2018 Leg, Reg Sess (Cal 2018).

Civil Rights Act passed by US Congress on 2 July 1964.

Clark County School District v Breeden 532 US 268 (2001).

Clark County School District v Breeden 532 US 268, 271 (2001).

AJ Colvin and DM Zorn 'The power of process: The role of the equal employment opportunity commission in employment discrimination litigation' (2019) 53/3 *Law and Society Review* 719–750.

Constitution of Kenya, 2010 establishes the Employment and Labour Relations Court.

Constitution of the United States Constitution, signed and adopted on 17 September1787.

Dos Santos v Preview Services LTD ET/2700170/10.

Eliminating Violence and Harassment in the World of Work Convention No 190, Recommendation No 206, and the accompanying Resolution, convened at Geneva by the Governing Body of the International Labour Office and having met in its 108th (Centenary) Session on 10 June 2019.

ELR Act No 20 of 2011. Date of assent, 27 August 2011. Date of commencement, 30 August 2011.

Employment Act No 11 of 2007. Date of assent, 22 October 2007. Date of commencement, 2 June 2008.

Employment Protection (Consolidation) Act of 1978 ch 44 (UK). Date of assent, 31 July 1978.

Employment Tribunals Act of 1996 ch 17. Date of assent, 22 May 1996.

Equal Employment Opportunity Commission 'Harassment' www.eeoc.gov/harassment (accessed on 24 April 2023).
Faragher v City of Boca Raton 524 US 775 (1998).
Faragher v City of Boca Raton 524 US 775 787 (1998).
W Fischel 'The political economy of American federalism' (2015) 9 *Journal Economic Survey* 800.
Government Gazette, 18 March 2022 No. 46056, replaced the Amended Code of Good Practice on the Handling of Sexual Harassment Cases in the Workplace, published in 2005.
Harris v Forklift Systems Inc 510 US 17 (1993).
Harris v Forklift Systems Inc 510 US 17, 21–22 (1993).
In situ Cleaning Co Ltd and Anor v Heads [1994] UKEAT 576/92/0505/ 1995 IRLR 4. Appeal No EAT/576/92.
JWN v Securex Agencies (K) Limited Civil Case No 359 of 2007.
CA MacKinnon 'Sexual harassment of working women: A case of sex discrimination' (1979) *Yale Law Journal* 891–932.
Meritor Savings Bank v Vinson 477 US 57 (1986).
Meritor Savings Bank v Vinson 477 US 57, 67 (1986).
New York State Department of Labour 'Sexual Harassment Prevention' *New York*. www.ny.gov/programs/combating-sexual-harassment-workplace/sexual-harassment-prevention.
New York State Human Rights Law § 292 et seq. (McKinney 2019), as amended by NYL 2019.
New York State Senate, Assembly Bill A8421 (2019). https://legislation.nysenate.gov/pdf/bills/2019/A8421.
Ntsabo v Real Security CC (2003) 24 ILJ 2341 (LC).
Oncale v Sundowner Offshore Services Inc 523 US 75 (1998).
Oncale v Sundowner Offshore Services Inc 523 US 75, 78 (1998).
Oncale v Sundowner Offshore Services Inc 523 US 75, 82 (1998).
Perry v Slensby No 19–2706 (2d Cir Jun 3, 2020). Find the original case here: https://pospislaw.com/wp-content/uploads/2018/03/Perry-v.-Slensby-SDNY-16-cv-8947-Feb.-28–2018.pdf.
Perry v Slensby, No 19–2706 at 3–4 (2d Cir. Jun. 3, 2020).
POV v Board of Trustees, AF and 2 Others [2014] EKLR.
Pryor v Jaffe and Asher, LLP 992 F Supp 2d 252 (SDNY 2014).
Senate Bill 1300 (enacted), 2018 Cal Stats ch 955 (West).
Sex Discrimination Act of 1975 ch 65 (UK). Date of assent, 12 November 1975.
Tanzania, Employment and Labour Relations Act, of 2004 (No 6 of 2004) [CAP. 366 R.E. 2019].
Tanzania Sexual Offences Special Provisions Act, Act No 4 of [1998], 1 July 1998, www.refworld.org/docid/3ae6b5098.html.
The Labour Court of South Africa, C 886/17and C627/2018.
The Sexual Offences Act No 3 of 2006 Date of assent, 14 July 2006 Date of commencement, 21 July 2006.
Title VII of the Civil Rights Act of 1964, 42 USC §§ 2000e et seq (1964).
Uganda Employment Act, 2006 Employment (Sexual Harassment) Regulations, 2012 Statutory Instrument 15 of 2012, Published in Uganda Gazette No 21 on 20 April 2012, Assented to on 28 April 2011, Commenced on 20 April 2012.

United Kingdom Equality Act of 2010 ch 15 (UK). Date of assent, 8 April 2010. Date of Commencement, 1 October 2010.

KE Whittington 'The constitution and federalism' (2014) 13 *The Georgetown Journal of Law & Public Policy*.

Zimbabwe, Labour Act [Chapter 28:01][short title amended by section 2 of Act 17 of 2002].

5 A Critical Analysis of Vicarious Liability for Sexual Harassment in South Africa

Yondela Ndema

Introduction

In this chapter, I analyse the historical development of the common-law remedy of vicarious liability through case law and legislation on sexual harassment in South Africa. The principle of vicarious liability in the context of the employer–employee relationship is a remedy that finds the employer liable for the wrongful acts committed by its employee and thus is an 'exception' to a general rule that 'a person is not liable for the unlawful actions of others'.[1] I conclude that the law on sexual harassment in South Africa has progressed with the courts' initiative in developing the common law[2] to correspond with the Constitution of the Republic of South Africa 1996 (South African Constitution), thereby giving hope and protection to the victims of sexual harassment.[3] The courts did this by broadening the 'scope of employment' test to include: approaches compatible with an abuse of power and trust, 'frolic of one's own',[4] enterprise risk, mismanagement of duties, and abuse of supervisory authority.

I place emphasis on statutory vicarious liability in terms of Section 60 of the Employment Equity Act 1998 (EEA) because it (unlike the common law) creates an element of deemed personal liability on the part of the employer for failure to take steps to ensure the eradication of gender discrimination. This is in harmony with the Code of Good Practice on the Prevention and Elimination of Harassment Cases (2022 Code), which creates an obligation for employers to manifest an attitude and climate of 'zero tolerance' to sexual harassment in the workplace.[5]

South African Legislation on Sexual Harassment

The Constitution

According to the Constitution, sexual harassment constitutes gender discrimination. The Constitution further prohibits unfair discrimination against any citizen based on sex, gender, and sexual orientation.[6] Sexual harassment can also be construed as being an affront to dignity and equality of workers

DOI: 10.4324/9781003373308-5

in the workplace; rights that are entrenched under Sections 9 and 10 of the Constitution and are critical founding democratic values in terms of Section 7(1) of the Constitution. Victims of sexual harassment have a claim to fair labour practices as provided for under Section 23(1) of the Constitution. When interpreting the Bill of Rights as enshrined in the Constitution, Section 39 enjoins the courts to consider international law and when developing common-law vicarious liability to promote the spirit, purport, and objects of the Bill of Rights, thereby protecting the rights of women in the workplace.

The Employment Equity Act

In labour law, the legal basis of a claim for sexual harassment is established under Sections 6(1) and 6(3) of the EEA. The EEA, in terms of Section 9(4) of the Constitution, gives effect to and regulates the constitutional prohibition of unfair discrimination in the employment context, and thus becomes the primary (in practice, exclusive) point of reference in dealing with discrimination in this context. Section 60 of the EEA creates a unique type of statutory vicarious liability and contains an element of deemed personal liability on the part of the employer for failure to take steps and ensure compliance with the EEA. The EEA must be interpreted 'taking into account any relevant code of good practice issued in terms of this Act or any other employment law'.[7] The 2022 Code is a 'code of good practice' issued by the minister of Employment and Labour in terms of Section 54 of the EEA.

In June 2019, ILO C190, which is the 'first international law to establish the right of everyone to a world of work free from discrimination and violence, including gender-based violence and harassment' and its accompanying Recommendation (No 206) were adopted.[8] Convention 190 enjoins members to adopt an 'inclusive, integrated and gender-responsive approach for the prevention and elimination of violence and harassment in the world of work'.[9] South Africa is the tenth member of the ILO, which ratified Convention 190 in November 2021 in compliance with its international obligations.[10] The ratification of ILO C190 led to the promulgation of the 2022 Code in March 2022, which repealed the 2005 Code of Good Practice on the Handling of Sexual Harassment Cases (2005 Code), forms part of the EEA, 'attempts to cover gaps in the legislation' and came into effect.[11] The 2022 Code is instructive as a 'guide' only on the prevention and elimination of sexual harassment and does not give rise to legally enforceable rights and obligations.[12] The scope of protection for the victims of sexual harassment under the EEA applies to all employees in their place of employment.[13] The 2022 Code applies to all employers and employees, as provided for in the EEA, and has widened the ambit of the perpetrators and victims of sexual harassment for the purposes of the EEA to include job seekers, volunteers, and persons in training, internship, apprenticeship and learnership, thereby extending the scope of the sexual harassment claim and remedy of vicarious liability.[14]

Remedies that are available in the EEA since sexual harassment is a form of unfair discrimination in terms of Section 6(1) include the Labour Court making an order that is 'just and equitable in the circumstances', including payment of compensation and damages by the employer to the employee, and an order directing the employer to take steps to ensure that deter the recurrence of unfair discrimination in the workplace.[15]

Labour Relations Act 1995 (LRA)

The LRA aims to ensure that the employer takes disciplinary action against employees who engage in sexual harassment, in accordance with the Code of Good Practice: Unfair Dismissal, particularly in cases of employees resigning against the backdrop of sexual harassment which is reported to employers but not addressed, thereby making continued employment intolerable to the employees and leading to constructive dismissal.[16] Different types of harassment, inclusive of sexual harassment, may also constitute an unfair labour practice in terms of Section 186(2) of the LRA and an automatically unfair dismissal in terms of Section 187(1)(f).[17] Remedies for unfair dismissal and unfair labour practices include reinstatement, reemployment, and compensation of an employee by the employer.[18]

Occupational Health and Safety Act 1993 (OHSA)

In terms of OHSA, employers have an obligation to take appropriate steps to 'protect employees against any harassment which would endanger the health or safety of an employee'.[19] The employer 'shall provide and maintain, as far as is reasonably practicable, a working environment that is safe and without risk to the health of his employees'[20] including 'taking such steps as may be reasonably practicable to eliminate or mitigate any hazard or potential hazard to the safety or health of employees' in the workplace.[21] In the context of sexual harassment in the workplace, 'safety means much more than physical security' but also covers 'freedom from sexual harassment and its psychological effects'.[22] Convention 190 also implores members to adopt national legislation creating obligations for employers to take appropriate steps to prevent violence and harassment, taking 'into account violence and harassment and associated psychological risks in the management of occupational health and safety'.[23]

Protected Disclosures Act 2000 (PDA)

The PDA provides for whistle-blower protection against retaliation and does not tolerate any form of an occupational detriment against whistle-blowers for reporting sexual harassment in good faith when the information is or appears accurate based on the facts available to the whistle-blower. Therefore, where an employee makes a protected disclosure of sexual harassment in good faith, they cannot be punished for it.[24]

Protection from Harassment Act 2011 (PHA)

The complainant can use one or more of the available remedies, including a protection order against harassment from the Magistrate's Court.[25] This Act 'covers harassment in all spheres of life including the workplace' and harassment is broadly defined to include sexual harassment and 'physical conduct as well as electronic and other communications which may cause mental, psychological, physical, or economic harm'.[26]

Statutory Vicarious Liability in Terms of Section 60 of the EEA

In this section, I discuss court judgments that have dealt with the labour law remedy of statutory vicarious liability in terms of Section 60 of the EEA, which is a strict liability where the wrongful acts of an employee during the course and scope of employment are imputed to the employer and is distinct from common-law vicarious liability. The relevant subsections of Section 60 of the EEA are the following:

(1) If it is alleged that an employee, while at work, contravened a provision of this Act, or engaged in any conduct that, if engaged in by that employee's employer, would constitute a contravention of a provision of this Act, the alleged conduct must immediately be brought to the attention of the employer.
(2) The employer must consult all relevant parties and must take the necessary steps to eliminate the alleged conduct and comply with the provisions of this Act.
(3) If the employer fails to take the necessary steps referred to in subsection 2, and it is proved that the employee has contravened the relevant provision, the employer must be deemed also to have contravened that provision.
(4) Despite subsection (3), an employer is not liable for the conduct of an employee if that employer is able to prove that it did all that was reasonably practicable to ensure that the employee would not act in contravention of this Act.

I now provide an overview of judgments, where complainants sought recourse under Section 60 of the EEA. The principle of the employer's non-delegable duty to ensure a non-discriminatory environment is also echoed in the 2022 Code, which states that employers are duty bound to 'take proactive and remedial steps to prevent all forms of harassment in the workplace'[27] and 'create and maintain a working environment in which the dignity of employees is respected'.[28] Any breach of this duty thus makes the employer personally liable for breach of both the letter and spirit of the EEA, which promotes equality and fair treatment in the workplace, and for breach of its non-delegable duty to ensure a working environment free from harassment, indignity, and unfair discrimination.

Ntsabo v Real Security CC

Relief in terms of Section 60 of the EEA was sought in *Ntsabo*,[29] where the applicant, a security guard, resigned after being sexually harassed by her supervisor, Dlomo, who had suggested that they engage in an intimate relationship. Upon her refusal, she stated, her supervisor (Dlomo) threatened to tender a 'negative work performance' report about her and indeed carried out that threat. She alleged that Dlomo had also touched her breasts, thighs, buttocks, and genital area when they were in the guardroom, as well as pulling up her skirt and simulating sexual intercourse, during which he ejaculated on her dress. He had a firearm and threatened to shoot her if she told anyone about the incident. Dlomo was thus 'enacting and thereby reinforcing and perpetuating gender norms that positioned him as a supervisor, as a masculine sexual conqueror' and his subordinate, Ntsabo, as a 'feminine sexual conquest'.[30] The court held that since sexual harassment was brought to the attention of the employer who did not attend to the issue as envisaged in Sub-Section 60(2) of the EEA, the employer's actions contravened the provisions of Section 60(3) of the EEA.[31] The failure of Ntsabo's employer to deal with her being mistreated contravened the provisions of Sections 6(1) and 6(3) of the EEA, since the conduct she experienced was sexual harassment in terms of the EEA.[32]

It is for this reason that the court rightly held that the employer 'did or, at best, ought to have foreseen the development of a hostile and intolerable working environment in the circumstances' and was directly liable for its failure to act on allegations of sexual harassment and for constructive dismissal.[33] The court concluded that, for the purpose of the EEA, the failure of the respondent to attend to the problem of sexual harassment brought the incident within the bounds of unfair discrimination on the grounds of gender.[34] This case highlights 'vertical harassment'[35] in that sexual harassment would not have occurred but for the supervisor's dominant authority and organisational power. It is clearly far easier to stand up to a harassing co-worker than to stand up to a supervisor who is in a superior position in the organisation and in whose hands one's livelihood, performance appraisal, and career direction and progress lie. Therefore, the affirmative defence in terms of Section 60(4) of the EEA provides immunity from vicarious liability if that employer can prove that it did all that was reasonably practicable to ensure that its employees would not act in contravention of Section 6(1) of the EEA.

Mokoena and Another v Garden Art (Pty) Ltd and Another

The case deals with a claim for vicarious liability of the employer under the EEA and defines sexual harassment to mean:

> sexual attention becomes sexual harassment if the behaviour is persisted in, although a single incident of harassment may constitute sexual harassment; the recipient has made it clear that the behaviour is

> considered offensive, and the perpetrator should have known that the behaviour would be regarded as unacceptable.[36]

I argue that the court erred in stating that sexual harassment must be persistent, as this is not part of the test for sexual harassment and sends an unintended message that victims must endure a hostile environment of recurring conduct of sexual harassment contrary to the employer's obligation to create a safe workplace and fostering a climate characterised by zero-tolerance towards sexual harassment.[37] Furthermore, the 2022 Code states that 'a single incident of unwelcome sexual conduct may constitute sexual harassment'.[38] Convention 190 recognises sexual harassment as a form of gender-based violence and harassment irrespective of whether the incident is singular or repeated.[39] Women are therefore not expected to tolerate any level of unfair discrimination. It is my view that a single act of sexual harassment is sufficient to constitute gender discrimination because women have the right to work in a discrimination-free environment and every single instance of gender discrimination is unfair discrimination, and therefore warrants legal and employer intervention.

Liberty Group Limited v Margaret Masango

In *Liberty Group Limited*,[40] the Labour Appeal Court found the appellant employer, Liberty Group Limited, vicariously liable under Section 60 of the EEA for having failed to take reasonable steps to protect the respondent, Margaret Masango, on becoming aware of her sexual harassment at work by her manager, Andrew Mosesi. In dismissing the appeal with costs against the appellant employer, the Labour Appeal Court held that:

> a failure to recognise the seriousness of the conduct complained of; a lack of interest in resolving the issue in the manner required; a failure to consult and take the necessary steps to eliminate the conduct complained of; and a failure to do all that was reasonably practicable to ensure that its employee would not act in a manner contrary to the provisions of the EEA.[41]

Section 60 of the EEA holds the employer vicariously liable for failure to act, address the complaint of sexual harassment, and remedy gender discrimination and a hostile environment once the alleged wrongful conduct was brought to its attention by the complainant.

National Union of Metal Workers of South Africa (NUMSA) and Another v Passenger Rail Agency of South Africa (PRASA)

The *NUMSA* case[42] deals with an applicant who was sexually harassed by two of her managers at PRASA, but the incident was not reported and only lodged three years after its occurrence. The applicant alleged that PRASA contravened the provisions of Section 60 of the EEA in that it failed to take steps as compelled by Section 60(2) of the EEA. The court highlighted the significance of reporting 'immediately' in that once an incident has been reported, a statutory obligation arises for an employer to eliminate the conduct of unfair discrimination and, thus, an employee should act with the necessary haste.[43] A delay of three years is not considered a limited delay, and the court held that 'the upshot of this delay is that for a period of three years, PRASA was deprived of its statutory duty to eliminate unfair discrimination'.[44] The shortcoming with the EEA requirement that sexual harassment be reported 'immediately' is that there is no legal guidance on what timeframe suffices as a reasonable delay and it appears to be decided on a case-by-case basis and, hence, caution that 'it is imperative to carefully evaluate the context of the situation, the reasons for the complainant's failure to report the matter "immediately", and the power imbalance between the parties'.[45]

The court concluded that the alleged conduct was not 'reported' as contemplated by Section 60(1) of the EEA in that it was not immediately brought to the attention of the employer to serve the statutory purpose. In addition, the court held that PRASA did not contravene Section 60 of the EEA because it took the necessary steps to eliminate the conduct, but the second applicant thwarted the steps by flatly refusing to participate and cooperate in the investigation. It is noteworthy that in reaching the conclusion that PRASA did not fail to take steps, the court found that the employer had taken preventative steps contemplated in Section 60(4) in that it had adopted a sexual harassment policy and circulated it at PRASA to ensure that its employees do not act in contravention of the EEA. This case illustrates that an employer cannot be held liable in terms of Section 60 of the EEA for failure to act on an incident that it did not have knowledge of.

Common-Law Vicarious Liability in South Africa

I turn now to the common-law remedy of vicarious liability, which is distinguishable from statutory vicarious liability enshrined in Section 60 of the EEA. The earliest case on the principle of vicarious liability in the context of the employee–employer relationship appears to be *Gifford v The Table Bay Dock and Breakwater Management Commission*, where De Villiers CJ stated the principle of vicarious liability as enunciated by Story and Pothier is as follows:

> The principal is liable to third persons for the torts, negligences, and other malfeasances or misfeasances and omissions of his servant or agent in the course of his employment, although the principal did not authorize or justify or participate in, or indeed know of such misconduct, or even if he forbade the acts or disproved of them. 'In all such cases', he adds, 'the rule applies *respondeat superior*; and it is founded upon public policy and convenience'.[46]

In South Africa, establishing common-law vicarious liability on the part of the employer for sexual harassment by its employees is a two-step test of who is an employee and what is meant by the course and scope of employment.[47] The paramount importance of distinguishing between an 'employee' and an 'independent contractor' is less evident in an epoch of increasingly 'atypical' employment and an expanded definition in the 2022 Code.[48] One of the considerations that the courts take into account in deciding whether an act was performed in the course of employment is a two-step test comprised of subjective and objective elements. This principle was established in *Minister Police v Rabie*, wherein the court held that the enquiry of whether conduct is within the scope of employment entails looking at the subjective state of mind of the employee and the objective test of a sufficiently close link between the servant's acts and the business of the master.[49]

The ruling in *Rabie*[50] was endorsed in *K v Minister of Safety and Security*,[51] where the Constitutional Court held that the approach to vicarious liability raises both a subjective and an objective enquiry. When assessing whether there is a sufficiently close nexus between the wrongful conduct and the business of the master, the court is under a constitutional mandate to give effect to the 'spirit, purport and objects of the Bill of Rights'.[52] In *Stallion Security (Pty) Limited v Van Staden*,[53] the Supreme Court of Appeal expanded the interpretation of the scope of employment by recognising the creation of the risk of harm perpetrated by the business of the employer. Giving effect to the 'spirit, purport and objects of the Bill of Rights' means that the courts, when interpreting any legislation or developing common-law vicarious liability, must endeavour to vindicate the constitutional rights of the plaintiff and deliver the promise of protection of rights entrenched in the Constitution.

Grobler v Naspers Bpk en 'n ander

The problem with the traditional test of vicarious liability is that the courts have battled to develop consistent rules on what amounts to the scope of employment. This is exacerbated by the perception that sexual harassment is not within the scope because it is an independent act which does not serve the master, even though it occurs within the course of employment. In *Grobler*,[54] Nel J sought guidance from the Constitution and found that the Constitution empowered the court to be creative and develop the common law to give effect to the Bill of Rights.[55] The employer had employed the perpetrator, Samuels, as a trainee manager, thus placing him in a position of authority over the plaintiff. The special relationship between Samuels and Grobler materially aided him in committing sexual harassment, thereby creating a sufficiently close link between the employment and the wrongful conduct. Judge Nel's judgment used the constitutional directives to protect and uphold the dignity of women, their right to freedom and bodily security, and their right to physical and psychological integrity[56] and held as follows:

> Section 173 of the Constitution provides that the Constitutional Court, the Supreme Court of Appeal and the High Courts have inherent power to develop the common law taking into account the interests of justice. Just as the courts in common-law jurisdictions have been prepared to adapt the vicarious liability rule on the grounds of policy considerations, so too should the South African courts adapt the rule in order to fulfil the duty imposed on them to protect and promote the right to inherent dignity, the right to freedom and security of the person and the right to bodily and psychological integrity of women in the workplace.[57]

He concluded that the common-law rules of vicarious liability must be adapted to give effect to the constitutional rights and consequently held the employer vicariously liable for sexual harassment. In *Grobler* (C),[58] Judge Nel developed the law on sexual harassment based on enterprise risk, finding that the traditional test of the scope of employment was too restrictive and left the victims of sexual harassment unable to secure vicarious liability on the part of the employer.

Media 24 Limited, Gasant Samuels v Sonja Grobler[59]

The protection of the psychological welfare of the employee is relevant in light of the psychological trauma that the victim suffers because of sexual harassment. The Supreme Court of Appeal developed the common-law duty of the employer to its employees to take reasonable care for their safety[60] in *Grobler* (SCA)[61] and held that the employer owes a common-law duty to its employees to protect them from not only physical harm caused by what may be called physical hazards, but includes a 'duty to protect employees from psychological harm caused, for example, by sexual harassment by co-employees'.[62]

The court established that the employer is under a general delictual duty to protect the psychological welfare of the employee, and that this duty stems not from the contract of employment or the statute, but from the legal convictions of the community.[63] The court held that the failure of Van As, the manager, to deal with the sexual harassment when it was reported to him by Grobler made him 'culpable'[64] and 'his employer, was clearly vicariously liable for his failure to act in this regard'[65] (as opposed to Samuel's wrongful conduct of sexual harassment). This distinguishes common law from labour law in that, 'the reluctance of a harassed employee to take formal steps does not absolve the employer from their duty to provide a safe working environment'.[66] It has thus been established in *Grobler* (SCA)[67] that the basis of the employer's duty to prevent and remedy sexual harassment arises out of the contract of employment, corporate governance, the common-law duty of care, a statutory remedy, and the legal convictions of the community.

K v Minister of Safety and Security

The appellant (K) was raped by three police officers, on duty and in uniform, who had offered her a lift from a night shop. K sued the employer for damages, asserting it was vicariously liable for the criminal acts of its policemen. The Supreme Court of Appeal dismissed the appellant's claim because the deviation of the police officers from the course of employment was 'to such a degree' that there was no justification upon which the court could find the employer vicariously liable.[68]

K appealed to the Constitutional Court and argued that the common-law test of vicarious liability be developed in terms of Section 39(2) of the Constitution, as the outcome did not accord with the spirit, purport, and objects of the Bill of Rights. The Constitutional Court agreed, holding that the question of protecting K's 'rights to security of the person, dignity, privacy and substantive equality are of profound constitutional importance'.[69] The court then went on to enquire whether the police officers' conduct was sufficiently close to their employer's business to render them vicariously liable. The court relied on several factors in finding a close nexus between the rape and the employment. The three police officers' work and constitutional obligations were to ensure the protection, safety, and security of all South Africans and to prevent crime.[70] These obligations are a creation of the statute in the South African Police Service Act 1995 and the Constitution.[71] In addition, the police officers had offered to assist K by giving her a lift home and she had accepted their offer in good faith. She placed her trust in them by virtue of their capacity as police officers and the police mandate.[72]

The court adopted a two-step test, comprising both a subjective and objective element, which was applied and developed in *Rabie*[73] and held that in committing rape, the police officers not only failed to protect K but also infringed on her rights to dignity and security of person.[74] The crime of rape was thus a failure by police to perform their duties to serve and protect K. It was committed within the scope of employment at a time and place when the police officers were on duty as law enforcement agents and agents of the master. This creates a close nexus between the rape and the employment. The police officers had not abandoned their scope of employment, but merely deviated from the instructions of the master within the sphere of employment.

Erasmus v Ikwezi Municipality and Another

In the *Eramus* case,[75] the High Court used judicial creativity in line with our constitutional democracy and considered whether the common law should be developed to hold an employer vicariously liable where a superior employee subjects another employee to sexual harassment. The basis of the action arose out of an alleged sexual assault committed upon the plaintiff by the perpetrator in the course of his duties to the employer.

The plaintiff was employed by Ikwezi Municipality as an archives clerk. Her supervisor was stationed at the Klipplaat office, but his duties required him to visit the Jansenville office regularly. On one such visit, the supervisor forcibly attempted to kiss the plaintiff. She reported the incident. As a result, steps were taken to prevent or limit contact between the plaintiff and the supervisor, and it was arranged that the plaintiff would be warned that the supervisor would be visiting the Jansenville office so that she could take steps to avoid contact with him. She was severely traumatised by the incident and suffered from post-traumatic stress disorder. However, the perpetrator remained in the service of the employer, and she would still meet him in the offices. She reported these meetings, but the response was that there was nothing that they could do to keep him away from her.

The court stated that 'there has been in recent years, a growing realisation and appreciation of the prevalence and the devastating effects of sexual harassment in the workplace, both in South Africa and in other jurisdictions'.[76] Pickering J found the perpetrator and employer jointly and severally liable for such damages as the plaintiff may prove she has suffered in consequence of the sexual assault, and held that the perpetrator 'by his gross actions, infringed plaintiff's rights in both respects' and 'created an offensive and intimidating work environment that undermined plaintiff's dignity, privacy, and integrity'.[77] This case demonstrated that the perpetrator was not furthering the employer's purposes or objectives, rather the incident took place as the perpetrator rendered services to the employer.[78]

The judgments in *Erasmus*

> together with decisions such as *Campbell Scientific Africa (Pty) Ltd v Simmers and Others* (2016) 37 *ILJ* 116 (LAC) and *Gaga v Anglo-Platinum Ltd and Others* (2012) 33 *ILJ* 329 (LAC), to which the High Court referred, indicate that the courts continue to view sexual harassment in a very serious light . . . [and that] employers will find it quite difficult to escape vicarious liability for the acts of sexual harassment of supervisors on their subordinates unless it can be shown that they have taken all reasonable steps to prevent this type of activity.[79]

Conclusion

I argue that the law on sexual harassment offers sufficient protection and remedies to victims of sexual harassment. Recommendation 206 contains a key provision that when members are adopting Convention 190 in terms of Article 4.2, they should similarly introduce legislative amendments that 'address violence and harassment in the world of work in labour and employment, occupational safety and health, equality and non-discrimination law, and in criminal law, where appropriate'[80] to promote the right to equality and non-discrimination in the world of work. While positive strides have been made in South Africa through legislation dealing with sexual harassment, it is my view that the interrelated pieces of legislation are at the risk of being disjointed and should therefore be amended to give clarity and effect to the letter and spirit of Convention 190, and thereby ensure consistent interpretation of laws on sexual harassment.

Section 60 of the EEA and the 2022 Code contain a legislative scheme and underlying zero tolerance policy to deter and outlaw sexual harassment in the workplace on the grounds of gender discrimination. This is done by extending legal responsibility beyond the guilty employees to their employers and supplying them with the affirmative defence under Section 60(4). In light of the recent judicial precedents in South Africa, the common-law principle of vicarious liability can no longer be rigidly applied while ignoring the constitutional mandate[81] and the rationale behind vicarious liability. The effect of the broadening of the scope of employment was thus to enhance legal recourse and protection, thereby bringing to fruition justice and the constitutional promise to the victims of sexual harassment.

If an employee acts promptly by reporting sexual harassment 'immediately', she enables the employer to take steps to address the complaint and eliminate sexual harassment in accordance with the 2022 Code.[82] This is critical because it will be an affirmative defence for an employer under Section 60(4) of the EEA when considering whether the employer has discharged its obligations in terms of Section 60(2), including adoption and communication of a sexual harassment policy.[83] Employers can mitigate the risk of vicarious liability through the following interventions to help curb sexual harassment in the workplace:[84]

a) Tone at the top for an ethical culture;[85]
b) A culture of speaking up that encourages employees to report sexual harassment in good faith, without subjecting employees to an occupational detriment;[86]
c) Confidential, independent, and speedy handling of 'gender-sensitive' investigations on sexual harassment;
d) A wellness programme through human resources that furnishes psychological support and counselling to victims of sexual harassment;[87]
e) Consequence management for sexual harassment in terms of the sanctions guide and disciplinary policy;[88]
f) Raising awareness on sexual harassment as part of induction and ongoing mandatory training;
g) Reporting cases of sexual harassment to the relevant governance structures under a 'standalone' category of sexual harassment versus general misconduct;[89]
h) An independent anonymous ethics line for reporting of sexual harassment;[90]

i) A plain-language and understandable sexual harassment policy that should be adopted by the employer and communicated groupwide to all employees;[91] and
j) Promotion of the letter and 'spirit' of the law against gender discrimination, such that sexual harassment would not only be in breach of the laws but would also be tantamount to a breach of an employer's values and ethics.

In addition to reducing the risk of legal liability, employers may wish to regard such interventions as part of being an ethical and good corporate citizen.

Notes

1 JPA Swanepoel *Introduction to Labour Law*, 3rd ed (Lexicon Publishers, 1993) 25. See also *Hirsch Appliance Specialists v Shield Security Natal (Pty) Ltd* 1992 (3) SA 643 (D) 644, Booysen J held that there are two grounds for holding the employer vicariously liable: Firstly, the breach by defendant's employees of its non-delegable duty to guard the premises and the goods therein; and, secondly, the abandonment of the defendant's work by said employees, which amounted not only to misconduct for their own benefit, but constituted mismanagement in the performance of their work, and was in itself the cause of harm to the plaintiff.
2 Common law is law that comes from Roman-Dutch law and English law, brought to South Africa by the Dutch and English settlers.
3 See ss 173 and 39(2) of the Constitution, which enjoin the courts when developing common-law to promote the spirit, purport, and objects of the Bill of Rights, thereby protecting the rights of women in the workplace.
4 The 'frolic of one's own' cases deal with the wrongful acts of an employee which did not serve the business of the employer, and thus excluded from the scope of employment. The landmark decision for extending wrongful acts committed in dereliction of duty was considered in *Feldman (Pty) Ltd v Mall* 1945 AD 733, to hold the employer vicariously liable when its employee, while driving his employer's motor vehicle deviated to run his personal errands, drank alcohol, and got involved in a car accident. Watermeyer CJ concluded at 743 that 'his departure from the path of duty did not take him so completely away from the functions entrusted to him as a servant as to exonerate his master from legal responsibility for his negligence'.
5 Item 8.2 2022 Code. Sect 5 of the EEA.
6 Sect 9(3).
7 Sect 3 of the EEA.
8 See www.lrs.org.za/2022/12/07/implementing-c190-lessons-from-south-africa-on-ending-violence-in-the-world-of-work/ (accessed on 27 April 2023).
9 Art 4.2 of Convention 190.
10 See also https://africa.businessinsider.com/apo/minister-thulas-nxesi-submits-international-labour-organization-convention-to-deal/z7b8yy2 (accessed on 18 April 2023).
11 *Ibid.*
12 Item 1.1 of the 2022 Code.
13 'Employee' is broadly defined in section 1 of the EEA, Labour Relations Act 66 of 1995, Basic Conditions of Employment Act 75 of 1997 and Skills Development Act 97 of 1998 to mean: 'any person, excluding an independent contractor

who-a) works for another person or for the State and who receives, or is entitled to receive, any remuneration; and b) in any manner assists in carrying on or conducting the business of an employer . . .'

14 Item 2.2 of the 2022 Code.
15 Sect 50(2) of the EEA.
16 Item 7.4.1 of the 2022 Code.
17 *Ibid* Items 7.4.2–3.
18 Sect 193(1) of the LRA.
19 Item 7.5.1 of the 2022 Code.
20 Sect 8(1) of the OHSA.
21 *Ibid* Sect 8(2)(b).
22 K Lux Lesley 'Understanding the law on sexual harassment in the workplace (through a case law lens): A classic fool's errand' (2020) 41 *Obiter* 88, 93.
23 Art 9(b) of Convention 190.
24 Sect 4 and 5 of the PDA.
25 Sect 2(1) of the PHA. See also AA Landman and MM Ndou 'The Protection from Harassment Act and its implications for the workplace' (2013) 22/9 *CLL* 81 that this remedy 'applies to everyone including an employer and employee and it may have an effect on a workplace, management and personnel issues'.
26 Sect 1 of the PHA. See also Item 7.7 of the 2022 Code.
27 Item 8.1 of the 2022 Code.
28 *Ibid* Item 8.2.
29 (2004) 25 ILJ 1907.
30 MF Katherine 'What is wrong with sexual harassment' (1997) 49/4 *The Stanford Law Review* 691, 766.
31 *Ibid* 94.
32 *Ibid* 95.
33 *Ibid* 93.
34 *Ibid* 95.
35 Item 4.7.8 of the 2022 Code defines vertical harassment as involving 'use of formal power (i.e., title, position, or supervisory control) or material leverage (i.e., financial, informational, resource or legal) to intimidate, threaten, harass, or harm an employee or to dominate and control the complainant'.
36 [2008] 5 BLLR 428 (LC).
37 Item 8.2 2022 Code.
38 Item 5.2.7 2022 Code.
39 Art 1 of Convention 190.
40 *Ibid.*
41 *Ibid* Para 63.
42 (JS1071/18) [2021] ZALCJHB 312 (2 September 2021).
43 *Ibid* 24.
44 *Ibid* 27.
45 P Karmini 'Employer liability when sex pests treat the workplace as a lonely-hearts club: Lessons to be learnt from *Liberty Group Limited v M* (2017) 38 ILJ 1318 (LAC)' (2019) 31/2 *SA Mercantile Law Journal* 201, 225.
46 (1874) 4 Buch 96 (Supreme Court of the Cape of Good Hope) at 114 citing *Story on Agency* §§ 308, 452–456 and *Pothier on Obligations* n.n. 121 and 453.
47 *Mkize v Martens* 1914 AD 382, 390.
48 Item 2.2 of the 2022 Code.
49 1986(1) SA 117 (A) Para 134C-E.
50 *Ibid.*
51 [2022] 8 BLLR 749 (CC) Para 32.
52 *Ibid* Para 17, O'Regan J held that the overall purpose of Section 39(2) is: to ensure that our common law is infused with the values of the Constitution. The

obligation imposed upon courts by Section 39(2) of the Constitution is thus extensive, requiring courts to be alert to the normative framework of the Constitution not only when some startling new development of the common law is in issue, but in all cases where the incremental development of the rule is in issue.

53 [2019] 40 ILJ 2695 (SCA) Para 32.

54 [2004] 2 All SA 160 (C). Nel J at 441cited *Bazley v Curry* [1999] 2 SCR 534 with approval, which reiterated that a court should determine whether there are precedents that determine on which side between vicarious liability and no liability the case falls. This Canadian precedent laid the foundation for expanding on constitutional and policy grounds the vicarious liability of employers for sexual harassment to include intentional wrongdoing.

55 Sect 39(2) of the Constitution.

56 Sect 12 of the Constitution.

57 *Ibid* (n 78) 441.

58 *Ibid.*

59 [2022] 7 BLLR 649 (SCA).

60 See also Sect 8(1) of the OHSA.

61 *Grobler* (n 54).

62 *Grobler* (n 54) Para 65.

63 *Ibid* (n 54) Para 70.

64 *Ibid.*

65 *Ibid.*

66 R Le Roux 'Sexual harassment in the workplace: A matter of more questions than answers or do we simply know less the more we find out?' (2006) 10/1 *Law, Democracy and Development* 49, 62.

67 *Grobler* (n 59).

68 *K v Minister of Safety and Security* [2022] 3 All SA 519 (SCA) Para 4–5.

69 *Ibid* Para 18.

70 *Ibid* Para 51.

71 Sect 205(3) of the Constitution.

72 *K v Minister of Safety and Security* (n 68) Para 51.

73 *Ibid* Para 134C-E.

74 *Ibid* Para 57.

75 (2016) 37 ILJ 1799 (ECG).

76 *Ibid* Para 57.

77 *Ibid* Para 75.

78 *Ibid* Para 72.

79 Le Roux PAK, 'Vicarious liability and sexual harassment: The risks of employer inaction' (2016) 26/1 *Contemporary Labour Law* 8.

80 Art 2 of the ILO Recommendation R206 – Violence and Harassment Recommendation, 2019 (No 206).

81 Sect 39(2) of the Constitution.

82 Items 10.1.1–10.1.2 of the 2022 Code.

83 Item 9.3 of the 2022 Code.

84 King IV Report on Corporate Governance in South Africa 2016 – Principles 3 and 13.

85 *Ibid.* King IV – Principle 1, 'The governing body should lead ethically and effectively'.

86 Sect 6 PDA; see also item 7.4.4 of the 2022 Code.

87 Item 10.5.2 2022 Code.

88 *Ibid* Item 7.4.1.

89 Landman and Ndou (n 25) 89 opine that 'sexual harassment is a form of misconduct. The employer may take disciplinary action against the alleged harasser and the alleged harasser may be fairly dismissed'.

90 Sect 159 of the Companies Act 2008.
91 Item 9.3 2022 Code, and Art 10 of the Convention 190.

References

https://africa.businessinsider.com/apo/minister-thulas-nxesi-submits-international-labour-organization-convention-to-deal/z7b8yy2 (accessed on 18 April 2023).

Bazley v Curry [1999] 2 SCR 534.

Campbell Scientific Africa (Pty) Ltd v Simmers& others (2016) 37 ILJ 116 (LAC).

Colonial Mutual Life Assurance Society v Macdonald (1931) AD 412.

Companies Act 71 of 2008.

Compensation for Occupational Injuries and Diseases Act 130 of 1993.

Constitution of the Republic of South Africa Act 108 of 1996.

Employment Equity Act 55 of 1998.

Erasmus v Ikwezi Municipality & another (2016) 37 ILJ 1799 (ECG).

KM Franke 'What is wrong with sexual harassment' (1997) 49/4 *The Stanford Law Review* 691–772.

Gaga v Anglo-Platinum Ltd & others (2012) 33 ILJ 329 (LAC).

Gifford v The Table Bay Dock and Breakwater Management Commission (1874) 4 Buch 96 (Supreme Court of the Cape of Good Hope).

Grobler v Naspers Bpk en 'n ander 2004 (5) BLLR 455 (C).

Hirsch Appliance Specialists v Shield Security Natal (Pty) Ltd 1992 (3) SA 643 (D).

www.lrs.org.za/2022/12/07/implementing-c190-lessons-from-south-africa-on-ending-violence-in-the-world-of-work/ (accessed on 27 April 2023).

K v Minister of Safety and Security [2005] 3 SA 179 (SCA).

K v Minister of Safety and Security [2005] 8 BLLR 749 (CC).

LL Kubjana 'Understanding the law on sexual harassment in the workplace (through a case law lens): A classic fool's errand' (2020) 41/1 *Obiter* 88–105.

Labour Relations Act 66 of 1995.

AA Landman and MM Ndou 'The Protection from Harassment Act and its implications for the workplace' (2013) 22/9 *Contemporary Labour Law* 81–90.

P Le Roux 'Vicarious liability and sexual harassment: The risks of employer inaction' (2016) 26/1 *Contemporary Labour Law* 8.

R Le Roux 'Sexual harassment in the workplace: A matter of more questions than answers or do we simply know less the more we find out?' (2006) 10/1 *Law, Democracy and Development* 49–67.

Liberty Group Limited v Margaret Masango (Case no: 105/2015) (7 March 2017).

C MacKinnon and R Siegel *Directions in Sexual Harassment Law* (Yale University Press, 2004).

Media 24 Limited, Gasant Samuels v Sonja Grobler [2005] 7 BLLR 649 (SCA).

Minister Police v Rabie [1986] 1 SA 117 (A).

Mkize v Martens [1914] AD 382.

Mokoena and Another v Garden Art (Pty) Ltd and Another [2008] 5 BLLR 428 (LC).

National Union of Metal Workers of South Africa (NUMSA) and Another v Passenger Rail Agency of South Africa (JS1071/18) [2021] ZALCJHB 312 (2 September 2021).

Ntsabo v Real Security CC [2004] 1 BLLR 58 (LC).

Occupational Health and Safety Act 85 of 1993.

K Pillay 'Employer liability when sex pests treat the workplace as a lonely-hearts club: Lessons to be learnt from *Liberty Group Limited v M* (2017) 38 ILJ 1318 (LAC)' (2019) 31/2 *South African Mercantile Law Journal* 201–238.
Promotion of Equality and Prevention of Unfair Discrimination Act 4 of 2000.
Protected Disclosures Act 26 of 2000.
Protection from Harassment Act 17 of 2011.
Rustenburg Platinum Mines Limited v UASA obo Pietersen and Others (2018) 39 ILJ 1330 (LC)
S v Makwanyane and Another [1995] 6 BCLR 665 (CC).
Stallion Security (Pty) Limited v Van Staden [2005] 8 BLLR 749 (CC).
JPA Swanepoel *Introduction to Labour Law*, 3rd ed (Lexicon Publishers, 1993).

6 Legal Protection of Women with Disabilities Against Sexual Harassment in Tanzania

Victoria Melkisedeck Lihiru

Introduction

Approximately one billion people (nearly 16% of the world's population) live with some form of disability.[1] In Tanzania, a 2008 Disability Survey which used the Washington Group Model[2] found a 7.8% prevalence rate of disability for people aged seven years and above.[3] The 2012 population and housing *census* identified 6% of Tanzania's population as living with some form of disability.[4] The 2022 national population census undertaken in August 2022, and with results yet unpublished, is expected to provide clarity on the current number of persons living with disability in Tanzania.[5]

Around 19% of the women in the world live with some form of disability.[6] The risk of disability for many women is also heightened by gender-based violence such as intimate partner violence and other forms of violence which occur in the workplace, public places, and health care institutions.[7] Other reasons include limited access to sexual and reproductive health services, exposure to harmful practices, and humanitarian and natural disasters.[8] Women exposed to abuse from an intimate partner are significantly more likely to report having a disability or chronic condition that impacts their daily lives.[9]

Sexual harassment is an expression and a reinforcement of existing inequalities which can cause disabilities and worsen conditions of persons living with disabilities.[10] Unlike men with disabilities, women and girls with disabilities are at four times a greater risk, both within and outside the home, of being subjected to violence, harassment, and exploitation.[11] Due to the intersection between disability and gender-based bias and discrimination, women and girls with disabilities experience higher levels of physical, sexual, and psychological violence for longer periods of time and with worse physical and mental outcomes than women without disabilities.[12] Women and girls with disabilities are often portrayed as weak, worthless, and, in some cases, subhuman by their societies.[13] They are also deemed asexual, unsexy, easily sexually accessible, and undesirable. They are expected to feel grateful if someone shows a sexual interest in them, even when it's harassment.[14] Girls and women with disabilities often depend on others to manage their lives and face multiple barriers in accessing sexual and reproductive health education

DOI: 10.4324/9781003373308-6

and, therefore, may be conflicted to react against acts of sexual harassment.[15] Accordingly, in this chapter I discuss the effectiveness of Tanzania's legal framework in addressing the problem of sexual harassment against women with disabilities. I start by providing statistics pertaining to the prevalence of sexual harassment against women with disabilities. I then present Tanzania's obligations under the international, regional, and sub-regional human rights conventions related to the protection of women with disabilities against sexual harassment. I further discuss the adequacy and gaps in Tanzanian national laws in protecting women with disabilities against sexual harassment. Conclusion and recommendations mark the end of this chapter.

Prevalence of Sexual Harassment against Women with Disabilities

Women who are deaf, blind, autistic, or living with psychosocial or intellectual disabilities are five times more vulnerable to violence, including acts of sexual harassment.[16] Furthermore, specific kinds of disabilities may attract specific forms of sexual harassment. For instance, women living with blindness have reported unwelcome physical sexual touching from people who offer them help.[17] With respect to women with a cognitive or speech disability, their lack of understanding of the situation during a sexual harassment incident and their inability to say no to sexual advances can be perceived as consent.[18]

The socio-economic conditions of women living with disabilities can be harmful, as it negatively impacts their productivity, safety, and psychological welfare and can lead to further trauma and reinforce other forms of disability,[19] thus preventing them from accessing income-generating opportunities in the labour market.[20] While campaigns such as #Metoo and Time's Up were instrumental in exposing the agony of sexual harassment among women, the plight of women with disabilities exposed to sexual harassment received less attention.[21] Accurate prevalence rates do not exist given the scant attention paid to disability-related sexual harassment. However, survey data depict women and girls with disabilities experiencing sexual harassment at higher rates than those without disabilities.[22]

In the European Union, for instance, 61% of women with disabilities experienced sexual harassment since the age of 15, as opposed to 54% of women without disabilities.[23] In the United Kingdom, a survey conducted in England and Wales showed that women with disabilities aged 16 are twice as likely to be subjected to sexual assault than women without disabilities.[24] In the case of Tanzania, there is more information on sexual harassment regarding women in general, whilst data on the sexual harassment of women with disabilities is limited. For instance, a report by the Tanzania Media Women's Association (TAMWA) estimates that between 75% and 89% of women in Tanzania have experienced some form of sexual harassment.[25] A Human Rights Survey conducted by the Legal and Human Rights Centre of Tanzania[26] depicts sexual harassment as a common form of violence against women, with 35% of the community members saying it is a serious problem in the community while (43%) say it is a moderate problem.[27] These reports, however, were silent on the extent to which sexual harassment is an issue for women with disabilities in Tanzania.

Research conducted by Action for Disability and Development International[28] (ADD) and the Federation for Disabled People Organisations (SHIVYAWATA) in Tanzania[29] shows a high incidence of sexual violence, including acts of sexual harassment committed against women and girls with disabilities with striking frequency and brutality by intimate partners, family members, and strangers.[30] The report points towards girls with intellectual and hearing disabilities being at a significantly higher risk of experiencing sexual harassment and violence.[31] According to the report, nine out of ten girls and women with intellectual disabilities were sexually abused, often frequently, without intervention from family or community.[32] Although this data is for three districts and calls for further research, it suggests a need for inspection of Tanzanian laws to assess their adequacy in protecting women with disabilities against acts of sexual harassment. This is because the country has already committed to a number of international, regional, and subregional conventions on protection of human rights, including the women- and disability-specific conventions.

Tanzania's Obligations under International, Regional, and Sub-Regional Human Rights Conventions

Tanzania has committed to several international, regional, and sub-regional instruments which call for promotion and protection of human rights, including the rights of persons with disabilities. In particular, in 1976 Tanzania ratified the general human rights documents, including the 1966 International Covenant on Economic, Social and Cultural Rights (ICESCR)[33] and, in 1966, the International Covenant on Civil and Political Rights (ICCPR).[34] Also, in 1985, the country ratified the Convention on the 1979 Elimination of All Forms of Discrimination against Women (CEDAW),[35] as well as the 1989 Convention on the Rights of the Child (CRC) in 1991.[36] Whilst these international instruments do not directly mention sexual harassment or refer to women with disabilities, they do recognise and respect the inherent integrity and dignity of all humans.[37] In general, these instruments recognise the right to life,[38] prohibit all forms of discrimination,[39] and call for equality of men and women in the enjoyment of economic, political, social, and cultural rights.[40] The instruments also call for the right to an adequate standard of living and free-consent marriages.[41] Under these instruments, all persons are equal before the law and are entitled, without any discrimination, to equal protection of the law.[42] Protection of privacy of the family and home and from unlawful attacks on honour and reputation are guaranteed.[43] The right to seek, receive, and impart information is also protected.[44] The CRC and the African Charter of the Rights and Welfare of Children,[45] which Tanzania ratified in 2003, contain specific provisions for children with disabilities requiring state parties to take all appropriate measures to ensure they are protected against all forms of discrimination.[46]

On women-specific international instruments, CEDAW is silent on the rights of women and girls with disabilities but prohibits any form of discrimination against women in general.[47] The CEDAW General Recommendation No 19, which was adopted by the Committee on the Elimination of Discrimination Against Women (CEDAW Committee) in 1992, recognises sexual harassment as a form of gender-based violence.[48] Likewise, the CEDAW General Recommendation No 39 on the Rights of Indigenous Women and Girls identifies patterns of discrimination faced by indigenous women and girls.[49] It notes that such discrimination is often intersectional and based on factors such as sex, gender, indigenous origin, status or identity, race, ethnicity, disability, age, language, socio-economic status, and HIV/AIDS status. It calls for states parties to take action to prevent and address discrimination against Indigenous women and girls; and to integrate a gender perspective, an intersectional perspective, an indigenous woman and girls' perspective, an intercultural perspective, and a multidisciplinary perspective. An intersectional perspective requires states parties to consider the multitude of factors that combine to increase and exacerbate the exposure of Indigenous women and girls to unequal and arbitrary treatment based on sex, gender, Indigenous origin, status or identity, race, ethnicity, disability, age, language, socio-economic status, and HIV/AIDS status, among other factors. The recommendations call on states parties to take steps to prevent discrimination, racism, stereotypes, gender-based violence, and sexual harassment against Indigenous women, including those with disabilities.

The Beijing Declaration and Platform for Action, 1995,[50] recognises sexual harassment as part of a continuum of violence against women. The declaration also calls upon governments and organisations to take special measures to eliminate violence and harassment against women with disabilities. Similarly, the Protocol on the Rights of Women in Africa (Maputo Protocol), which Tanzania ratified in 2007, recognises violence against women as a violation of the rights to dignity, life, integrity, and security of persons. The Protocol requires the states parties to take specific measures to prevent and prosecute violence, including sexual abuse and discrimination based on disability, and recognises the right to be treated with dignity, whether in public or private.[51]

Tanzania has also ratified disability-specific instruments, including the 2006 United Nations Convention for Persons with Disabilities (UNCRPD) in 2009, as well as its Optional Protocol to the Convention in 2009.[52] The UNCRPD does not create new rights but applies the existing human rights legal framework to the context of disability and guides states parties on how human rights law should apply to the lives of persons with disabilities. UNCRPD recognises that women with disabilities are subject to multiple forms of discrimination and calls states parties to take appropriate measures to ensure their full development, advancement, and empowerment.[53] Article 16 of UNCRPD similarly obliges states parties to take all appropriate measures to prevent and protect persons with disabilities by ensuring that appropriate gender and age-sensitive assistance and support is provided. Under the General Comment No 3 on Women and Girls with Disabilities, the CRPD Committee explicitly addresses sexual harassment at the workplace.[54] It notes that besides the general barriers that persons with disabilities face when trying to exercise their right to work, women with disabilities face unique barriers to their equal participation in the workplace, including the problem of sexual harassment.[55]

At the sub-regional level, Tanzania, together with other members of the East Africa Region, adopted the East African Policy on Persons with Disabilities in 2012.[56] The Policy outlines joint commitments in line with the UNCRPD and country-level recommendations addressing challenges facing persons with disabilities, including women.[57] Further, as a member of the United Nations, Tanzania joins the world towards realising Sustainable Goals number One (Ending Poverty), Three (Good Health and Wellbeing), Four (Quality Education), Five (Gender Equality), Eight (Decent Work and Economic Growth), Ten (Reduced Inequalities), Eleven (Sustainable Cities and Communities) and Sixteen (Peace, Security, and Strong Institutions).[58] These goals have specific disability indicators and components which call for the protection of women and girls with disabilities against sexual harassment.

With the ratification of these conventions, Tanzania is required to take legal, administrative, and institutional efforts to protect its people, including persons with disabilities, against any human rights violations and to protect against acts of sexual harassment. However, several gaps are noted when the Tanzanian laws are mirrored against the international and regional conventions with regard to the protection of women with disabilities against sexual harassment.

Adequacy of Tanzanian National Laws in Protecting Women with Disabilities against Sexual Harassment

The first problem I note regarding the protection of women with disabilities against sexual harassment in Tanzania is how the term disability is defined. The word 'disability' has been termed as a complex and evolving concept.[59] The UNCRPD defines persons with disabilities as 'People with long-term physical, mental, intellectual or sensory impairments, which in interaction with various barriers may hinder their full and effective participation in society on an equal basis with others'.[60] The barriers can be attitudinal, environmental, and/or institutional.[61] Within the disability discourse, there is a growing recognition of the intersectionality approach to understanding and addressing disability-related challenges.[62] The approach calls for recognition of the heterogeneity among persons living with disabilities and challenges concepts of disability as a homogeneous group. It also demands an end to the marginalisation of persons with disabilities whose oppression is shaped by intersecting structural and social inequalities.[63]

The intersectionality approach is also reflected in the UNCRPD, where the preamble identifies discrimination faced by persons with disabilities as a result of intersectionality of their race, colour, sex, gender, language, religion, political or other opinion, national, ethnic, indigenous or social origin, property, birth, age, or other status.[64] Women with disabilities are not a homogenous group; they experience multiple forms of discrimination cutting across gender, age, education, economic status, and disability at a higher rate in comparison to men with disabilities.[65] Cognisant with this fact, the UNCRPD acknowledges that the intersection of disability- and gender-based discrimination causes women and girls with disabilities to experience higher levels of marginalisation. Article 6 recognises that women and girls with disabilities are subject to multiple discriminations. This recognition is further reinforced by the CRPD Committee[66] which acknowledges that women with disabilities experience discrimination not as 'a homogeneous group but, rather, as individuals with multidimensional layers of identities, statuses and life circumstances'.[67]

In Tanzania, Section 2 of the Persons with Disability Act, 2010, defines 'disability' as a loss or limitation of opportunities for an individual to take part in the normal life of the community on an equal level with others due to physical, mental, or social factors.[68] Section 4(f) of the Persons with Disability Act recognises equality between men and women with disabilities, while Section 6 requires the government to ensure equality and non-discrimination for persons with disabilities of all genders and ages.[69] The Act is however silent on how disability intersects with other forms of social inequalities, and how such intersectionality compounds discrimination against women and girls with disabilities. This legal gap is the evidence of inadequate awareness amongst policy-makers, self-advocates, and civil society on intersectional barriers which exacerbate discrimination against women with disabilities.[70] Although there have been calls to acknowledge the intersection between disability and other marginalised identities, the calls have been largely ignored.[71] The African Disability Protocol, 2018 (which Tanzania is yet to ratify), has different provisions for girls, women, children, and youth with disabilities, and so actively addresses the issue of intersectional discrimination for persons with disabilities.[72] Sexual harassment intersects with all structural social inequalities, such as disability, race, ethnicity, age, social status, economic status, gender, sexual orientation, and other status. The intersection of these social dynamics influences who becomes a target for sexual harassment, brutality levels, as well as how or if perpetrators are held accountable.[73] Failure of the Persons with Disability Act to stipulate the ways disability intersects with other forms of social inequalities distorts the understanding of contributing factors towards the discrimination faced by women with disabilities, including acts of sexual harassment.

I also find challenges in the existing legal definition of the term sexual harassment, particularly in the context of disability. Tanzania does not have a standalone law governing sexual harassment. Key legislations such as Persons with Disabilities Act and the Employment and Labour Relations Act[74] only make reference to and prohibit harassment in general. Section 34(d) of the Persons with Disabilities Act provides for the protection of employees with disabilities against harassment but does not state what harassment entails. The Employment and Labour Relations Act prohibits discrimination on multiple grounds, including disability.[75] The Act specifically prohibits harassment which it also describes as a form of discrimination.[76] Similar to the Persons with Disabilities Act, the Employment and Labour Relations Act does not define and expound on what constitutes harassment.

A definition of sexual harassment is provided for under the Code of Ethics and Conduct for Public Service.[77] Section 3 of the Code prohibits a public official from discriminating or harassing a member of the public or a fellow employee on the grounds of sex, tribe, religion, nationality, ethnicity, marital status, or disability.[78] In addition, Section 6 of the Code prohibits a public servant from having sexual relationships in the workplace. Public servants are to avoid all types of conduct which may constitute sexual harassment, which includes: pressure for sexual activity or sexual 'favours' with a fellow employee; rape, sexual battery, and molestation or any sexual assault; intentional physical conduct which is sexual in nature, such as unwelcome touching, pinching, patting, grabbing, and/or brushing against another employee's body, hair, or clothes; sexual innuendos, gestures, noises, jokes, comments, or remarks to another person about one's sex or body; and offering or receiving preferential treatment, promises, or rewards and offering or submitting to sexual 'favours'.[79] The Code of Ethics and Conduct for Public Service, however, applies to only acts committed by public officials against their fellow employees or members of the public, including those with disabilities.[80] It does not regulate sexual harassment perpetrated by non-public officials. Further, the protection does not extend beyond formal employment conditions and contractual status. This anomaly is, however, partly cured by Section 25 of the Prevention and Combating of Corruption Act.[81] Its definition of sexual harassment covers victims with no contractual status. It provides that:

> Anybody being in the position of power or authority, who in the exercise of his authority, demands or imposes 'sexual favours', or any other 'favours' on any person as a condition for giving employment, a promotion, a right, a privilege, or any other preferential treatment, commits an offence and shall be liable, on conviction, to a fine of not exceeding five million shillings or to imprisonment for a term not exceeding three years or both.

Although the definition covers victims with no contractual status, only perpetrators in a position of power or authority can be subjected to the law.

There is a timid attempt under the Sexual Offences Special Provisions Act (SOSPA) to categorise certain acts committed by unemployed perpetrators or those 'not in the position of power or authority' as potentially acts of sexual harassment. Section 138 D of SOSPA provides that:

(1) Any person who, with intention, assaults or by use of criminal force, sexually harasses another person, or by the use of words or actions, causes sexual annoyance or harassment to such other person, commits the offence of sexual harassment . . .
(2) Whoever, intending to insult the modesty of any woman utters any word, makes any sound or gesture, or exhibits any object including any organ whether male or feminine, intending that such word or sound shall be heard, or that the gesture or object shall be seen, by the woman or intrudes upon the privacy of the woman, commits the offence of sexual harassment.

Although the definition of sexual harassment under SOSPA covers acts committed by unemployed perpetrators or those 'not in the position of power or authority', the definition is disability insensitive. It assumes that all women can see, hear, comprehend acts done to them, and can express what they have seen or heard. This legal limitation makes it challenging and almost impossible for women who are blind, have intellectual challenges, and those with deafness to successfully challenge acts of sexual harassment in courts. As sexual harassment is defined as an unwelcome act, the perception of the victim could be a critical determinant to establish whether sexual harassment occurred.[82] However, a perpetrator may equally argue that they believed that their conduct was not unwelcome.

Either way, the situation of women with disabilities places them in a precarious position, for instance, an inability to react or reject (including verbalising the rejection or physically moving away) sexual harassment could be construed as consent by both the perpetrators and witnesses.[83] At times, the reaction by a woman with disability to sexual harassment acts may not be understood by the perpetrators as well as the witnesses. In most incidences the reaction by a woman with disability is used to mock her further.[84] Similarly, the Penal Code punishes anyone who knowingly has or attempts to have sexual intercourse with a woman who is an imbecile or idiot with 14 years' imprisonment, with or without corporal punishment.[85] The reference to women with disabilities as imbeciles and idiots is culturally and disability insensitive, and reinforces stereotypes that can increase the risk of violence and sexual harassment.

I also note situations where the decision to seek justice by women with disabilities against acts of sexual violence is influenced by their financial status, as well as the availability of disability-sensitive judicial services.[86] In 2017 and 2018, Tanzania enacted the Legal Aid Act and the Legal Aid Regulations,[87] respectively, requiring the judicial officers, legal aid providers, and paralegals to offer legal aid to all indigent people.[88] Also, in 2019, the Chief Justice of Tanzania issued specific rules for procedures and practice for cases involving vulnerable groups, including persons with disabilities.[89] Rule 4 of The Judicature and Application of Laws (Practice and Procedure of Cases of vulnerable Groups) Rules, 2019,[90] requires any case involving vulnerable groups to be determined and concluded within six to nine months. Rule 6 allows deaf people involved in a case to have access to free sign language interpretation payable from the Judicial Fund. In addition, Rule 9 permits that judgment, decree, and proceedings may be made in braille format when a case involves a visually impaired person. Rule 8 obliges every court to designate a desk officer to handle court matters involving vulnerable groups.

These legislative commitments are, however, merely rhetorical and without adequate resources and prioritisation of implementation. Even with availability of legal aid services and disability-sensitive services on paper, most women and girls with disabilities are unaware or constrained to reach the legal aid services or the courts due to technical and physical accessibility challenges.[91] A human rights survey by the Legal and Human Rights Centre showed that 67% of those surveyed did not know where to get help if they or a friend were subjected to sexual harassment or abuse.[92] The survey also found that lawyers and legal aid providers find it difficult to handle cases involving persons with disabilities because of inaccessible court buildings, a shortage of sign language and other disability experts, lengthy legal procedures, and corruption. Also, legal aid services are not available in all parts of the country due to the remoteness of some areas.[93]

The disability-sensitive rules are hardly practiced by courts of law due to the minimum technical capacity of judicial officers and accessibility challenges.[94] When trying to access justice following an encounter with acts of sexual violence, women with disabilities may encounter hostile police officers who may encourage them to settle such issues outside of the judicial system. The established gender and children's desks within the police posts fall short of knowledgeable staff handling cases involving women with disabilities.[95] In addition to the legal loopholes, access to justice for women with disabilities is also hindered by social and cultural norms. A patriarchal society, for instance, undermines women's bodily autonomy and makes it more societally acceptable for sexual harassment allegations to be taken less seriously.[96] Sometimes acts of sexual harassment are committed by family members who may or may not be responsible for the welfare and wellbeing of women with disabilities. Under these circumstances, women with disabilities exposed to family-related sexual harassment fear the loss of care and support from them and worry about possible vengeance.[97] When employed or engaged in an informal business, women with disabilities fear losing jobs and entitlements, business, revenge, and being perceived as troublemakers.[98] When this is compounded by information and communication barriers, it may result in a protracted response by women with disabilities to report sexual harassment.

Conclusion

The legal analysis that I have presented in this chapter suggests that while there is a global appreciation of the intersectionality principle in defining disability and its related rights, Tanzania's disability law is silent on the ways in which disability intersects with other forms of social inequalities. This lacuna limits the appreciation of causative factors for the discrimination and marginalisation faced by women with disabilities. My legal analysis further shows that Tanzania's legal framework does not offer a comprehensive definition of sexual harassment to protect women with disabilities against sexual harassment in a non-employment context. The offered protection is disability insensitive and makes it challenging for women with disability to challenges acts of sexual harassment through judicial process. Further, although the law allows for legal aid and calls for inclusive judicial process, its utilisation is hindered by both technical and accessibility challenges encountered by the victims, legal aid providers, and the courts of law. These findings and the respective recommendations in the following section are critical guidelines for disability advocates and lawmakers to work towards desirable reforms to guarantee effective legal protection for women with disabilities against acts of sexual harassment.

Recommendations

Tanzania's legal framework has not adequately addressed the nexus of sexual harassment and disability, and thus offers minimum protection to women with disabilities against acts of sexual harassment. It is paramount for Tanzania to strengthen its commitment to protect women with disabilities against acts of sexual harassment. This can be done through signing, ratification, and domestication of the 2019 International Labor Organisation's Convention No 190 on Violence and Harassment (C190) as well the African Union's Protocol to the African Charter on Human and Peoples' Rights on the Rights of Persons with Disabilities (African Disability Rights Protocol). The two instruments cover the nexus of disability, the related social inequalities parameters, and sexual harassment extensively, thus are key in reforming the Tanzania's disability law. Also, the enactment of a comprehensive law on gender-based violence in line with the guidance from C190, African Disability Rights Protocol, should be prioritised.[99]

The gender-based violence law should entail a harmonised definition of gender-based violence, including sexual harassment, depicting how the intersection of gender with other structural social inequalities such as disability, age, and economic status compounds the problem of marginalisation of women, including women with disabilities. Gender-based violence law should also incorporate an inclusive, integrated, and gender-responsive approach to tackle the underlying causes and risk factors for sexual harassment, including gender stereotypes, multiple and intersecting forms of discrimination, and unequal gender-based power relations that work against women and girls with disabilities. The law should further offer protection against sexual harassment for persons working in both private and public sectors beyond formal employment, and irrespective of their contractual status. Protection against sexual harassment in public spaces should be strengthened through accommodating the unique dynamics of women and girls with disabilities.[100]

Although robust disability- and gender-sensitive laws are paramount, strengthening the autonomy of women and girls with disabilities through training, community awareness raising, as well as an accessible, inclusive, and effective justice system is necessary to increase the protection of women with disabilities against sexual harassment. Similarly, there is also a need to influence the government and non-state actors to raise awareness on the Judicature and Application of Laws (Practice and Procedure of Cases involving vulnerable Groups) Rules, 2019, and the Legal Aid Act[101] to promote access to justice by women and girls with disabilities who are victims of sexual harassment. Nationwide research on the prevalence of sexual harassment for women with disability to further understand the risk and the desired interventions to tackle the problem of sexual harassment for women with disabilities in Tanzania should be prioritised.

Notes

1 World Health Organisation 'Disability factsheet' *Disability*, 2022, www.who.int/en/news-room/fact-sheets/detail/disability-and-health (accessed on 5 February 2022).
2 The Washington Group on Disability Statistics (WG) promotes and coordinates international cooperation in the area of health statistics focusing on the development of disability measures suitable for census and national surveys. The major objective of the WG is to provide information on disability that is comparable throughout the world.
3 It was based on a sample of 7,000 households.
4 National Bureau of Statistics 'Population and housing census' 2012, www.nbs.go.tz/index.php/en/census-surveys/population-and-housing-census/162-2012-phcpopulation-distribution-by-administrative-areas (accessed on 15 January 2022). Both the survey and census did not contain desegregated data and did not include information on forms of disabilities, magnitude, age, location and situation of the persons with disabilities.
5 Tanzania undertakes national population census after every ten years. The recent census took place in August 2022.
6 The UN Entity for Gender Equality and the Empowerment of Women (UN Women) 'Making the SDG count for women and girls with disabilities' 2017, www.un.org/development/desa/disabilities/wp-content/uploads/sites/15/2019/10/Making-SDGs-count-for-women-with-disabilities.pdf (accessed on 15 January 2022).
7 M Breiding, M Black and GW Ryan 'Chronic disease and health risk behaviors associated with intimate partner violence' (2008) 18/7 *Annals of Epidemiology* 538–544.
8 World Health Organisation (n 1).
9 Breiding, Black and Ryan (n 7).

10 UN Women (n 6).
11 *Ibid.*
12 Action for Disability and Development International 'Disability and gender-based violence: Peer research in Kibaha and Mkuranga, Tanzania' (2017) 4, www.humanrights.or.tz/assets/attachments/1627542868.pdf (accessed on 20 August 2021).
13 UN Women (n 6).
14 W Lu 'I'm disabled and I get sexually harassed: Here's why that matters' *Teen Vogue* 2017, www.teenvogue.com/story/disability-and-sexual-harassment (accessed on 20 August 2022).
15 T Mthembu and W Holness 'Criteria for law reform on comprehensive sexuality education for children with disabilities in South Africa' (2022) 10 *African Disability Rights Yearbook* 78–109.
16 The United Nations Population Fund (UNFPA) 'Five things you didn't know about disability and sexual violence' https://esaro.unfpa.org/en/news/five-things-you-didnt-know-about-disability-and-sexual violence#:~:text=Children%20who%20are%20deaf%2C%20blind,far%20more%20susceptible%20to%20bullying (accessed on 20 January 2022).
17 Lu (n 14).
18 Plan International 'Fact sheet: Violence against women and girls with disabilities' 2013, www.un.org/womenwatch/daw/csw/csw57/side_events/Fact%20sheet%20%20VAWG%20with%20disabilities%20FINAL%20.pdf (accessed on 15 January 2022).
19 UN Women (n 6).
20 UNFPA (n 16); see also the Preamble to the International Labour Organisation 'Violence and harassment in the world of work: A guide on convention No 190 and recommendation No 206' *International Labour Office* ILO, 2021. 1v ISBN 9789220350126 (web pdf).
21 E Flores 'The #MeToo movement hasn't been inclusive of the disability community' *Teen Vogue*, 2018, www.teenvogue.com/story/the-metoo-movement-hasnt-been-inclusive-of-the-disability-community (accessed on 7 February 2022).
22 SB Plummer and F Patricia 'Women with disabilities' experience with physical and sexual abuse. trauma violence abuse' (2012) 13/1 *Trauma, Violence and Abuse* 15–29.
23 M Uldry and P Mahlamaki 'Making women with disabilities visible' www.socialeurope.eu/making-women-with-disabilities-visible (accessed on 20 January 2022).
24 Office of National Statistics 'Disability and crime' UK, 2019, www.ons.gov.uk/peoplepopulationandcommunity/healthandsocialcare/disability/bulletins/disabilityandcrimeuk/2019#sexual-assault (accessed on 20 January 2022).
25 CB Camargo et al 'Behavioural influences on attitudes towards petty corruption: A study of social norms and mental models in Tanzania' 2017, www.baselgovernance.org/sites/default/files/2019-04/earf_tanzania_country_report_12_december_2017_final.pdf (accessed on 18 August 2020).
26 Legal and Human Rights Centre (LHRC) is a nongovernmental human rights organisation based in Dar es Salaam as its Head Quarters and having a sub-office in Arusha and Dodoma. It was founded and registered in 1995 under the Companies Ordinance, Chapter 212 of the laws of Tanzania as a company without shares limited by guarantee, https://humanrights.or.tz/en (accessed on 18th August 2022).
27 Legal and Human Rights Centre (LHRC), Human Rights and Business Report 2020/21 Tanzania Mainland, 2021, ISBN: 978-9987-740-60-4.

28 Action on Disability and Development (ADD International) fights for independence, equality and opportunity for disabled people living in poverty in Africa and Asia, https://add.org.uk/africa/ (accessed on 18 August 2020).
29 SHIVYAWATA is a Swahili short term for 'Tanzania Federation of Disabled People's Organisations' translated from Tanzania Federation of Disabled People's Organisations. SHIVYAWATA is a non-governmental federation which brings together ten national Disabled People's Organisations (PWDs) established by the DPOs in 1992, shivyawata.or.tz/about-us/?lang=en (accessed on 18 August 2020).
30 Action for Disability and Development International (n 12) 22.
31 *Ibid.*
32 *Ibid.*
33 UN General Assembly, International Covenant on Economic, Social and Cultural Rights of 16 December 1966, UN Treaty Series Vol 993, www.refworld.org/docid/3ae6b36c0.html (accessed on 5 February 2022).
34 UN General Assembly International Covenant on Civil and Political Rights of 16 December 1966, United Nations, Treaty Series Vol 999 171, www.refworld.org/docid/3ae6b3aa0.html (accessed on 5 February 2022).
35 UN General Assembly Convention on the Elimination of All Forms of Discrimination Against Women of 18 December 1979, UN Treaty Series, Vol 1249, www.refworld.org/docid/3ae6b3970.html (accessed on 5 February 2022).
36 UN General Assembly, Convention on the Rights of the Child of 20 November 1989, UN Treaty Series Vol 1577, www.refworld.org/docid/3ae6b38f0.html (accessed on 5 February 2022).
37 ICCPR, Art 1.
38 ICCPR, Art 6.
39 ICESCR, Art 2, and ICCPR, Art 2.
40 ICESCR, Art 3, and ICCPR, Art 3.
41 Art 11 of ECESCR and Art 23 of ICCPR.
42 ICCPR, Art 26.
43 Art 17 of the ICCPR.
44 ICCPR, Art 19.
45 Organisation of African Unity (OAU), African Charter on the Rights and Welfare of the Child of 11 July 1990, CAB/LEG/24.9/49 (1990), www.refworld.org/docid/3ae6b38c18.html (accessed on 17 October 2022).
46 CRC, Art 2, ICESCR, Art 9, and ICCPR Art 24.
47 Art 1 of the CEDAW defines 'discrimination' to mean any distinction, exclusion or restriction made on the basis of sex which has the effect or purpose of impairing or nullifying the recognition, enjoyment or exercise by women, irrespective of their marital status, on a basis of equality of men and women, of human rights and fundamental freedoms in the political, economic, social, cultural, civil or any other field.
48 UN Committee on the Elimination of Discrimination Against Women (CEDAW Committee), CEDAW General Recommendation No 19: Violence against Women, 1992, www.refworld.org/docid/52d920c54.html (accessed on 5 February 2022).
49 General Recommendation No 39, *On the Rights of Indigenous Women and Girls* 2022, CEDAW/C/GC/39.
50 United Nations Beijing Declaration and Platform of Action, adopted at the Fourth World Conference on Women, 27 October 1995, www.refworld.org/docid/3dde04324.html (accessed on 3 February 2022).
51 Art 23 of the Maputo Protocol.

52 UN General Assembly, Convention on the Rights of Persons with Disabilities of 13 December 2006, A/RES/61/106, Annex I, www.refworld.org/docid/4680cd212.html (accessed on 8 October 20122).
53 The Committee on the Rights of Persons with Disabilities (CRPD Committee) explained in General Comment No 3 of 2016
54 UN Committee on the Rights of Persons with Disabilities (CRPD), General comment No 3 of 2016, Art 6: Women and girls with disabilities, of 2 September 2016, CRPD/C/GC/3, www.refworld.org/docid/57c977344.html (accessed on 5 February 2022).
55 A/HRC/20/5, Para 40 and A/67/227, Para 67.
56 Adopted in March 2012, www.eac.int/gender/persons-with-disabilities (accessed on 19 May 2023).
57 Section 2.1.2, 3.0 and 4.7 of the East African Policy on Persons with Disabilities, 2012.
58 www.un.org/development/desa/disabilities/news/news/the-sustainable-development-goals-sdgs-and-disability.html (accessed on 21 September 2022).
59 R Young, M Reeve and G Nathan 'The functions of disabled people's organisations (DPOs) in low and middle-income countries: A literature review disability' (2016) 27/3 *Disability CBR and Inclusive Development* 45–71.
60 UNCRPD, Art 1.
61 World Health Organisation (n 8).
62 A Brinkman et al 'Shifting the discourse on disability: Moving to an inclusive, intersectional focus' (2023) 93/1 *American Journal of Orthopsychiatry* 50–62.
63 UN Women (n 6).
64 Preamble to the UNCRPD.
65 Action for Disability and Development International (n 30).
66 The CRPD Committee is the body of independent experts which monitors the implementation of the Convention by the States Parties. More information on the work of the Committee, www.ohchr.org/en/hrbodies/crpd/pages/crpdindex.aspx (accessed on 8 August 2020).
67 CRPD Committee General Comment No 3 on Women and Girls with Disabilities of 2016, UN Doc. CRPD/C/GC/3, Para 16, www. ohchr.org/EN/HRBodies/CRPD/Pages/GC.aspx (accessed on 9 August 2021).
68 Act No 9 of 2010.
69 *Ibid.*
70 P Roz 'Strengthening participation of people with disabilities in leadership roles in developing countries' (2018), K4D Helpdesk. Brighton, UK: Institute of Development Studies.
71 Brinkman (n 59).
72 T Mthembu and W Holness 'Criteria for law reform on comprehensive sexuality education for children with disabilities in South Africa' (2022) 10 *African Disability Rights Yearbook* 78–109.
73 Action for Disability and Development International (n 12).
74 Employment and Labour Relations Act, 2004 (No 6 of 2004) [CAP. 366 R.E. 2019].
75 The Employment and Labour Relations Act, Sect 7(4).
76 Employment and Labor Relations Act, Sect 7(5).
77 The Code of Ethics and Conduct for Public Service, www.policyforum-tz.org/sites/default/files/CodeEthics.pdf (accessed on 25 August 2022).
78 *Ibid.*
79 *Ibid.*
80 Sect 7(1) and 8(3) of the Code of Ethics and Conduct for Public Service.
81 CAP 329.
82 UN Women (n 6).

83 J Wamoyi, M Ranganathan and H Stöckl 'Male and female conceptualizations of sexual harassment in Tanzania: The role of consent, male power, and social norms' (2022) 37/19–20 *Journal of Interpersonal Violence*.
84 Action for Disability and Development International (n 12).
85 Sect 137 of Penal Code, [CAP. 16 R:E 2002].
86 LHRC (n 27).
87 Legal Aid Act, [Act No 1 of March 2017], Legal Aid Regulations (Government Notice 44 of 2018).
88 Section 22 of Legal Aid Act, [Act No 1 of March 2017].
89 The Judicature and Application of Laws (Practice and Procedure of Cases involving vulnerable Groups) Rules, 2019 (Government notes No 110, Published on 1 February 2022).
90 *Ibid*.
91 Action for Disability and Development International (n 12).
92 LHRC (n 27).
93 *Ibid*.
94 *Ibid*.
95 Action for Disability and Development International (n 12).
96 *Ibid*.
97 *Ibid*.
98 UN Women (n 6).
99 Article 7 of ILO C190.
100 Article 8 of ILO 190.
101 Act No 1 of March 2017.

References

Action for Disability and Development International 'Disability and gender-based violence: Peer research in Kibaha and Mkuranga, Tanzania' 2017, www.humanrights.or.tz/assets/attachments/1627542868.pdf (accessed on 20 August 2021).

M Breiding, M Black and G Ryan 'Chronic disease and health risk behaviors associated with intimate partner violence' (2008) 18/7 *Annals of Epidemiology* 538–544.

AH Brinkman 'Shifting the discourse on disability: Moving to an inclusive, intersectional focus' (2023) 93/1 *American Journal of Orthopsychiatry* 50–62.

CB Camargo et al 'Behavioural influences on attitudes towards petty corruption: A study of social norms and mental models in Tanzania' 2017, www.baselgovernance.org/sites/default/files/2019-04/earf_tanzania_country_report_12_december_2017_final.pdf (accessed on 18 August 2020).

CRPD Committee General Comment No 3 on Women and Girls with Disabilities of 2016, UN Doc. CRPD/C/GC/3, www. ohchr.org/EN/HRBodies/CRPD/Pages/GC.aspx (accessed on 9 August 2021).

East African Policy on Persons with Disabilities, 2012.

F Emily 'The #MeToo movement hasn't been inclusive of the disability community' *Teen Vogue* 2018, www.teenvogue.com/story/the-metoo-movement-hasnt-been-inclusive-of-the-disability-community (accessed on 7 February 2022).

Employment and Labour Relations Act, 2004 (No 6 of 2004) [CAP. 366 R.E. 2019].

General Recommendation No 39, *On the Rights of Indigenous Women and Girls* 2022, CEDAW/C/GC/39.

International Labour Organisation 'Violence and harassment in the world of work: A guide on Convention No 190 and Recommendation No 206' *International Labour Office* ILO, 2021. 1v ISBN 9789220350126 (web pdf).

Legal Aid Act, [Act No 1 of March 2017], Legal Aid Regulations (Government Notice 44 of 2018).

Legal and Human Rights Centre (LHRC), Human Rights and Business Report 2020/21 Tanzania Mainland, 2021, ISBN: 978-9987-740-60-4.

W Lu 'I'm disabled and I get sexually harassed: Here's why that matters' *Teen Vogue*, 2017, www.teenvogue.com/story/disability-and-sexual-harassment (accessed on 20 August 2022).

T Mthembu and H Willene 'Criteria for law reform on comprehensive sexuality education for children with disabilities in South Africa' (2022) 10 *African Disability Rights Yearbook* 78–109.

National Bureau of Statistics 'Population and housing census' www.nbs.go.tz/index.php/en/census-surveys/population-and-housing-census/162-2012-phcpopulation-distribution-by-administrative-areas (accessed on 15 January 2022).

Office of National Statistics 'Disability and crime' *UK*, 2019, www.ons.gov.uk/peoplepopulationandcommunity/healthandsocialcare/disability/bulletins/disabilityandcrimeuk/2019#sexual-assault (accessed on 20 January 2022).

Organisation of African Unity (OAU), African Charter on the Rights and Welfare of the Child of 11 July 1990, CAB/LEG/24.9/49 (1990), www.refworld.org/docid/3ae6b38c18.html (accessed on 17 October 2022).

Plan International 'Fact sheet: Violence against women and girls with disabilities' 2013, www.un.org/womenwatch/daw/csw/csw57/side_events/Fact%20sheet%20%20VAWG%20with%20disabilities%20FINAL%20.pdf (accessed on 15 January 2022).

S-B Plummer and P Findley 'Women with disabilities' experience with physical and sexual abuse. trauma violence abuse' (2012) 13/1 *Trauma, Violence and Abuse* 15–29.

P Roz 'Strengthening participation of people with disabilities in leadership roles in developing countries' (2018), K4D Helpdesk. Brighton, UK: Institute of Development Studies.

The Code of Ethics and Conduct for Public Service, www.policyforum-tz.org/sites/default/files/CodeEthics.pdf (accessed on 25th August 2022).

The Committee on the Rights of Persons with Disabilities (CRPD Committee) explained in General Comment No 3 of 2016.

The CRPD Committee is the body of independent experts which monitors the implementation of the Convention by the States Parties. More information on the work of the Committee, www.ohchr.org/en/hrbodies/crpd/pages/crpdindex.aspx (accessed on 8 August 2020).

The Judicature and Application of Laws (Practice and Procedure of Cases involving vulnerable Groups) Rules, 2019 (Government notes No 110, Published on 1 February 2022).

The UN Entity for Gender Equality and the Empowerment of Women (UN Women) 'Making the SDG count for women and girls with disabilities' 2017, www.un.org/development/desa/disabilities/wp-content/uploads/sites/15/2019/10/Making-SDGs-count-for-women-with-disabilities.pdf (accessed on 15 January 2022).

The United Nations Population Fund (UNFPA) 'Five things you didn't know about disability and sexual violence' 2018, https://esaro.unfpa.org/en/news/five-things-you-didnt-know-about-disability-and-sexual violence#:~:text=Children%20who%20are%20deaf%2C%20blind,far%20more%20susceptible%20to%20bullying (accessed on 20 January 2022).

M Uldry and P Mahlamaki 'Making women with disabilities visible' www.social-europe.eu/making-women-with-disabilities-visible (accessed on 20 January 2022).
www.un.org/development/desa/disabilities/news/news/the-sustainable-development-goals-sdgs-and-disability.html (accessed on 21 September 2022).
United Nations Beijing Declaration and Platform of Action, adopted at the Fourth World Conference on Women, 27 October 1995, www.refworld.org/docid/3dde04324.html (accessed on 3 February 2022).
United Nations Committee on the Elimination of Discrimination Against Women (CEDAW Committee), CEDAW General Recommendation No 19: Violence Against Women, (1992), www.refworld.org/docid/52d920c54.html (accessed on 5 February 2022).
United Nations Committee on the Rights of Persons with Disabilities (CRPD), General comment No 3 of 2016.
United Nations General Assembly Convention on the Elimination of All Forms of Discrimination Against Women of 18 December 1979, UN Treaty Series, Vol 1249, www.refworld.org/docid/3ae6b3970.html (accessed on 5 February 2022).
United Nations General Assembly, Convention on the Rights of Persons with Disabilities of 13 December 2006, A/RES/61/106, Annex I, www.refworld.org/docid/4680cd212.html (accessed on 8 October 20122).
United Nations General Assembly, Convention on the Rights of the Child of 20 November 1989, UN Treaty Series Vol 1577, www.refworld.org/docid/3ae6b38f0.html (accessed on 5 February 2022).
United Nations General Assembly International Covenant on Civil and Political Rights of 16 December 1966, United Nations, Treaty Series Vol 999 171, www.refworld.org/docid/3ae6b3aa0.html (accessed on 5 February 2022).
United Nations General Assembly, International Covenant on Economic, Social and Cultural Rights of 16 December 1966, UN Treaty Series Vol 993, www.refworld.org/docid/3ae6b36c0.html (accessed on 5 February 2022).
J Wamoyi, M Ranganathan and H Stöckl 'Male and female conceptualizations of sexual harassment in Tanzania: The role of consent, male power, and social norms' (2022) 37/19–20 *Journal of Interpersonal Violence*.
World Health Organisation 'Disability factsheet' *Disability*, 2022, www.who.int/en/news-room/fact-sheets/detail/disability-and-health (accessed on 5 February 2022).
R Young, M Reeve and G Nathan 'The functions of disabled people's organisations (DPOs) in low and middle-income countries: A literature review disability' (2016) 27/3 *Disability CBR and Inclusive Development* 45–71.

7 Silent but Pervasive

Sexual Harassment Against Women Lawyers in Uganda

Labila Sumayah Musoke

Introduction

In this chapter, I provide a detailed analysis of sexual harassment and the law in Uganda through the lens of women lawyers. Further, I draw upon existing literature to analyse the situational context in Uganda and examine sexual harassment-related legal and policy frameworks within Uganda. Furthermore, I look at the intersectionality between gender, power, and sexual harassment in the legal sector and I draw on the lived experiences of women lawyers subjected to sexual harassment by highlighting the well-know, case of Samantha Mwesigye. It is indeed a case that exposes critical flaws not only within the legal sector but also the judicial sector and, notably, the selection process of judges whose integrity is compromised as result of sexual harassment allegations and impropriety. I conclude with recommendations to address the problem of sexual harassment that cuts across key institutions in Uganda and society in general.

According to the longitudinal study conducted by the International Bar Association on gender disparity in the legal profession,[1] women in Uganda make up 49% of the legal profession with a mere 40% holding senior-level positions. Slight improvements on gender representation in the legal sector have not on its own been a sufficient deterrent against sexual harassment. Sylvia Tamale, a Ugandan academic and human rights activist, notes that sexual harassment remains a universal problem and that women, including lawyers, continue to grapple with workplace sexual harassment which makes the workplace hostile and unsafe.[2] Consequently, women lawyers struggle to attain the same level of success as their male counterparts and some are forced to resign or change their career field, thereby adversely impacting women's economic development and social participation. Sexual harassment repels organisational growth and carries significant costs for both the employer and employee in that it can reduce employee satisfaction, erode sustainability commitment, increase absenteeism, deteriorate co-worker relations, and cause ostracism and career stagnation. Whilst sexual harassment carries a broad negative workplace impact, it is women who are disproportionately affected and of which women within the legal profession are exposed. For this

DOI: 10.4324/9781003373308-7

reason, the scope of this chapter focuses on sexual harassment and women lawyers because, as Samaradiwakera observes, they are disproportionately vulnerable to sexual harassment in the legal profession.[3] The 2021 national labour survey report affirms that women are more likely than men to experience sexual harassment.[4] The report revealed that 1.6% of women and 0.2% of men had experienced workplace sexual abuse in the workplace. This translates into 196 male experiencing sexual abuse compared to 1,536 women.

According to the Uganda Demographic and Health Survey,[5] one in five women aged between 15 to 49 have experienced some form of sexual harassment. Sylvia Tamale[6] argues that ongoing current sexual harassment cases reflect pre-existing patterns of violence and abuse in several sectors where women work, indicating a systemic problem that has gone unchecked for years. However, the MeToo movement initiated by Tarana Burke in the United States of America which gained prominence in 2017[7] inspired civil society organisations and advocacy coalitions in Uganda to push back against sexual harassment. In Uganda, social justice activists turned to social media using hashtags such as #MeTooUg and #TimesUp. Some activists organised protests and dialogues demanding that employers take action to prevent sexual harassment and hold perpetrators to account.[8] Chapter Four Uganda,[9] the Uganda Association of Women Lawyers[10] (FIDA-U), Akina Mama wa Afrika (AMwA), Women Pro bono Initiative,[11] and the Center for Domestic Violence and Prevention[12] are a few such organisations. For instance, AMwA commissioned a study to assess the level of violence against women learners in higher education institutions of learning.[13] The study revealed that sexual harassment in the form of sex for marks, blackmail, and social media violence, among others, were the most prevalent forms of violence at institutions of higher learning.[14] In July 2020, AMwA published another study, *Tusikize! Listen to Us*, to document the voices and experiences of women at work.[15]

Similarly, the International Lawyers Assisting Workers Network (ILAW)[16] presented compelling policy recommendations to the Employment (Sexual Harassment) Regulations.[17] ILAW notes that the current definition of an employer in respect to sexual harassment in the Principal Employment Act is overly restrictive, thereby failing to account for certain relevant work-related relationships. To address the concern, ILAW recommended that the Amendment Bill[18] should provide for a broader interpretation of an 'employer' to encompass individuals who are not directly employed by the employer yet maintain a working or business relationship with the same. Additionally, ILAW also recommended the inclusion of other employee cadres, regardless of their level of authority, in the definition of an employee. It is against this stark background, that I propose and call for a comprehensive reform of existing laws to respond to sexual harassment in Uganda and, specifically, in the legal sector.

Context Analysis

In Uganda, the subjection of women lawyers to sexual harassment though prevalent is rarely spoken about.[19] This is in part due to the fact that Uganda's legal sector is male dominated.[20] Thus, without safeguard measures, disproportionate power held by male lawyers in the legal sector makes it more difficult for women lawyers subjected to sexual harassment to speak out.[21] Samaradiwakera[22] notes that this allows perpetrators to continue this vice with impunity.[23] The power dynamics between employer and employee coupled with a culture of silence has resulted in the under-reporting of sexual harassment-related cases in the legal sector.[24] According to a survey conducted by WAN-IFRA Women in News (a global organisation focused on gender equality), the low rate of formal reporting of sexual harassment cases is evident as only 12% of sexual harassment survivors choose to report,[25] citing reasons such as fear of job loss (14%), lack of admissible evidence (12.7%), or fear of victimisation (11.7%).[26]

Silence is normalised because of the gender and power disparities which embolden a toxic misogynistic workplace environment. Much of the silencing was shifted under the wave of defiance brought on by the MeToo Movement and this inevitably affected Ugandan women. This is demonstrated by the fact that in the wake of the MeToo movement, a *Daily Monitor* headline dated Monday, 12 May 2019,[27] 'Senior State Attorney accuses Deputy Solicitor General of sexual harassment' was the 'silence breaker' on issues of sexual harassment in the legal profession. Samantha Mwesigye, a former senior state attorney at the Ministry of Justice and Constitutional Affairs, publicly spoke out about her sexual harassment.[28] The incident gained nationwide traction and sparked debate on the prevalence of workplace sexual harassment for women, especially in the legal sector.

Subsequently, in 2019, under the stewardship of the Female Lawyers Committee, the Uganda Law Society developed and launched a pilot sexual harassment policy as a safeguard for adoption by law firms and legal departments across Uganda. However, since its launch in 2019, the policy has yet to be implemented and there is a need for the proactive engagement with women lawyers and judicial members to facilitate its effective implementation across the legal fraternity. Some politicians, including Chairman Norbert Mao (now the serving minister of Justice and Constitutional Affairs), expressed solidarity with professional and informal workers who had been subjected to sexual harassment and specifically showed support in Samantha's case.[29] Prominent Ugandan women leaders, including the likes of Winnie Byanyima, the UNAIDS Executive Director, demonstrated support for survivors of sexual harassment as well as to Samantha via social media. For instance, a Tweet dated 13 May 2019 was powerful. She wrote:

> I salute you Samantha Mwesigye for the courage to speak up against sexual harassment at work. It's not easy but you've done it for all

> women & girls. I believe you & support your demand for justice & protection against retaliation. Stay strong.[30]

Media spotlights of sexual harassment cases at Makerere University also created awareness of this pervasive problem.[31] In response to sexual harassment allegations, the vice-chancellor commissioned a five-member committee to investigate the cause of increasing cases of sexual harassment at the institution, review the existing sexual harassment policy, and draw recommendations. The investigation report was released in 2018 and it revealed a pervasive culture of sexual harassment and abuse at Makerere University. The investigation findings at Makerere University established that some male examiners deliberately omitted female students' marks from the class list in order to lure them into their offices and exploit them.[32]

According to a 2008 cross-sectional survey by Frank Kiwalabye, a researcher at Youth Crime Watch Uganda,[33] out of 1,437 women, two-thirds of whom were below the age of 35 years and about half of whom were low-ranking employees (58%, approximately) had been subjected to some form of sexual harassment by their employers, and 26% succumbed to engaging in sexual encounters with their bosses and were less likely to be fired or demoted even if they were under performing. Further, respondents reported that individuals in high-ranking positions had 28% less chance of being subjected to sexual harassment at the workplace. Only 13% of the respondents were aware of policies in the workplace that protect individuals from sexual harassment.[34]

Gender, Power, and Sexual Harassment: Fighting Three Battles from Three Different Fronts

Sexual harassment against women lawyers must be examined through an intersectional lens as this expands on a critical perspective on how multiple forms of oppressive behaviour shape a survivor's experience.[35] As previously noted, the legal profession in Uganda is a male-dominated sector; there are generally more men in senior legal positions of power than women.[36] Uganda is ranked 61st worldwide in respect to gender equality score, according to the Global Gender Gap 2022 report.[37] This power imbalance is problematic and reinforces patriarchal values that uphold male dominance while socially constructing women as subordinates.

Ugandan scholar Sylvia Tamale, in a report investigating sexual harassment at Makerere University, noted that the social construction of women as subordinates translates into a culture of male dominance that shrinks women's power and silences women.[38] Tamale further noted that such subordination practices have historically deprived women, including lawyers, from realising their full potential while victimising and traumatising women lawyers.[39] Tamale also argues that any serious discussion on sexual harassment must go beyond sexism and pay close attention to the impact of a gender-stratified society, because sexual harassment reinforces women's inferior labour market position.[40] In line with Tamale's notion, Cock *et al*[41] recognise that sexual harassment is a manifestation of gender inequality which is a primary product of deeply ingrained prejudice and harmful stereotypes. These prejudices and stereotypes are evident in many Ugandan workplaces[42] where a woman is reduced to an object with little voice or agency.[43]

In addition to gender, other intersecting identities like tribe, socio-economic status, and disability, among others, also create unique challenges for women lawyers in the workplace. These intersecting identities can impact an individual's ability to report or seek redress for sexual harassment. For example, a woman lawyer from a low societal background may face economic pressures that make it difficult for her to either report or resign from a job where she is sexually harassed, as she does not have financial security or other employment opportunities in the event the employer retaliates against her. During her presentation of the Makerere University sexual harassment investigation report, Sylvia Tamale[44] remarked that the association of women's bodies with sexuality and shame can be traced to alien traditions and religious values.

To effectively address sexual harassment against women lawyers in Uganda, it is important to fight all three battles of gender, power, and sexual harassment simultaneously. This calls for collaboration and coordination between legal experts, policy makers, cultural institutions, and civil society. It also requires acknowledging the intersecting identities and power dynamics. By so doing, Uganda would create a safe and equitable workplace for all women in the legal profession.

National Laws Relevant to Sexual Harassment

The 1995 Constitution of Uganda as the supreme law of the land has a binding force on all persons and authorities in Uganda.[45] In particular, Article 20 of the Constitution provides for the inherent right of every individual and enjoins state agencies to respect, protect, and uphold the same. Similarly, Article 21 provides for equality and freedom from discrimination before and under the law, while Article 24 calls for the protection of human dignity and protection from cruel and inhuman treatment. Additionally, Article 33 specifically provides for the rights of women. Beyond this normative framing, the state has an obligation to take positive measures to ensure the effectiveness of all related secondary legislation aimed at preventing and combating sexual harassment. One such step would be to review and amend all laws, policies, and practices related to sexual harassment to ensure that all secondary legislation adopts a human rights-based approach, is gender responsive, and addresses intersectional and structural discrimination.

At a subsidiary level, the Employment Act[46] governs employment relations between the employer and employee within the labour market, including the legal profession. In relation to sexual harassment, the Act, specifically

Section 7,[47] prohibits sexual harassment in the workplace and prescribes how employers should combat sexual harassment. The section further characterises sexual harassment as an act committed by the employer or a representative of that employer. In this context, Section 2 of the Employment Act defines an employer as 'Any person or group of persons, including a company or corporation, a public, regional or local authority . . . for whom an employee works or has worked, or normally works under a contract of service'.

In addition, Section 7(3) provides an interpretation of what constitutes an employer's representative. Specifically, Section 7(3) of the Employment Act (2006) states:

> an employer's representative is a person who is employed by that employer, who either has authority over the employee alleging sexual harassment, or is in a position of power over other employees in the workplace of the employee alleging sexual harassment.[48]

Section 7(3) provides inadequate protection to all employees because it assumes that a harasser must be in a supervisory position. Whilst this is a sad reality for many workers reporting to management, sexual harassment can occur across a horizontal spectrum, such as between co-workers, and it can be committed by a subordinate against a superior.

As alluded to in the previous section, the Employment Act[49] further compounds the problem of sexual harassment by stating that only an employer with more than 25 employees need provide a sexual harassment policy.[50] The implication being that an employer with less than 25 employees is not legally mandated to have any measures in place to protect their employees against sexual harassment, leaving vulnerable individuals, especially women lawyers, unprotected and without legal recourse to report sexual harassment-related incidents.

Also noteworthy is the definition of what constitutes sexual harassment in the workplace and the express and implicit limitations that come with that definition. According to the Employment (Sexual Harassment) Regulations of 2012,[51] sexual harassment arises where a direct or implicit request to a worker is made for any form of 'sexual favour' to get preferential treatment in the workplace or threaten the worker with detrimental treatment of the present or future employment status of the worker. This form of sexual harassment is called *quid pro quo* sexual harassment.

The Employment (Sexual Harassment) Regulations[52] explicitly prohibit retaliation against sexual harassment complainants. Specifically, Regulation 9(2)(c) provides that: 'An employer shall instruct the recipient of sexual harassment complaints to inform the complainant and the alleged perpetrator that the employer shall not tolerate any form of retaliation against the complainant'. In this context, retaliation means any unwarranted action against an employer, employee, or any other person who may be involved in a sexual harassment complaint. Regulation 13(1)(h) also provides that 'On receipt of a complaint, the labour officer shall promptly investigate a complaint and inform the employer that he or she will not engage in retaliation against the complainant or anyone else who cooperates with the investigation'.

Additionally, Regulation 17 outlines instances in which a sexual harassment survivor may consult on, report, file a complaint, testify as a witness, or cooperate during an investigation without fear of retaliation.[53] Notwithstanding the significance of these provisions, potential challenges exist in their implementation and enforcement where a labour officer is not trained to identify retaliatory behaviour. Lastly, there is an inadequate legal and policy environment which shrinks protection to survivors in pursuit of justice.[54]

The Employment (sexual harassment) Regulation[55] only places a duty on companies with 25 or more employees to develop a sexual harassment policy and condemn it in their respective organisations. The Regulations therefore create legal loopholes which have a causal effect and impact on increasing women's vulnerability to sexual harassment in the workplace and fails to consider that hundreds of women lawyers, for example, work in establishments with less than 25 employees.[56] Not only does such a legislative failure reinforce gender inequality, it increases impunity for sexual harassment perpetrators. From an equality lens, the regulation's narrow scope undermines constitutional fundamental principles of equal protection under the law and before the law, as guaranteed by Article 21.[57]

Criminalising Sexual Harassment in Uganda

Sexual harassment in Uganda is a labour law issue which creates civil liabilities and remedies to address violations thereof; however, aspects of sexually harassing behaviour can amount to a criminal offence. This is apparent from the Penal Code.[58] However, sexual harassment is not explicitly defined as a separate offence under the Penal Code. Instead, Section 128 is applied to address the offense of indecent assault, which is a form of sexual harassment, and the offender is liable to imprisonment for 14 years. Still, Section 128(3) provides:

> Any person who, intending to insult the modesty of any woman or girl, utters any word, makes any sound, gesture, intending that such word or sound shall be heard, or that such gesture or object shall be seen by such a woman or girl, or intrudes upon the privacy of such a woman or girl commits a misdemeanour and is liable to imprisonment of one year.

In addition, Section 128(3) frames unwanted behaviour and gestures as violations of a woman's modesty. That said, the Penal Code Act does not explicitly define modesty, but guidance can be drawn from Justice Musota's ruling in *Uganda v Olupot*.[59] In this case, the accused indecently assaulted the victim by raping her in front of her children. Justice Musota observed that the accused was insensitive, as he abused the victim's modesty and dignity.

Likewise, Surendra Chaher, an author from India, in her article 'outraging the modesty of a woman',[60] opines that modesty is an inherent characteristic of womanhood, independent of any individual's personality. Similarly, the Indian Supreme Court, in *Ramkripal Singh v State of Madhya Pradesh*, expounded on what outraging a woman's modesty encompasses.[61] The court stressed that the act of pulling a woman, removing her saree, and requesting sexual intercourse or any act likely to put her to shame could be an affront to her modesty. The Supreme Court interpreted modesty to mean a woman's decency and a virtue that she possesses as a result of her sex. The aforementioned perspectives view modesty as an integral virtue of womanhood that aligns with cultural norms and gender expectations.

Contrary to the aforementioned, Avantika Tewari, a feminist political theorist, researcher, and academic based in India, criticises the court's narrow interpretation of modesty in *Ram Kripal Singh v State of Madhya*[62] in her article, 'My modesty is not outraged, I am'. Tewari argues that framing sexual harassment as an attack on a woman's modesty reinforces the dominant narrative that a woman's worth is tied to her chastity and that any violation of her body is a violation of her dignity. Tewari further asserts that sexual harassment is not solely an attack on a woman's body, but rather an abuse of power by the perpetrator. In short, Tewari contends that such a gendered interpretation serves to entrench protective patriarchal notions of gender, culture, agency, and victimhood, all which consider women as 'second citizens', which limits their agency and autonomy. Tewari rather advocates for a nuanced understanding of modesty that recognises agency and bodily autonomy, paying particular attention to a given jurisdiction context.

The Story of Samantha Mwesigye

In this section, I highlight the victim blaming, character assassination, and intimidation experienced by Samantha when she reported the sexual harassment she was subjected to. The story of Samantha provides a real-life experience of the difficulties of speaking out. This is exacerbated by inadequate legal protections for those who wish to report sexual harassment as well as socio-cultural backlash embedded by patriarchal perceptions of women's place in society and in the legal sector. While sharing her experience before the labour tribunal, Samantha Mwesigye, a woman lawyer, recounted the sexual harassment that she had been subjected to:

> The alleged sexual harassment began while I was clerk student at the Ministry of Justice and Constitutional Affairs. The unwelcome behaviour continued through my employment as a state attorney for over 13 years. In 2018, I took a stand against it. Christopher Gashirabake (the then- Deputy Solicitor General) who was both my boss and supervisor, often texted me in an inappropriately flirtatious manner. He would end his texts with 'Samantha Gash' or 'with love from Gash'. He

> once demanded sex after learning I received a job offer from the sex in exchange for a job at Kampala Capital City Authority; and showed off the size of groin. On 28 September 2018, I sent him a letter demanding an end to his behaviour. I disclosed my concerns to several colleagues at work and subsequently, filed several complaints with Ministry of Justice and Constitutional Affairs (my employer) but to no avail. I was shocked to learn that the Ministry of Justice and Constitutional Affairs did not have an established sexual harassment committee to address my complaints against my harasser. I filed a complaint before the Kampala Capital City Authority Labour tribunal, but they did not hear it.[63]

Subsequently, Samantha had to institute a lawsuit at the Industrial Court against Christopher Gashirabake and the attorney general.[64] It must further be noted that on the 18 April 2023, the Industrial Court gave Justice Christopher Gashirabake leave to appeal. Samantha's story spurred public debate across Uganda. Activists like Rosebell Kagumire, a feminist writer and editor, took the struggle to her Twitter account and remarked as follows:

> Nowhere is safe! In a country where a state attorney is harassed out of a job, we know the situation is way dire for many women and girls. We must come together support those brave enough to speak. Demand #JusticeForSamantha.[65]

Samantha, like so many other sexual harassment survivors, was vilified for challenging a system that has for long normalised sexual harassment in all spheres of life.[66] The failure by the Ministry of Justice and Constitutional Affairs to promptly constitute a sexual harassment committee raises serious human rights concerns. By not taking immediate action as obligated under the Employment Act, the Ministry did not only infringe on Samantha's constitutional guarantee to equality and non-discrimination under Article 21 and the right to a fair and timely hearing under Article 28, but also sent a message to the other employees that sexual harassment is not taken seriously.

The Appointment of Christopher Gashirabake to the Court of Appeal

The hierarchy of courts in Uganda is constitutionally prescribed.[67] At the top of the hierarchy is the Supreme Court,[68] also called the final court of appeal. This is followed by the Court of Appeal/Constitutional Court,[69] charged with the duty of hearing appeals from the High Court and the High Court[70] which is headed by the Principal Judge (PJ) and such number of judges as Parliament may prescribe. One of the key mandates of the Judicial Service Commission (JSC) of Uganda is to provide recommendations to the president on suitable persons for appointment as judges and registrars.[71] Whilst the JSC receives and processes complaints or recommendations from the public about the judiciary and the general administration of justice, there is no process to allow for public scrutiny of the nominees nor does it involve public interviews.

The selection and nomination process of a judge is thereafter completed by a vetting process undertaken by Parliament and, specifically, the Parliament Appointments Committee.[72] On approval of Parliament, the nominee is appointed by the president. The selection and nomination and appointment of Christopher Gashirabake as a Justice of the Court of Appeal[73] took place amidst widespread public knowledge of the sexual harassment allegations as well as the sexual harassment complaint pending determination by the Labour Tribunal Court. Despite the obvious scandal, the president of Uganda, acting on the advice of the Judicial Service Commission[74] and upon approval by Parliament,[75] proceeded to appoint Christopher Gashirabake to this position of judicial influence.

Activists and concerned citizens took to social media[76] to express their discontent and demand a review of the appointment in order to uphold the integrity of the judiciary.[77] Samantha also protested the pending appointment of Christopher Gashirabake by submitting a letter to the Judicial Service Commission and Parliament.[78] She began her letter by stating the following:

> The appointment of Gashirabake Christopher to the Constitutional Court is desecration of the Constitutional Court and the Constitution of Uganda. This is someone with a sexual harassment claim brought against him in the Industrial Court-Labour Dispute Reference No 353 of 2019 [arising from Labour Dispute KCCA/RUB/LC/560/2019. That claim has been in the media so it is very hard to understand why the Judicial Service Commission (JSC) would recommend someone to such an office with a claim against him, one involving moral turpitude.[79]

Conclusion

In this chapter, I have argued that whilst both men and women are subjected to sexual harassment, it is women who are disproportionately affected and, further, that women lawyers are particularly vulnerable given the gender dynamics of the legal sector. The analysis of Uganda's legal and policy framework relating to sexual harassment exposes the inadequacy of the existing laws and policies to combat sexual harassment at the workplace. Further, the paucity of literature and insufficient publicly available data on sexual harassment within the legal profession in Uganda makes it difficult for survivors and stakeholders to appreciate its socio-economic impact and ultimately contributes to a culture of silence surrounding workplace sexual harassment, allowing the violations and inequalities to continue unchecked.

I noted specific legal loopholes, such as the Employment (sexual harassment) Regulation which only places a duty on companies with 25 or more employees to develop a sexual harassment policy. Such a position is rightly vulnerable to legal challenges around broad concepts of access to justice and equal protection before the law for those employed by companies with less than 25 employees. Indeed, very few law firms (if any) have 25 or more employees, and the lack of a sexual harassment policy has a direct impact on awareness, prevention, and intervention.

Another challenge lies in the selection, recruitment, or appointment of judges to the courts of Uganda. I have noted the specific challenges and the awkward situation of an alleged sexual harasser having been promoted with little resistance to a higher court in Uganda. It is appropriate to return to Angelou's poem as a dedication to all sexual harassment survivors, like Samantha Mwesigye. The poem is a reminder of the courage required to speak up against sexual harassment and the importance of supporting survivors in their journey towards healing and justice. To all survivors that are struggling to speak up, I believe you!

Did you want to see me broken?
Bowed head and lowered eyes?
Shoulders falling down like teardrops,
Weakened by my soulful cries
. . . . but still, like air, I rise.[80]

Recommendations

Parliament should fast-track the passing of the Employment (amendment) Bill 2022.[81] Although, the Bill in its present form offers an opportunity for Uganda to streamline her employment laws and regulations in accordance with internationally recognised human rights instruments, for instance, Goal 8, Target 8.5 of the Sustainable Development Goals, policy alone will not be enough to safeguard employees like women lawyers from sexual harassment at the workplace. Thus, it is crucial for the government to allocate sufficient resources to ensure effective implementation of the bill.

In addition, the Employment (amendment) Bill envisions a safe working environment by removing the requirement that only employers with 25 and more employees put in place measures to prevent sexual harassment at the workplace. The proposed provision falls short of protecting women employees in informal settings. This legislative oversight is likely to lead to a lack of accountability for informal businesses that employ most women, thereby putting them at risk of experiencing sexual harassment without recourse. It is, therefore, important that both formal and informal workplaces put in place measures to prevent sexual harassment.

The justice system, including quasi-judicial institutions, should lower the standard of proof by shifting the burden of proof from the survivor to the perpetrator. This approach would address gaps that have led to survivors bring re-victimised. Civil society and grass-root organising should strengthen the existing movements and amplify the campaign as to increase public awareness about the social and economic impact of sexual harassment. One way would be through identification of champions that most people relate with and strongly believe in. However, the campaign should go to the root causes of workplace sexual harassment and unsettle the existing gender hierarchies that have for so long maintained and normalised sexual harassment.

Lastly, it is imperative for the Judicial Service Commission and Parliament to ensure inclusive participation in the selection process of judicial officers, going beyond the current practice of limited public participation. This broader participation will not only foster accountability among judicial officers but also rebuild public confidence in the judiciary.

Notes

1 International Bar Association. 50:50 by 2030: A longitudinal Study into Gender Disparity in Law: Uganda results report, www.ibanet.org/document?id=Uganda-Report-2022-5050-by-2030 (accessed on 24 February 2023).

2 S Tamale 'Making sure the issue becomes the story: Problematizing media coverage of sexual harassment at Makerere University' *Konrad Adenauer Stiftung (KAS), Women in Media, Kweeta*, 17 August 2018, www.kas.de/en/web/uganda/veranstaltungsberichte/detail/-/content/making-sure-the-issue-becomes-the-story-problematizing-the-media-coverage-of-sexual-harassment-at-makerere-university (accessed on 27 February 2023).

3 C Samaradiwakera-Wijesundara 'Reframing corporate subjectivity: Systemic inequality and the company at the intersection of race, gender and poverty' (2022) 7/1 *Business and Human Rights Journal* 100–116.

4 Uganda Bureau of Statistics (UBOS) 'The national labour force survey' (2021) *Main Report*. The survey was carried out between July and November 2021, www.ubos.org/national-labour-force-survey-2021-main-report/ (accessed on 27 February 2023).

5 Uganda Bureau of Statistics 'Uganda demographic and health survey' (2016) *Kampala*, https://dhsprogram.com/pubs/pdf/FR333/FR333.pdf (accessed on 27 February 2023).

6 S Tamale 'The right to culture and the culture of rights: A critical perspective on women's sexual rights in Africa' (2008) 16/1 *Feminist Legal Studies* 47–69.

7 The MeToo movement is a global campaign against sexual harassment that Tarana Burke started in 2006. It gained international recognition in 2017. The movement aimed to a safe forum for women and girls to share their personal sexual harassment stories and experiences.

8 Some tweet links. https://twitter.com/amwaafrika/status/124346744983768269 8?s=20; https://twitter.com/arkwesi/status/1146876374575132672?s=20; https://twitter.com/SarahBireete/status/1146783290541727744?s=20.

9 Chapter Four Uganda, an indigenous organisation that seeks to become a vocal and principled defender of constitutionally guaranteed rights across a spectrum without limitation based on ethnic, religious, or other group identity, political affiliation, or sexual orientation.

10 FIDA-Uganda Association of Women Lawyers, https://fidauganda.org/ (accessed on 10 May 2023).

11 A Mama wa Afrika, this is a Pan-African feminist leadership development organisation based in Uganda.

12 Women Pro Bono Initiative, 'Women Pro Bono Initiative, is a civil society organisation founded in July 2018 to advance access to justice for women and girls in Uganda through awareness creation, legal representation, research and knowledge sharing, https://womenprobono.org/ (accessed on 10 May 2023).

13 A Mama wa Afrika 'Uganda baseline study report on violence against young women' www.akinamamawaafrika.org/wp-content/uploads/2019/10/AMwA-Baseline-report-FINAL-1.pdf (accessed on 25 February 2023).
14 *Ibid* No 9.
15 A Mama wa Afrika 'Tusikize! Listen to Us' July 2020.
16 International Lawyers Assisting Workers Network 'Views and recommendations on the Employment (Amendment) Bill of 2022, https://voicesforlabour.org/wp-content/uploads/2023/02/Opinion-on-the-Employment-Bill-Uganda-1–1.pdf (accessed on 8 May 2023).
17 The Employment (Sexual Harassment) Regulations [2012] Statutory Instrument No 15 of 2012, commenced on 20 April 2012, https://ulii.org/akn/ug/act/si/2012/15/eng@2012-04-20 (accessed on 08 May 2023).
18 Employment (Amendment) Bill, 2022, www.parliament.go.ug/cmis/views/8c16ae2f-8ce0-4590-88b6-a4cda1dbdbaa%253B1.0 (accessed on 8 May 2023).
19 P Nyamishana 'Breaking the silence to end workplace sexual harassment in Uganda, African feminism' https://africanfeminism.com/breaking-the-silence-to-end-wokplace-sexual-harassment-in-uganda (accessed on 14 May 2023) Prudence is a Ugandan Human Rights blogger.
20 *Ibid* No 2, 6. In addition, as of 11 May 2023, unofficial data provided by an officer at the Uganda Law Society indicated that male lawyers comprise of about 60% while female lawyers are approximately 40%. This difference is suggestive of a male dominated legal fraternity in Uganda (data unpublished).
21 A Mama wa Afrika *Experiences of Women in the World of Work in Uganda, Sexual-Harassment-Study.pdf*, akinamamawaafrika.org (accessed on 30 July 2021).
22 *Ibid* No 11, 3
23 A Moretti 'Sexual harassment in the legal profession: An analysis of the current legislative framework' (2022) 47/2 *Alternative Law Journal* 95–100.
24 A Mama wa Afrika 'Understanding sexual harassment in the world of work' 3, 16 October 2019, https://docs.google.com/document/d/15ka4rnJ5CDpJoOf6bod AyazCZMFEYOTw/edit (accessed on 25 February 2023).
25 World Association of News 'Women in news. sexual harassment in the Media' *Africa Report*, 38–39, https://womeninnews.org/wp-content/uploads/2021/07/20210704_Sexual-Harassment-in-The-Media-Low-Res.pdf (accessed on 27 February 2023).
26 *Ibid* No 28.
27 'Senior state attorney accuses deputy solicitor general of sexual harassment' *The Daily Monitor*, 12 May 2019, www.monitor.co.ug/uganda/news/national/senior-state-attorney-accuses-deputy-solicitor-general-of-sexual-harassment-1825234 (accessed on 22 December 2021).
28 'Solicitor General breaks silence on harassment allegations' *The Observer*, 14 May 2019, https://observer.ug/news/headlines/60677-solicitor-general-breaks-silence-on-sexual-harassment-allegations (accessed on 09 May 2023).
29 N Mao 'Samantha Mwesigye's Agony: Has Uganda's #MeToo movement' *The Daily Monitor*, 18 May 2019, www.monitor.co.ug/uganda/oped/commentary/samantha-mwesigye-s-agony-has-uganda-s-metoo-moment-arrived–1826490 (accessed on 22 December 2021).
30 W Byanyima 13 May 2019. See tweet at: https://twitter.com/Winnie_Byanyima/status/1127970417224953856?s=20 (accessed on 25 February 2023).
31 'Victims of sexual harassment at Makerere speak out' *The Daily Monitor*, 6 May 2017, www.monitor.co.ug/uganda/video/victims-of-sexual-harassment-at-makerere-speak-out-1699894 (accessed on 13 May 2023); see also 'Three Makerere University lecturers suspended for alleged sexual harassment' *The Independent*, 16 July 2019, www.independent.co.ug/three-makerere-university-lecturers-suspended-for-alleged-sexual-harassment/ (accessed on 13 May 2023).

32 Makerere University, Report on Investigating Sexual Harassment at Makerere University, June 2018, https://afi.la.psu.edu/wp-content/uploads/sites/21/2021/09/Makerere-Committee-Investigating-Sexual-Harassment-FINAL-Report-June2018.pdf (accessed on 27 February 2023).
33 F Kiwalabye 'Effects of sexual harassment at the workplace: A Ugandan case study' *Youth Crime Watch Uganda/ Ignites Worldwide Uganda*, 2008, https://svri.org/forums/forum2011/EffectsHarassment.pdf (accessed on 16 September 2020).
34 *Ibid* No 25.
35 T Mogapaesi 'Sexual harassment in the workplace and women's access to justice: Lessons for Botswana from a South Africa perspective' (2019) 45/3 *Commonwealth Law Bulletin* 431–453.
36 Presently, the Uganda Law Society Executive Council is composed of mainly men (https://uls.or.ug/executive-council/) with male president and a male CEO. Other Legal Institutions like the Uganda Law Reform Commission- the commission is fairly balanced (www.ulrc.go.ug/content/staff) with a female as the head.
37 World Economic Forum 'Global gender gap report, 2022' 13 July 2022, www.weforum.org/reports/global-gender-gap-report-2022/?DAG=3&gclid=CjwKCAjw3ueiBhBmEiwA4BhspA4xODztFvPAXEf2lGxlcjccYGiOF-UcHLGa9dNRfgR-f8QLR_Bwi4RoCL3sQAvD_BwE (accessed on 9 May 2023).
38 Makerere University 'Report on investigating sexual harassment at Makerere University' June 2018, https://afi.la.psu.edu/wp-content/uploads/sites/21/2021/09/Makerere-Committee-Investigating-Sexual-Harassment-FINAL-Report-June2018.pdf (accessed on 27 February 2023).
39 S Tamale *When Hens Begin to Crow: Gender and Parliamentary Politics in Uganda*, 1st ed (Fountain Publishers, 2008).
40 *Ibid* No 34.
41 R Cook and S Cusack *Gender Stereotyping: Transnational Legal Perspectives* (University of Philadelphia Press, 2010).
42 J Aloka 'Prevalence and management of sexual harassment at the workplace: The case study of Uganda prison service' (Masters thesis, Makerere University 2009), www.mak.ac.ug/documents/Makfiles/theses/Aloka_Julias.pdf (accessed on 13 May 2023); However, it is worth noting that both the professional regulatory (Uganda Law Council) and membership (Uganda Law Society) bodies lack aggregated readily available data on the gender composition of law firms or legal departments.
43 R Kagumire 'Ads about bus stop harassment and 'bonus wives' normalise sexism' *The Guardian*, 1 April 2019, www.theguardian.com/global-development/2019/apr/01/ugandan-ads-bus-stop-harassment-bonus-wives-normalise-sexism (accessed on 13 May 2023).
44 Tamale (n 2) 3.
45 Constitution of the Republic of Uganda, Art 2, 22 September 1995, www.parliament.go.ug/documents/1240/constitution (accessed on 13 May 2023).
46 The Employment Act, 2006. Laws of Uganda, https://ulii.org/system/files/legislation/act/2006/2006/employment_act_2006_pdf_50549.pdf (accessed on 18 September 2020).
47 *Ibid* No 53, Sect 7.
48 *Ibid* No 35.
49 Sect 7(4) of Employment Act.
50 *Ibid* No 35; 'Every employer who employs more than twenty-five employees is required to have in place measures to prevent sexual harassment in the workplace'.
51 Employment (Sexual Harassment) Regulations, 20 April 2012, Statutory Supplementary Instrument, Uganda Gazette No 21, Vol CIV, https://ulii.org/akn/ug/act/si/2012/15/eng%402012-04-20 (accessed on 18 February 2023). These

Regulations give effect to the provisions on sexual harassment in the Employment Act of 2006.

52 Ibid No 23, Regulation 9(2)(c), Regulation 1(1)(h), and Regulation 17.

53 Ibid No 23, Regulation 17.

54 L Blumell and D Mulupi 'Sexual harassment is rife in many African media workplaces' *The Conversation*, 19 July 2021, https://theconversation.com/sexual-harassment-is-rife-in-many-african-media-workplaces-163451 (accessed on 27 February 2023).

55 Employment (Sexual Harassment) Regulations, 2012. Statutory Instrument No 15 of 2012, commenced on 20 April 2012, https://ulii.org/akn/ug/act/si/2012/15/eng@2012-04-20 (accessed on 8 April 2023).

56 *Ibid* no 18.

57 The 1995 Constitution of the Republic of Uganda. Laws of Uganda. Article 21(1) 'All persons are equal before and the law in all spheres in political, economic, social and cultural life and in every other respect and shall enjoy equal protection of the law. The position of the law is likely to change as the Employment (Amendment) Bill of 2022 proposes to provide protection against sexual harassment to all employees by extending the obligation to all employers, regardless of the number of employees, making it necessary to fast-track its passage into law.

58 The Penal Code Act 1950 (Uganda) 15 June 1950, https://ulii.org/akn/ug/act/ord/1950/12/eng@2014-05-09 (accessed on 10 May 2023).

59 [HCt-04-CR-SC-0066–2008] 21 April 2011(HC).

60 S Chaher 'Outraging the modesty of a woman: Inter-spousal perspective' (1990) 32/4 *Journal of the Indian Law Institute* 527–535.

61 *Ramkripal Singh v State of Madhya Pradesh*, AIR (2007) SC India, Criminal Appeal No 370/2007, delivered by Hon Judge Dr Arijit Pasayat, 19 March 2007, www.legitquest.com/case/ramkripal-v-state-of-mp/2F8E3 (accessed on 19 September 2020).

62 A Tewari 'My modesty is not outraged, I am! Patriarchy in the language of law' 28 August 2017, https://feminisminindia.com/2017/08/28/modesty-outraged-patriarchy-law/ (accessed on 18 September 2020).

63 *Samantha Mwesigye* [KCCA/RUB/560/2019] Labour Complaint.

64 *Samantha Mwesigye v Attorney General and Gashirabake Christopher* [Labour Dispute Reference No 353 of 2019] The Industrial Court at Kampala.

65 R Kagumire, a feminist writer and activist. Twitter handle, @RosebellK, 11 May 2019, https://twitter.com/RosebellK/status/1127269978510643200?s=20 (accessed on 27 February 2023.

66 The Daily Monitor 'Attorney in sexual harassment case scrapped off government pay roll' *Kampala*, 1 September 2019, www.monitor.co.ug/uganda/news/national/attorney-in-sexual-harassment-case-scrapped-off-government-payroll-1845680 (accessed on 27 February 2023).

67 Constitution of Uganda. Art 129(2).

68 Art 132.

69 Art 134.

70 Art 138.

71 Art 142, 1995 Constitution of Uganda '. . . the Justice of Appeal shall be appointed be appointed by the president acting on the advice of the Judicial Service Commission and upon approval of parliament'.

72 Committees of Parliament, www.parliament.go.ug/page/committees-parliament (accessed on 3 June 2023).

73 The Judiciary Uganda 'The honourable justices of court of appeal' http://judiciary.go.ug/data/incourt/18/The%20Honorable%20Justices%20of%20the%20Court%20of%20Appeal%20.html; see also 'Museveni appoints Gashirabake and Justice Eve Luswata to Court of Appeal' www.homelandmedia.co.ug/news/

museveni-appoints-gashirabake-and-justice-eve-luswata-to-court-of-appeal/; see also 'Museveni appoints seven justices to court of Appeal' https://allafrica.com/stories/202108190543.html.

74 Judicial Service Commission [Rules No 87 of 2005] Rule 11, 12, and 13, https://old.ulii.org/ug/legislation/statutory-instrument/2005/87 (accessed on 15 May 2023). In the appointment of judicial officers, the Commission may consult with any other organisation, department or person or seek the advice of selection board.

75 Article 142, 1995 Constitution (Uganda) '. . . the Justice of Appeal shall be appointed be appointed by the president acting on the advice of the Judicial Service Commission and upon approval of parliament'.

76 R Kagumire [@RosebellK] 25 August 2021 'The fact that the president has appointed Christopher as a Judge of the Court of Appeal, a man who is facing sexual harassment charges tells what patriarchal violence at the heart of the state is https://twitter.com/RosebellK/status/1430475801565306881?s=20? (accessed on 16 May 2023) also see Kugonza Isaac [@Kisaac63] 20 August 2021 'Kaguta Museveni appoints Christopher as court of appeal judge, his victim Samantha is horrified' https://twitter.com/kisaac63/status/1428665261884727301?s=20 (accessed on16 May 2023).

77 According to Art 126 of the Constitution judicial power is derived from the people and should be exercised according to the aspirations of the people.

78 Gashirabake Christopher's Appointment – Desecration of the Constitutional Court/Court of Appeal. Letter dated 22nd August 2021.

79 *Ibid.*

80 A Maya *Still I Rise' from and Still I Rise: A Book of Poems* (Poetry Foundation, 1978), https://poets.org/poem/still-i-rise (accessed on 14 September 2020).

81 Employment (Amendment) Bill 2022, https://parliamentwatch.ug/bills/employment-amendment-bill-2022/ (accessed on 27 February 2023). The Bill proposes prohibition of mistreatment, violence and harassment at the workplace. The bill further proposes that it is mandatory for all employers to put in place measures to prevent sexual harassment and it makes an offense to an employer who does not comply.

References

Akina Mama wa Afrika *Experiences of Women in the World of Work in Uganda*, Sexual-Harassment-Study.pdf (akinamamawaafrika.org) (accessed 30 July 2021).

Akina Mama wa Afrika, this is a Pan-African feminist leadership development organisation based in Uganda.

Akina Mama wa Afrika 'Uganda baseline study report on violence against young women' www.akinamamawaafrika.org/wp-content/uploads/2019/10/AMwA-Baseline-report-FINAL-1.pdf (accessed on 25 February 2023).

Akina Mama wa Afrika 'Understanding sexual harassment in the world of work' 3. 16 October 2019, https://docs.google.com/document/d/15ka4rnJ5CDpJoOf6bodAyazCZMFEYOTw/edit (accessed on 25 February 2023).

A Alana Moretti 'Sexual harassment in the legal profession: An analysis of the current legislative framework' (2022) 47/2 *Alternative Law Journal* 95–100.

J Aloka 'Prevalence and management of sexual harassment at the workplace: The case study of Uganda prison service' (Masters Thesis, Makerere University 2009), www.mak.ac.ug/documents/Makfiles/theses/Aloka_Julias.pdf (accessed on 13 May 2023).

Byanyima, Winnie 13 May 2019. See tweet at: https://twitter.com/Winnie_Byanyima/status/1127970417224953856?s=20 (accessed on 25 February 2023).
Committees of Parliament, www.parliament.go.ug/page/committees-parliament (accessed on 3 June 2023).
R Cook and S Cusack *Gender Stereotyping: Transnational Legal Perspectives* (University of Philadelphia Press, 2010).
Employment (Amendment) Bill, 2022, www.parliament.go.ug/cmis/views/8c16ae2f-8ce0-4590-88b6-a4cda1dbdbaa%253B1.0 (accessed on 08 May 2023).
Employment (Sexual Harassment) Regulations, 2012. Statutory Instrument No 15 of 2012, commenced on 20 April 2012, https://ulii.org/akn/ug/act/si/2012/15/eng@2012-04-20 (accessed on 8 April 2023).
Employment (Sexual Harassment) Regulations, 20 April 2012, Statutory Supplementary Instrument, Uganda Gazette No. 21, Vol. CIV, https://ulii.org/akn/ug/act/si/2012/15/eng%402012-04-20 (accessed on 18 February 2023). These Regulations give effect to the provisions on sexual harassment in the Employment Act of 2006.
FIDA-Uganda Association of Women Lawyers, https://fidauganda.org/ (accessed on 10 May 2023).
www.homelandmedia.co.ug/news/museveni-appoints-gashirabake-and-justice-eve-luswata-to-court-of-appeal/; see also 'Museveni appoints seven justices to court of Appeal' https://allafrica.com/stories/202108190543.html.
International Bar Association. 50:50 by 2030: A longitudinal Study into Gender Disparity in Law: Uganda results report, www.ibanet.org/document?id=Uganda-Report-2022-5050-by-2030 (accessed on 24 February
International Lawyers Assisting Workers Network 'Views and recommendations on the Employment (Amendment) Bill of 2022, https://voicesforlabour.org/wp-content/uploads/2023/02/Opinion-on-the-Employment-Bill-Uganda-1–1.pdf (accessed on 08 May 2023).
Judicial Service Commission [Rules No 87 of 2005] Rule 11, 12, and 13 https://old.ulii.org/ug/legislation/statutory-instrument/2005/87 accessed 15 May 2023. In the appointment of judicial officers, the Commission may consult with any other organisation, department or person or seek the advice of selection board.
R Kagumire [@RosebellK] 25 August 2021 'The fact that the president has appointed Christopher as a Judge of the Court of Appeal, a man who is facing sexual harassment charges tells what patriarchal violence at the heart of the state is https://twitter.com/RosebellK/status/1430475801565306881?s=20? (accessed on 16 May 2023) also
R Kagumire a feminist writer and activist. Twitter handle, @RosebellK, (11 May 2019) https://twitter.com/RosebellK/status/1127269978510643200?s=20 (accessed on 27 February 2023).
R Kagumire 'Ads about bus stop harassment and 'bonus wives' normalise sexism' *The Guardian*, 1 April 2019, www.theguardian.com/global-development/2019/apr/01/ugandan-ads-bus-stop-harassment-bonus-wives-normalise-sexism (accessed on 13 May 2023).
F Kiwalabye 'Effects of sexual harassment at the workplace: A Ugandan case study' *Youth Crime Watch Uganda/Ignites Worldwide Uganda*, 2008, https://svri.org/forums/forum2011/EffectsHarassment.pdf (accessed on 16 September 2020).
I Kugonza [@Kisaac63] 20 August 2021 'Kaguta Museveni appoints Christopher as Court of Appeal Judge, his victim Samantha is horrified' https://twitter.com/kisaac63/status/1428665261884727301?s=20 (accessed on16 May 2023).

B Linsey and M Dinfin 'Sexual harassment is rife in many African media workplaces' *The Conversation*, 19 July 2021, https://theconversation.com/sexual-harassment-is-rife-in-many-african-media-workplaces-163451 (accessed on 27 February 2023).

Makerere University 'Report on investigating sexual harassment at Makerere University' June 2018, https://afi.la.psu.edu/wp-content/uploads/sites/21/2021/09/Makerere-Committee-Investigating-Sexual-Harassment-FINAL-Report-June2018.pdf (accessed on 27 February 2023).

A Maya *Still I Rise' from and Still I Rise: A Book of Poems* (Poetry Foundation, 1978), https://poets.org/poem/still-i-rise (accessed on 14 September 2020).

M Norbert 'Samantha Mwesigye's Agony: Has Uganda's #MeToo movement' *The Daily Monitor*, 18 May 2019, www.monitor.co.ug/uganda/oped/commentary/samantha-mwesigye-s-agony-has-uganda-s-metoo-moment-arrived–1826490 (accessed on 22 December 2021).

P Nyamishana 'Breaking the silence to end workplace sexual harassment in Uganda, African feminism' https://africanfeminism.com/breaking-the-silence-to-end-wok-place-sexual-harassment-in-uganda (accessed on 14 May 2023) Prudence is a Ugandan Human Rights blogger.

Ramkripal Singh v State of Madhya Pradesh, AIR (2007) SC India, Criminal Appeal No 370/2007, delivered by Hon Judge Dr Arijit Pasayat, 19 March 2007, www.legit-quest.com/case/ramkripal-v-state-of-mp/2F8E3 (accessed on 19 September 2020).

Regulation 9(2)(c), Regulation 1(1)(h), and Regulation 17.

Samantha Mwesigye [KCCA/RUB/560/2019] Labour Complaint.

Samantha Mwesigye v Attorney General and Gashirabake Christopher [Labour Dispute Reference No 353 of 2019] The Industrial Court at Kampala.

C Samaradiwakera-Wijesundara 'Reframing corporate subjectivity: Systemic inequality and the company at the intersection of race, gender and poverty' (2022) 7/1 *Business and Human Rights Journal* 100–116.

'Senior State Attorney accuses deputy solicitor general of sexual harassment' *The Daily Monitor*, 12 May 2019, www.monitor.co.ug/uganda/news/national/senior-state-attorney-accuses-deputy-solicitor-general-of-sexual-harassment-1825234 (accessed on 22 December 2021).

'Solicitor general breaks silence on harassment allegations' *The Observer*, 14 May 2019, https://observer.ug/news/headlines/60677-solicitor-general-breaks-silence-on-sexual-harassment-allegations (accessed on 9 May 2023).

Some tweet links, https://twitter.com/amwaafrika/status/124346744983768269 8?s=20.

C Surendra 'Outraging the modesty of a woman: Inter-spousal perspective' (1990) 32/4 *Journal of the Indian Law Institute* 527–535.

T Sylvia *When Hens Begin to Crow: Gender and Parliamentary Politics in Uganda*, 1st ed (Fountain Publishers, 2008).

S Tamale 'Making sure the issue becomes the story: problematizing media coverage of sexual harassment at Makerere University' *Konrad Adenauer Stiftung, Women in Media*, 17 August 2018, www.kas.de/en/web/uganda/veranstaltungs-berichte/detail/-/content/making-sure-the-issue-becomes-the-story-problematizing-the-media-coverage-of-sexual-harassment-at-makerere-university (accessed on 27 February 2023).

S Tamale 'The right to culture and the culture of rights: A critical perspective on women's sexual rights in Africa' (2008) 16/1 *Feminist Legal Studies* 47–69.

A Tewari 'My modesty is not outraged, I am! Patriarchy in the language of law' 28 August 2017 https://feminisminindia.com/2017/08/28/modesty-outraged-patriarchy-law/ (accessed on 18 September 2020).

The Daily Monitor 'Attorney in sexual harassment case scrapped off government pay roll' *Kampala*, 1 September 2019, www.monitor.co.ug/uganda/news/national/attorney-in-sexual-harassment-case-scrapped-off-government-payroll-1845680 (accessed on 27 February 2023).

The Employment (Sexual Harassment) Regulations [2012] Statutory Instrument NO 15 of 2012, commenced on 20 April 2012, https://ulii.org/akn/ug/act/si/2012/15/eng@2012-04-20 (accessed on 08 May 2023).

The Employment Act, 2006. Laws of Uganda, https://ulii.org/system/files/legislation/act/2006/2006/employment_act_2006_pdf_50549.pdf (accessed on 18 September 2020).

The Judiciary Uganda 'The honourable justices of court of appeal' http://judiciary.go.ug/data/incourt/18/The%20Honorable%20Justices%20of%20the%20Court%20of%20Appeal%20.html; see also 'Museveni appoints Gashirabake and Justice Eve Luswata to Court of Appeal';

The Penal Code Act 1950 (Uganda) 15 June 1950, https://ulii.org/akn/ug/act/ord/1950/12/eng@2014-05-09 (accessed on 10 May 2023).

'Three Makerere University lecturers suspended for alleged sexual harassment' *The Independent*, 16 July 2019, www.independent.co.ug/three-makerere-university-lecturers-suspended-for-alleged-sexual-harassment/ (accessed on 13 May 2023).

M Tsepho 'Sexual harassment in the workplace and women's access to justice: Lessons for Botswana from a South Africa perspective (2019) 45/3 *Commonwealth Law Bulletin* 431–453.

Uganda Bureau of Statistics (UBOS) 'The national labour force survey' *Main Report*, July and November 2021, www.ubos.org/national-labour-force-survey-2021-main-report/ (accessed on 27 February 2023).

Uganda Bureau of Statistics 'Uganda demographic and health survey' *Kampala*, 2016, https://dhsprogram.com/pubs/pdf/FR333/FR333.pdf (accessed on 27 February 2023).

Uganda, Constitution of the Republic of Uganda, Art 2, 22 September 1995, www.parliament.go.ug/documents/1240/constitution (accessed on 13 May 2023).

Uganda v Olupot HCt-04-CR-SC-0066–2008] 21 April 2011(HC).

'Victims of sexual harassment at Makerere speak out' *The Daily Monitor*, 6 May 2017, www.monitor.co.ug/uganda/video/victims-of-sexual-harassment-at-makerere-speak-out-1699894 (accessed on 13 May 2023).

Women Pro Bono Initiative 'Women Pro Bono Initiative, is a civil society organisation founded in July 2018 to advance access to justice for women and girls in Uganda through awareness creation, legal representation, research and knowledge sharing, https://womenprobono.org/ (accessed on 10 May 2023).

World Association of News 'Women in news. sexual harassment in the Media' *Africa Report*, 38–39, https://womeninnews.org/wp-content/uploads/2021/07/20210704_Sexual-Harassment-in-The-Media-Low-Res.pdf (accessed on 27 February 2023).

World Economic Forum 'Global gender gap report, 2022' 13 July 2022, www.weforum.org/reports/global-gender-gap-report-2022/?DAG=3&gclid=CjwKCAjw3ueiBhBmEiwA4BhspA4xODztFvPAXEf2lGxlcjccYGiOF-UqHLGa9dNRfgRf8QLR_Bwi4RoCL3sQAvD_BwE (accessed on 9 May 2023).

8 The Cost of Workplace Sexual Harassment

A Critique of the Ethiopia Labour Law

Wubrest F. Adamu

Introduction

In this chapter, I provide a synopsis of the concept of gender equality and women empowerment in Ethiopia within the context of sexual harassment and interrogate relevant laws. I describe the significant gains achieved by Ethiopia in the past few years in terms of advancing gender equality and women's empowerment, including the ratification of several international treaties, gender-sensitive policy reforms, and increasing women's participation in the decision-making capacities. I also assess the Ethiopian revised labour Proclamation No 1156/2019 and discuss how its approach to workplace sexual harassment has enhanced or failed to prevent predatory sexually harassing conduct against anecdotal data developed to expose the prevalence of workplace sexual harassment in Ethiopia. In this regard, I attempt to show how the newly enacted law fails to strongly contemplate the prevention, mitigation, and response to sexual harassment through the provision of appropriate procedures to deal with the problem and prevent its recurrence in a specific manner by providing a comparison with and recommendation of selected best practices of other countries. I question whether this new law provides the answers we seek given the cultural and socio-economic challenges beguiling women's enjoyment of equality in the workplace.

In June 2019 at the Centenary Conference of the International Labour Organisation (ILO), the Violence and Harassment Convention (No 190) and its accompanying Recommendation (No 206) were adopted.[1] The global community has made it clear that violence and harassment in the workplace will not be tolerated and must end. As an ILO member state, Ethiopia attended the 108th International Labour Conference (Centenary Conference 1919–2019) under the theme 'the Future of Work We Want' in July 2019 and witnessed at the adoption of the Violence and Harassment Convention (No 190) and its accompanying Recommendation (No 206).[2] However, the country is yet to sign the ILO international conventions as C 190, C 182, and C 183. In this regard, a recently held workshop by the Friedrich-Ebert-Stiftung Ethiopia Office[3] in cooperation with the NGO Ethiopian Labour Rights Watch[4] stressed why Ethiopia needs to sign the ILO conventions and help strengthen already existing laws dealing with labour/employment.[5]

DOI: 10.4324/9781003373308-8

Convention No 190 and Recommendation No 206 are the first international labour standards to provide a common framework to prevent, remedy, and eliminate violence and harassment in the world of work, including sexual harassment. The Convention includes the specific recognition, for the first time in international law, of the right of everyone to a world of work free from violence and harassment, and sets out the obligation to respect, promote, and realise this right (Art 4[1]).[6] These landmark instruments were developed by the world of work actors (representatives of governments, employers, and workers) and set out a common framework to prevent and address violence and harassment based on an inclusive, integrated, and gender-responsive approach. The Convention recognises that everyone has the right to a world of work free from violence and harassment, including gender-based violence and harassment. It offers broad protection and applies to the public and private sectors, the formal and informal economies, and urban and rural areas. The Convention defines violence and harassment as 'a range of unacceptable behaviours and practices, or threats thereof, whether a single occurrence or repeated, that aims at, result in, or are likely to result in physical, psychological, sexual, or economic harm, and includes gender-based violence and harassment'.[7]

Similarly, following the adoption of the sustainable development goals (SDGs) 2030 Agenda in 2015 as a roadmap for enhancing economic, social, and environmental outcomes in all nations worldwide by 2030, Ethiopia has proactively mainstreamed and aligned the SDGs with the country's Second Growth and Transformation Plan (GTP II), which spans from 2015/16 to 2019/20. Likewise, the government of Ethiopia has recently formulated a 10-year perspective development plan for the period 2019/20 to 2029/30 which is aligned to the 2030 agenda and SDGs. Ethiopia has also volunteered and participated in the 2017 Voluntary National Review (VNR) on SDGs[8] which undertook the review of how the SDGs are mainstreamed into national and sub-national development plans and being implemented. In 2022, the country submitted a Voluntary National Review (VNR) and reported on their progress towards the Sustainable Development Goals (SDGs).[9]

Significant achievements have also been made in relation to SDG 5, achieving gender equality and empowering all women and girls in terms of promoting women's political participation, with women occupying 50% of the cabinet of ministers. As of 2020, women make up 39% of seats in the national parliament, compared to 8% in 2004,[10] and 42% of legal frameworks that promote, enforce, and monitor gender equality under the SDG indicator, with a focus on violence against women. Nevertheless, Ethiopia still has a long way to go to ensure equal occupation of men and women in political, socio-economic, and decision-making spaces and other institutions. According to the UN Women Data on Ethiopia, as of December 2020, only 38% of indicators needed to monitor the SDGs from a gender perspective were available, with gaps in key areas – in particular, key labour market indicators such as the gender pay gap, gender and poverty, physical and sexual harassment, among others, lack comparable methodologies for regular monitoring. Closing these data gender gaps is essential for achieving gender-related SDG commitments in Ethiopia.[11]

Studies show that sexual harassment is one of many manifestations of power imbalances in the workplace. It affects women and men across industries and occupations, and negatively impacts women's workplace opportunities and career decisions. For instance, a study conducted in North America shows that sexual harassment can impede a woman's job performance, workplace advancement, and earnings. Hence, women who experience sexual harassment at work often avoid reporting it for fear of retaliation, termination, or inaction and, among women who do report sexual harassment to their employers, nearly half report being dissatisfied with the response.[12] In addition, many women who experience sexual harassment at work report increased anxiety and depression, which is associated with lower productivity and poorer performance at work. Some report experiencing a decline in job involvement and satisfaction, as well as increases in absenteeism, turnover, early retirement, and a range of negative health outcomes. Furthermore, women in workplaces that do not address sexual harassment may feel less empowered to negotiate salaries and raises, depressing their long-term earnings and advancement.[13] Another study shows that sexual harassment contributes to sex segregation and pay inequality in the labour market and may contribute to gender inequality. As a result, workplace harassment contributes to inequality through deterring women from applying for jobs in workplaces where they are the gender minority or/and by making workplace gender minorities leave their workplaces for new jobs.[14] Preventing and effectively addressing workplace sexual harassment is one way to help close the gender wage gap and promote women's financial security.

Ethiopia is no exception; workplace sexual harassment undermines equality between men and women broadly and has contributed to the marginalisation of working women. Sexual harassment particularly affects women and reinforces gender stereotypes which have proved to be harmful and lead to other gender-based violence of criminal nature. For instance, a systematic review and meta-analysis study on the prevalence and associated factors of sexual violence experienced by housemaids in Ethiopia discovered, after conducting eight studies involving 3,324 housemaids, that the pooled prevalence was 55% for sexual harassment, 39% for attempted rape, and 19% for rape. In conclusion, the study revealed that the prevalence of sexual violence against housemaids in Ethiopia is high and one of the major attributing factors is the prevalence of sexual harassment amongst housemaids, with male employers being the vast majority of perpetrators of their housemaids.[15]

It also contributes to fewer women entering or remaining in the labour market and to women being paid less than men, thus exacerbating the gender gap, as discussed in the previous research studies.[16] For instance, in a study conducted back in 2018 on women's experience of workplace sexual harassment and their coping mechanisms in the capital, Addis Ababa,[17] most of the informants claimed that sexual harassment has a negative impact over their psychological wellbeing and work environment which led to loss of enjoyment of life. The respondents in this study somehow experienced all forms of psychological impacts ranging from hating their situation, being unable to perform their duties properly, up to being forced to lose their job and suffer from lack of income. The following are extracts of the experiences of some of the respondents from the research interviews conducted by Bethelehem Fiseha:

> 'Sometimes you start hating your job; you will say what if I don't do this job anymore. Why do I subject myself to such abuse? Aren't I a human? Why do they keep humiliating me just because I do this job?'
>
> 'It makes me mad for the time being but since it is my job and I need it to cover my school expenses I let it go, because this won't be my life forever'.
>
> 'It is very exhausting emotionally and physically; it drains your energy. I was a waitress first now I am a bartender see how I am moving away from having any contact with the customers. If I move on to other positions, it has to be a position that has zero to little contact with the customer. This is the effect the job it has on you don't wish it on anyone really'.
>
> 'When a person disrespects you in front of other customers or touches you inappropriately, it is very humiliating. It makes you really hate your job. In various occasions I went home with bad mood and find it hard to be happy for the rest of the day. In days like this I feel worthless. It makes me hate my job so much. I would never advice anyone to work with customers in settings like this'.[18]

The Prevalence of Workplace Sexual Harassment in Ethiopia

Workplace sexual harassment is a serious human rights issue in Ethiopia. There has been no government-initiated national study to date which assesses the prevalence of sexual harassment in Ethiopia workplace settings. There have, however2, been individual studies which have provided differing prevalence rates of sexual harassment in various occupations. One cause for the poor implementation of sexual harassment prevention and control programs in workplaces might be the absence of nationally summarised statistics. In this regard, a study conducted in 2020 showed that there was a high prevalence of sexual harassment in Ethiopian workplaces. The study indicated that sexual harassment was particularly high among female university staff, accounting for 49%, and 28% among commercial sex workers[19] and employees of governmental institutions.[20] There is an unacceptably high prevalence of sexual violence and harassment in workplace settings.

Concerned stakeholders must design and implement effective interventions to prevent workplace sexual violence in Ethiopia and provide the necessary support and care to the victims and survivors of this heinous problem. Moreover, the researchers recommend that governmental organisations, non-governmental organisations, and other stakeholders develop effective programs and interventions to reduce workplace sexual violence prevalence in different Ethiopian workplaces.[21] For instance, the Ethiopian Labour Rights Watch (ELRW)[22] set up a civic organisation that works on labour-related issues in Ethiopia which is committed to facilitating the provision of labour rights training to workers, union leaders, law enforcement officials, and local association representatives and free legal aid. It also undertakes more formal training and capacity-building activities in collaboration with other civic organisations and law schools in addition to researching and advocating labour rights.

A multicentre cross-sectional study in 2022 on the prevalence of workplace sexual harassment among midwives and nurses working in Northwestern Ethiopia referral hospitals found that sexual harassment in the workplace is a systemic and pervasive problem within the healthcare sector in Ethiopia. In this research, the prevalence of sexual harassment was found to be 17.4%.[23] Initiators of sexual harassment towards nurses and midwives in this research were found to be patients' families, physicians, patients themselves, and other colleagues. In this study, young midwives and nurses (18–25 years old) had 7.2 times higher probabilities of sexual harassment in the workplace than the other groups.[24] Additionally, having less than five years of work experience in hospitals increases the likelihood of workplace sexual harassment. This might be because senior male nurses and doctors have more control or influence over less-experienced nurses and midwives, or it may be because they have fewer career-related soft skills and have adapted to the health system less.[25] The aforementioned studies agreed over two key points: firstly, that workplace sexual harassment usually remains concealed, as victims cannot report such offenses; secondly, that concerned stakeholders should develop and implement interventions that could empower workers – particularly female workers – in their struggle towards the elimination of sexual harassment, create awareness to prevent and control the implementation of sexual harassment legislation and policies, and ensure prompt punishment of the perpetrators.

An Overview of the Ethiopian Revised Labour Proclamation No 1156/2019

Ethiopia has no clear legal definition of sexual harassment. The 1995 FDRE Constitution, criminal law, the law of torts, and the recently revised labour law are all general areas of law that ban sex discrimination and are potentially able to be used as a basis for accusations of sexual harassment to be brought before the courts and less formal structures. However, it is difficult to envision a successful case being lodged under the aforementioned general laws, as they are insufficient to protect sexual harassment victims. The

Criminal Code[26] prohibits sexual harassment and prescribes simple imprisonment for the perpetrator. The provision[27] underscores the issue of sexual harassment by stating that whoever solicits sexual intercourse or any other indecent act from a woman by taking advantage of her material or mental distress or of the authority he exercises over her by his position, function, or capacity as protector, teacher, master, or employer, or by any other like relationship, is punishable, upon complaint, with simple imprisonment. Hence, it can be reasonably deduced from the prescribed Criminal Act that it is unlawful for an employer, manager, or employee to commit sexual harassment or sexual assault at a workplace.

In 2019, Ethiopia adopted a new proclamation which replaces the Labour Proclamation[28] that had been in existence for 16 years prior and introduced new rules governing workplace sexual harassment that were non-existent in previous legal frameworks. The previous labour proclamation[29] provided no definition for sexual harassment. This increased the likelihood that sexual harassment in the workplace would remain undetected, normalised, or trivialised. This approach by the previous proclamation created several legal loopholes, not only in respect to capturing the meaning of sexual harassment, but also by leaving room to allow anyone to be sexually harassed at work by anyone else. The revised labour proclamation[30] was enacted to reformulate the existing labour law in accordance with and in conformity with the international conventions and other legal commitments to which Ethiopia is a party.

The highly stressed generic objective of this law is to ensure worker-employer relations are governed by basic principles of rights and obligations and lay down a working system that guarantees the rights of workers and employers. This proclamation consists of 193 articles dealing with 12 main subsections that deal with standard definitions and a range of issues such as employment relations, wages, hours of work, leave days, working conditions of women and young workers, occupational safety and health, the working environment, collective relations, and administrative measures.[31] The article that deals with working conditions for women stipulates that women shall not be discriminated against in all respects based on their sex and further underlines that assigning women to work that may be listed by the ministry as particularly dangerous to women or hazardous to their health is prohibited.[32]

Under the revised labour proclamation, sexual harassment is defined as an act to persuade or convince another, through utterances, signs, or any other manner, to submit for sexual favour without his or her consent.[33] The proclamation further defines 'sexual violence' as sexual harassment accompanied by force or an attempt thereof.[34] Furthermore, 'discrimination' is defined as any distinction, exclusion, or preference made based on nation, race, colour, sex, religion, political opinion, national extraction, social origin, HIV/AIDS status, disablement, and others that have the effect of nullifying or impairing equality of opportunity or treatment in employment or occupation.[35] Sexual harassment is defined in a very generic manner in that it excludes the different forms it entails by only stating the conduct as an act of persuading or convincing a person to submit for sexual favour without consent.

In terms of Article 2(11), 'sexual harassment' means to persuade or convince another through utterances, signs, or any other manner to submit for sexual favour without his/her consent. Nevertheless, sexual harassment is beyond an act of persuading or convincing another, it rather encompasses a range of unacceptable behaviours, practices, or threats thereof, whether a single occurrence or repeated, that aim at, result in, or are likely to result in physical, psychological, sexual, or economic harm, and includes sexual violence and harassment.[36] The second element where the definition falls short is the aspect of a hostile work environment, whereby such conduct creates an intimidating, hostile, offensive, or humiliating working environment.

This could appear in circumstances where acceptance of such conduct is made a requirement of employment, either explicitly or implicitly, or where acceptance or rejection of such conduct is used as the basis for any decision regarding the employee's employment, such as a promotion, pay increase, job security, or benefits; or such conduct has the purpose or the effect of interfering with a person's work performance. For instance, such an act would impair the employee's rights or privileges under existing labour laws; or result in an intimidating, hostile, or offensive environment for the employee. The other crucial point is that any demand, request, or to otherwise require any sexual favour from the other should be considered unlawful, regardless of whether the demand, request, or requirement for submission is accepted by the object of said act.

The prohibition of sexual harassment in connection with the workplace should be expanded to protect all forms of sexual harassment in the employment recruitment process, education, or training environment. An expansion of what constitutes the workplace would demonstrate the state's commitment to protecting workplace equality and would affirm that it is sensitive to protect all people, in particular women, at the various stages of the employment process. This would also enhance the development of human resources functionality, whilst also guaranteeing full respect for human rights, and would uphold the dignity of workers including employees, applicants for employment, contractors, volunteers, students, or those undergoing training, instruction, or education. Hence, the scope should be defined in a way that encompasses sexual harassment committed by an employer, employee, manager, supervisor, agent of the employer, teacher, instructor, professor, coach, trainer, or any other person who, having authority, influence, or moral ascendancy over another in a work or training or education environment. In the meanwhile, the provisions under the revised labour proclamation should also apply, *mutatis mutandis*, to institutions that provide academic or vocational training.

There is a clear intersection of sexual harassment as a civil and as a criminal offence. A workplace sexual harassment case may include acts that meet the legal definition of criminal sexual assault. In this scenario, the incident may be reported internally, reported to law authorities, or pursued in civil or criminal court. For instance, if a supervisor rapes a worker at work, this could amount to both sexual harassment and a criminal offense of rape.[37] Certainly, sexual harassment under Ethiopia law is a civil matter, and the provisions of the civil code and the revised labour proclamation therefore would apply. To this end, the revised proclamation categorised sexual harassment by the employer or a managerial employee as one of the good causes to terminate a contract of employment without prior notice.[38] Furthermore, it asserts that a worker shall have the right to receive severance pay from the employer where the worker resigned due to sexual harassment or sexual violence by the employer or managerial employee, or where such an act was committed by a co-worker and the incident was reported to the employer, but the latter failed to take appropriate measures in due time.[39] The law provides that workers forced to terminate their contract without notice for reasons of sexual harassment shall be entitled, in addition to the severance pay referred to in Article 40 of this Proclamation, to a payment of compensation.[40]

Acts of sexual harassment encompass criminally recognised conduct such as stalking, sexual assault, indecent exposure, or rape. Nonetheless, the revised proclamation does not impose criminal liability where a person harasses another sexually, whether in the form of a fine, incarceration, restitution, or imprisonment. The fact that sexual harassment is not criminalised does not and cannot prevent a victim from filing a lawsuit against the harasser or employer. By outlining guidelines within which state agencies, employers, or unions should develop policies, rules, and procedures based on their different roles and unique situations, the proclamation has fallen short of serving as a roadmap for action. State agencies are unclear about the implications of their current duty to defend human rights and provide practical assistance to organisations on what steps they should take to guarantee that they respect internationally recognised human rights and resolve any damage.

According to the UN Guiding Principles on Business and Human Rights,[41] employers should, as a rule, establish and uphold a workplace where employees' dignity is respected. It states as follows:

> A culture should be established and fostered in the workplace where victims of sexual harassment won't experience feelings of dismissal, indifference, or fear of retaliation. Employers, management, and staff are all expected to refrain from sexual harassment and have a collective responsibility for helping to establish and uphold a workplace where sexual harassment is prohibited. They should take care to prevent offending others with their standards of behaviour, and they should dissuade others from engaging in inappropriate behaviour. Employers and management should make an effort to prevent sexual harassment by the employer or its employees from happening to people who interact with the business. Additionally, when cases of sexual harassment in the workplace are brought to their knowledge, they are expected to take the proper legal action.[42]

However, these guiding principles are not included in the revised proclamation, and the concept of human rights-centred responsive assessment, transformative measures, and remedies that state, employers, and other stakeholders could use to prevent, mitigate, and respond to workplace sexual harassment is completely missed.

Does Ethiopia Need a Separate Law to Deal with Workplace Sexual Harassment?

The last two decades have witnessed significant legislative reform concerning the protection of the rights of women in Ethiopia. In addition to the Federal Democratic Republic of Ethiopia (FDRE) Constitution with several provisions relevant to women's rights, many other laws have been enacted and the existing ones have been revised in a particularly gender-sensitive manner. The FDRE Constitution provides under Article 9(4) that all international treaties ratified by the country are integral parts of the law of the land. Article 13(2) further affirms that the fundamental rights and freedoms specified in the constitution shall be interpreted in a manner conforming to the principles of the Universal Declaration of Human Rights, International Covenants on Human Rights, and international instruments adopted by Ethiopia.

Ethiopia has a good track record of ratifying international and regional human rights treaties. Among those treaties are the International Convention on Civil and Political Rights;[43] the International Convention on Economic, Social, and Cultural Rights;[44] the Convention on Elimination of Discrimination against Women;[45] the African Charter on Human and Peoples' Rights;[46] the Beijing Platform of Action;[47] and the Convention on the Rights of the Child.[48] More recently, in Ethiopia, the African Charter on Human and Peoples' Rights on the Rights of Women in Africa, also known as the Maputo protocol (2018),[49] will serve as an additional framework for gender equality related to workplace sexual harassment with several reservations. However, the country did not put any specific reservation on sections which require state parties to adopt and enforce legislative and other measures to guarantee women equal opportunities in work and career advancement and other economic opportunities, including ensuring transparency in recruitment, promotion, and dismissal of women, and combat and punish sexual harassment in the workplace.

The Ethiopian Constitution allows for both dualistic and monistic procedures and does not rigidly stick to one method of incorporation when it comes to the domestication of international human rights treaties. Although the Ethiopian Constitution favours both methods of implementing human rights treaties, neither the dualistic approach's requirement for domestic law transformation into treaty provisions, including amendments and repeals, nor the monistic approach's requirement for a single translation and publication of the treaty's actual provisions have been met. Due to the lack of access to international human rights treaties and rulings as a result, drafters and other authorities in the drafting process were forced to concentrate only on the constitution and its provisions.[50]

Ethiopia integrated gender equality into the constitution and ratified international and regional human right instruments; these were and continue to be viewed as part and parcel of the law and specific laws prohibited gender-based discrimination. Still, the implementation thereof was problematic. For instance, the country somehow failed to adopt and enforce legislative measures to combat and punish sexual harassment in the workplace. The new labour proclamation which replaces the one that has been in existence for 16 years prior fails to provide a clear definition of gender harassment and regulate the protection of women's equality in the workplace. In this regard, one of the recommendations set by the Committee on the Elimination of Discrimination against Women[51] is that state parties implement preventive measures through the adoption and implementation of effective legislative and other appropriate preventive measures to address the underlying causes of gender-based violence against women, including patriarchal attitudes and stereotypes, inequality in the family, and the neglect or denial of women's civil, political, economic, social, and cultural rights. Likewise, Article 13 of the Maputo Protocol reaffirms that state parties shall adopt and enforce legislative and other measures to guarantee women's equal opportunities in work, career advancement, and other economic opportunities. In this respect, they shall ensure transparency in the recruitment, promotion, and dismissal of women, combat and punish sexual harassment in the workplace, and protect them from exploitation by their employers who violate and exploit their fundamental rights as recognised and guaranteed by conventions, laws, and regulations in force.

The current revised legal framework remains too general and lacks definitions and specific indicators to determine what type of behaviour constitutes sexual harassment. To lay the legal groundwork for a safe and healthy work environment, the country needs more than a broad labour law and I stress that Ethiopia needs a context-specific and detailed sexual harassment law in line with international standards. For instance, whilst the revised law clearly prohibits the commission of sexual harassment or sexual assault at the workplace, the details concerning measures that should be taken by employers to effectively prevent sexual harassment at the workplace and how employers should respond promptly to any accusation of sexual harassment and the process of receiving complaints remain unclear. Instead, the law could explore specific and detailed rules concerning the role and responsibility of every employer to create and maintain a working environment that is free from sexual harassment through ensuring that information on sexual harassment is included in their staff orientation, education, and training programs. Similarly, all workers, regardless of their sex, age,[52] position, type of contract, or status have a responsibility to ensure that the workplace is free from sexual harassment, to discourage and report unacceptable behaviour, and to comply with the company's sexual harassment policy.[53]

The Canadian approach could be a good model. An employer and the applicable partner (policy committee or, if there is no policy committee, a workplace committee) identify risk factors internal and external to the workplace that contribute to harassment and violence in the workplace. Such a process of identification of risk factors could be undertaken by taking into account the culture, conditions, activities, and organisational structure of the workplace; circumstances external to the workplace, such as family violence, that could give rise to harassment and violence in the workplace including any reports, records, and data that are related to harassment in the workplace, the measures that are in place to protect psychological health and safety in the workplace.[54] The other element of the Canadian law is prevention and protection measures, and one of them is a workplace assessment jointly carried out by an employer and the applicable partner that consists of the identification of risk factors and the development and implementation of preventive measures.

Furthermore, an employer and the applicable partner must jointly monitor the accuracy of the workplace assessment and, if necessary, update it to reflect a change to the information set out in the assessment, including a change to the risk factors identified under sections and any change that compromises the effectiveness of a preventive measure developed and implemented under sections. In addition, the act requires a jointly reviewed workplace assessment by the employer and the applicable partner every three years and, if necessary, an update.[55]

Within the Ethiopian labour law sphere, the revised proclamation enshrines the rights of workers and employers to establish and organise trade unions or employers' associations, respectively, and actively participate.[56] In particular, Article 115 of the proclamation gives employers' associations specific functions such as, but not limited to, observing working conditions and fulfilling legal obligations, protecting their members' rights and interests, ensuring that laws are known to and implemented by members; initiating laws and regulations pertaining to labour relations and actively participating in their formulation and implementation. Moreover, a trade union has the capacity to represent members at any level and to undertake any lawful act necessary for the attainment of its objectives, among other things.[57] However, the trade union's responsibility to participate in the development and implementation of a company's policy, including a sexual harassment policy, and ensure that issues related to sexual harassment in the workplace are negotiated in a fair and transparent manner are not cited. The law should also include the responsibility of both trade unions and employers' associations to provide information, advice, and representation to workers who have been sexually harassed, as well as to workers against whom allegations of sexual harassment have been made and include such information on sexual harassment in their regular education and training programs.

Another good practice is an Israelite labour law on the prevention of sexual harassment which places the responsibility to prevent on the employer. Employers must take steps that are reasonable under the circumstances in order to prevent sexual harassment within the realm of labour relations by their employee or by a person who has been put in charge on his behalf.[58] Hence, the law extends protection from sexual harassment not only from employers directly, rather it governs cases of sexual harassments perpetrated by a person who has been put in charge on behalf of an employee. Here, the employer's civil liability is in addition to the harasser's individual civil and criminal liability. To avoid liability, an employer must take all the measures prescribed by the sexual harassment law (including, inter alia, establishment of policy and serious, prompt, and efficient treatment of a victim's complaint).

> Wherefore, the employer shall provide an effective method for the submission of complaints of sexual harassment or persecution and the investigation of such complaints, take effective action in cases of sexual harassment or persecution of which he is aware, and do all that he can to prevent a repetition of the aforesaid acts and to make good any harm caused to the complainant as a result of such sexual harassment or persecution.[59]

The other element where the law falls short is on the issue of lability. Under the revised proclamation, liability is recognised only where the workers have been victims of sexual harassment or sexual violence by the employer or a managerial employee. The law does not recognise instances where an organisation has contributed to the sexual harassment either knowingly, recklessly, or through wilful blindness or where an organisation is an accessory to sexual harassment. However, the law should grant protection for victims and extend accessory liability employers or managerial employees were aware or should have been aware that sexual harassment was occurring, or that there was a real possibility of it occurring, did nothing to address it and thereby allowed the harassment to take place. One example in this regard is the Australian Sex Discrimination Act which holds individuals and employers liable under Section 105 of the act if they 'caused, instructed, induced, aided or permitted' an individual to commit an unlawful act. For example, a manager who is aware that an employee is being sexually harassed and does nothing about it may be held liable as an accessory to the harassment. There is no defence available for this type of liability.[60]

Conclusion

Like many other countries in the world, Ethiopia has inadequately defined sexual harassment. As was addressed in this chapter, the 1995 FDRE Constitution, criminal law, the law of torts, and the recently revised labour law are all general areas of legislation that prohibit sex discrimination. Notably, the revised labour proclamation introduced new rules governing workplace sexual harassment that were non-existent in previous legal frameworks. Under the previous labour proclamation, there was no definition for sexual harassment or sexual violence. The lack of recognition as an illegal act by law whereby cases related to these issues are treated as squabbles at the workplace. This approach by the previous proclamation created several crises, not only by falling short of capturing the meaning of sexual harassment, but also simply by leaving a room to allow anyone to be sexually harassed at work by anyone else. Likewise, the revised criminal code lacks clear provisions specifically dealing with sexual harassment.

The only applicable provision by virtue of interpretation is Article 625, an act of procuring sexual intercourse from a woman or any other indecent act by taking advantage of her material or mental distress, or of the authority he exercises over her by virtue of his position, function, or capacity. However, the new law is not free from shortcomings and lacks some basic principles, including but not limited to a wide-ranging definition of sexual harassment, prohibition of different acts of sexual harassment, formal and informal complaints procedures, outside complaints mechanisms, sanctions and disciplinary measures, civil and criminal liability, monitoring, and evaluation. I have stressed the need for a specific law on sexual harassment that clearly explains what constitutes sexual harassment by providing a comprehensive definition of sexual harassment. The definition should clearly specify the standardised elements set by the ILO, mainly the *quid pro quo* and hostile environment elements of sexual harassment and expand the prohibition of sexual harassment to protect all forms of sexual harassment in the employment, education, or training environment.

Furthermore, guiding principles and parameters should be placed and defined to ensure that states and employers develop policies, rules, and processes based on their respective roles and particular circumstances within the parameters and internationally recognised standards governing workplace sexual harassment. However, a specific workplace sexual harassment law consisting of guiding principles informed by the concept of human rights-cantered responsive assessment, transformative measures, and remedies for states, employers, and other stakeholders should be designed to guarantee the prevention, mitigation, and response to the growing issue of workplace sexual harassment.

Notes

1 www.ilo.org/wcmsp5/groups/public/–dgreports/–gender/documents/briefingnote/wcms_738114.pdf
2 https://m.facebook.com/MFAEthiopia/posts/the-centenary-conference-of-the-ilc-opens-in-geneva-the-108th-international-labo/2844165885610636/?locale=ar_AR.
3 https://ethiopia.fes.de/about/friedrich-ebert-stiftung
4 www.ethiopianlabour.org/index.php/en/home
5 https://ethiopia.fes.de/e/instituting-reporting-mechanisms-on-violation-of-workers-rights-in-the-workplace
6 www.ilo.org/wcmsp5/groups/public/–dgreports/–gender/documents/briefingnote/wcms_738114.pdf
7 Gender-based violence and harassment is then defined as 'violence and harassment directed at persons because of their sex or gender or affecting persons of a particular sex or gender disproportionately and includes sexual harassment'.

8 Ethiopia 2017 Voluntary National Review on SDGs Government Commitments, National Ownership and Performance Trends www.undp.org/ethiopia/publications/ethiopia-2017-voluntary-national-review-sdgs.
9 Ethiopia 2022 Voluntary National Review on SDGs https://hlpf.un.org/sites/default/files/vnrs/2022/VNR%202022%20Ethiopia%20Report_1.pdf.
10 B Mesfin 'Women's participation in political leadership and decision making in Ethiopia: A research note' (2004) 2/2 *Ethiopian Journal of the Social Sciences and Humanities* 81–99.
11 https://data.unwomen.org/country/ethiopia.
12 www.eeoc.gov/data/sexual-harassment-our-nations-workplaces.
13 www.ncbi.nlm.nih.gov/books/NBK519461/.
14 O Folke and J Rickne 'Sexual harassment and gender inequality in the labor market' (2022) 137/4 *The Quarterly Journal of Economics* 2163–2212.
15 BD Mekonnen, ZH Lakew and EB Melese 'Prevalence and associated factors of sexual violence experienced by housemaids in Ethiopia: a systematic review and meta-analysis' (2022) 19/162 *Reproductive Health* 1–14.
16 www.ilo.org/wcmsp5/groups/public/–dgreports/–gender/documents/briefingnote/wcms_738115.pdf
17 A Tasew *Causes, Effects and Challenges of Sexual Harassment on Waitresses: The Case of Bole Sub City, Addis Ababa* (Lap Lambert Academic Publishing, 2012).
18 *Ibid.*
19 Worke, Mulugeta Dile et al 'Prevalence of sexual violence in Ethiopian workplaces: Systematic review and meta-analysis' (2020) 17/196 *Reproductive Health* 1–15.
20 Workplace sexual violence (WSV) results in negative organisational culture, long-term health and psychological impacts on employees, damage to research integrity, and a costly loss of skilled workforce. It mainly affects workers in the most vulnerable work situations who have poor access to labour rights such as freedom of association, collective bargaining, decent work, non-discrimination, and access to justice. It also increases the likelihood of sexually transmitted infections, unintended pregnancies, and unsafe abortion. In Ethiopia, workplace sexual violence is one of the high burdens of sexual and reproductive health problems. The prevalence of workplace sexual violence varies from workplace to workplace and from occupation to occupation in Ethiopia. Poor knowledge of the impacts of workplace sexual violence prevention mechanisms, transactional sex practices, and poverty are the major contributors to WSV.
21 *Ibid.*
22 Voluntary National Review on SDGs Government Commitments (n 8).
23 EH Dagnaw, Eyaya et al 'Sexual harassment at the workplace is still a hindrance among midwives and nurses working in Northwester Ethiopia referral hospitals: A multicentre cross-sectional study' (2022) 15 *Journal of Multidisciplinary Healthcare* 2453.
24 *Ibid.*
25 The researchers disclaim that their finding is in line with research done in southern Ethiopia (13.5%), due to the similarity of settings and sociocultural makeup. On the contrary, their finding is much higher than studies in Gambia and Uganda, where prevalence was about 10% and 8.1%, respectively. This also could be due to differences in catchment population, security protocols, and cultural characteristics. This might be due to differences in the cultural nature of abusers and participants. On the other hand, the finding of this scientific paper is much lower than a systematic meta-analysis done in 2020 of 22 peer-reviewed articles on health-care workers in Africa, which found 7.2%–84.6%. This could be due to the approach or study-design difference, as this report is of a single study, whereas that study used pooled prevalence.

26 Ethiopia: Criminal Code [Ethiopia], Proclamation No 414/2004, 9 May 2005, www.refworld.org/docid/49216b572.html.
27 Article 625 of the Criminal Code.
28 National Legislative Bodies/National Authorities, Ethiopia: Labour Proclamation No 377/2003 of 2003, 26 February 2004, www.refworld.org/docid/4fcc47712.html.
29 *Ibid.*
30 National Legislative Bodies/National Authorities, Ethiopia: Labour Proclamation No 1156/2019 of 9 May 2019, www.ilo.org/dyn/natlex/natlex4.detail?p_isn=109825&p_lang=en.
31 *Ibid.*
32 Art 87.
33 Art 2(11).
34 Art 2(12).
35 Art 2(15).
36 Art 1(1) of the ILO.
37 K Lonsway and P Wendy 'Sexual harassment and sexual assault: Understanding the distinctions and intersections' (2022) *End Violence Against Women International* 1–14.
38 Art 32(1)(b).
39 Art 39.
40 Art 41.
41 The Guiding Principles on Business and Human Rights are the global standard for preventing and addressing the risk of adverse impacts on human rights involving business activity, and they provide the internationally accepted framework for enhancing standards and practices regarding business and human rights. They were developed by the Special Representative of the Secretary-General on the issue of human rights and transnational corporations and other business enterprises. The Human Rights Council unanimously endorsed the Guiding Principles in its resolution 17/4 of 16 June 2011.
42 Guiding Principles on Business and Human Rights (n 41).
43 UN General Assembly, International Covenant on Civil and Political Rights, 16 December 1966, United Nations, Treaty Series Vol 999, 171, www.refworld.org/docid/3ae6b3aa0.html.
44 UN General Assembly, International Covenant on Economic, Social and Cultural Rights, 16 December 1966, United Nations, Treaty Series, Vol 993, 3, www.refworld.org/docid/3ae6b36c0.html.
45 UN General Assembly, Convention on the Elimination of All Forms of Discrimination Against Women, 18 December 1979, United Nations, Treaty Series, Vol 1249, 13, www.refworld.org/docid/3ae6b3970.html.
46 Organisation of African Unity (OAU) African Charter on Human and Peoples' Rights (Banjul Charter), 27 June 1981, CAB/LEG/67/3 rev. 5, 21 I.L.M. 58 (1982).
47 United Nations, Beijing Declaration and Platform of Action, adopted at the Fourth World Conference on Women, 27 October 1995, www.refworld.org/docid/3dde04324.html.
48 UN General Assembly, Convention on the Rights of the Child, 20 November 1989, United Nations, Treaty Series Vol 1577, 3, www.refworld.org/docid/3ae6b38f0.html.
49 African Union Protocol to the African Charter on Human and People's Rights on the Rights of Women in Africa, 11 July 2003, www.refworld.org/docid/3f4b139d4.html.
50 L Worku 'Legislative proposals and application of human right treaties in Ethiopia' (2015) *Abyssinian Law* 1–12, www.abyssinialaw.com/blog/categories/legislative-drafting-blog.

51 In 1992, the UN Committee on the Elimination of Discrimination against Women (CEDAW) has adopted its first guidance on violence against women commonly known as General Recommendation No 19. In 2017, General Recommendation No 35 were adopted to provide more comprehensive guidance to accelerate the elimination of gender-based violence against women and girls, https://undocs.org/Home/Mobile?FinalSymbol=CEDAW%2FC%2FGC%2F35&Language=E&DeviceType=Desktop&LangRequested=False.
52 As per the Labor proclamation No 1156/2019, minimum age for employment has been raised from 14 years to 15 years under the 2019 Labour Proclamation and the minimum Age for Hazardous Work is set as 18 years. Workers between the ages of 15 to 18 years are classified as young workers.
53 Under the Philippines Anti-Sexual Harassment Act 7877 of 1995, an employer or head of office is required by the law to prevent the occurrence of sexual harassment acts and to provide the procedures for the resolution, settlement, or prosecution of sexual harassment. Towards this end, the employer or head of office shall promulgate appropriate rules and regulations in consultation with and jointly approved by the employees or student or trainees, through their duly designated representatives. The employer or head of office also has a duty to create a Committee on Decorum and Investigation (CODI) of cases on sexual harassment. The committee shall conduct meetings or as the case may be, with officers and employees, teachers, instructors, professors, coaches, trainers and students or trainees to increase understanding and prevent incidents of sexual harassment. It shall also conduct the investigation of alleged cases constituting sexual harassment.
54 Canada Gazette, Part II, Volume 154, Number 13. Workplace Harassment and Violence Prevention Regulations: SOR/2020–130, 2020.
55 *Ibid.*
56 Art 113.
57 Art 114.
58 Labour Laws, 2000–01, State of Israel, Ministry of Labour and Social Affairs. Division of Labour Relations, Jerusalem, Israel, 105–111. Prohibits sexual harassment to protect human dignity, liberty, and privacy and promote equality between the sexes. Enumerates acts constituting sexual harassment. Regulates sexual harassment as offenses and civil wrongs, steps to be taken by an employer, labour court jurisdiction, and related matters.
59 *Ibid.*
60 Australia: Act No 4 of 1984, Sex Discrimination Act 1984 [Australia], 21 March 1984, www.refworld.org/docid/4e01b6dd2.html.

References

African Union Protocol to the African Charter on Human and People's Rights on the Rights of Women in Africa, 11 July 2003, www.refworld.org/docid/3f4b139d4.html.

Australia: Act No 4 of 1984, Sex Discrimination Act 1984 [Australia], 21 March 1984, www.refworld.org/docid/4e01b6dd2.html.

Canada Gazette, Part II, Volume 154, Number 13. Workplace Harassment and Violence Prevention Regulations: SOR/2020–130. 2020.

EH Dagnaw et al 'Sexual Harassment at the workplace is still a hindrance among midwives and nurses working in Northwester Ethiopia referral hospitals: A multicentre cross-sectional study' (2022) 15 *Journal of Multidisciplinary Healthcare* 2453–2459.

Ethiopia 2017 Voluntary National Review on SDGs Government Commitments, National Ownership and Performance Trends, www.undp.org/ethiopia/publications/ethiopia-2017-voluntary-national-review-sdgs.

Ethiopia 2022 Voluntary National Review on SDGs, https://hlpf.un.org/sites/default/files/vnrs/2022/VNR%202022%20Ethiopia%20Report_1.pdf.

Ethiopia: Criminal Code [Ethiopia], Proclamation No 414/2004, 9 May 2005, www.refworld.org/docid/49216b572.html.

O Folke and J Rickne 'Sexual harassment and gender inequality in the labour market' (2022) 137/4 *The Quarterly Journal of Economics* 2163–2212.

Guiding Principles on Business and Human Rights developed by the Special Representative of the Secretary-General, endorsed by the Human Rights Council in Resolution 17/4 of 16 June 2011.

Labour Laws, 2000–01, State of Israel, Ministry of Labour and Social Affairs. Division of Labour Relations, Jerusalem, Israel, 105–111.

K Lonsway and W Patrick 'Sexual harassment and sexual assault: Understanding the distinctions and intersections' (2022) *End Violence Against Women International* 1–14.

B Mekonnen, Z Lakew and E Melese 'Prevalence and associated factors of sexual violence experienced by housemaids in Ethiopia: A systematic review and meta-analysis' (2022) 19/162 *Reproductive Health* 1–14.

B Mesfin 'Women's participation in political leadership and decision making in Ethiopia: A research note' (2004) 2/2 *Ethiopian Journal of the Social Sciences and Humanities* 81–99.

National Legislative Bodies/National Authorities, Ethiopia: Labour Proclamation No 377/2003 of 2003, 26 February 2004, www.refworld.org/docid/4fcc47712.html.

National Legislative Bodies/National Authorities, Ethiopia: Labour Proclamation No 1156/2019 of 9 May 2019, www.ilo.org/dyn/natlex/natlex4.detail?p_isn=109825&p_lang=en.

Organisation of African Unity (OAU) African Charter on Human and Peoples' Rights (Banjul Charter), 27 June 1981, CAB/LEG/67/3 rev. 5, 21 I.L.M. 58 (1982).

A Tasew Causes, *Effects and Challenges of Sexual Harassment on Waitresses: The Case of Bole Sub City, Addis Ababa* (Lap Lambert Academic Publishing, 2012).

UN General Assembly, Convention on the Elimination of All Forms of Discrimination Against Women, 18 December 1979, United Nations, Treaty Series, Vol 1249, 13, www.refworld.org/docid/3ae6b3970.html.

UN General Assembly, Convention on the Rights of the Child, 20 November 1989, UN Treaty Series, Vol 1577, 3, www.refworld.org/docid/3ae6b38f0.html.

UN General Assembly, International Covenant on Civil and Political Rights, 16 December 1966, UN Treaty Series, Vol 999, 171, www.refworld.org/docid/3ae6b3aa0.html.

UN General Assembly, International Covenant on Economic, Social and Cultural Rights, 16 December 1966, UN Treaty Series, Vol 993, 3, www.refworld.org/docid/3ae6b36c0.html.

United Nations, Beijing Declaration and Platform of Action, adopted at the Fourth World Conference on Women, 27 October 1995, www.refworld.org/docid/3dde04324.html.

MD Worke et al 'Prevalence of sexual violence in Ethiopian workplaces: Systematic review and meta-analysis' (2020) 17/196 *Reproductive Health* 1–15.

L Worku 'Legislative proposals and application of human right treaties in Ethiopia' (2015) *Abyssinian Law* 1–12, www.abyssinialaw.com/blog/categories/legislative-drafting-blog.

9 Sexual Harassment and the Law in Kenya

Broadening Employee Rights in the World of Work

Wycliffe Nyachoti Otiso

Introduction

Regardless of where it occurs, whether in formal or informal workspaces, sexual harassment represents a pervasive form of gender-based violence which disproportionally affects women. The problem is not unique to Kenya, as evidenced by global reports which indicate that almost one in three women (30%) having been victims of sexual violence at least once in their lifetime.[1] In sub-Saharan Africa, the statistics on violence against women are marginally higher than the global average, at 33%.[2] In keeping with international trends to address violence against women and sexual harassment specifically, the government of Kenya has, through various pieces of legislation, dealt with this issue. For instance, the enactment of the Penal Code[3] is an early example of legislative response to violence against women broadly.

Under the Penal Code, acts of sexual violence and harassment were dealt with as 'offences against morality'.[4] Definitions of sexual offences in the Penal Code did not make reference to sexual harassment. The law had not been revised to capture nuance behaviour, one behaviour in society.[5] There was an acknowledgement that offences had to be redefined beyond traditional categories like rape and defilement[6] in order to include behaviour which was subtle, verbal, and psychological as conduct that amounts to harassment within the workplace.[7] Penalties also needed to be revised to be more punitive to deter perpetrators as existing sanctions under the Penal Code were lenient.[8] The gaps in the Penal Code noted here led to the introduction of Section 23 of the Sexual Offences Act.[9]

The implementation of the Sexual Offences Act in 2006 repealed Sections 139 to 145 and Sections 147 to 149 of the Penal Code which related to the offences of rape, indecent assault, and defilement.[10] Recognising that the Penal Code did not adequately cover 'sexual offences', the Sexual Offences Act was enacted to address the legislative gap. This was followed by the passing of the Employment Act in 2007 providing robust mechanisms for the protection of employee rights at the workplace.[11] Section 6 of the Employment Act introduced provisions that specifically prohibit sexual harassment at the workplace to include direct or indirect sexual advances with promises

DOI: 10.4324/9781003373308-9

of preferential treatment in employment or threat to future employment. The Act prohibits the use of words, materials, or behaviours of a sexual nature which are unwelcome or offensive to an employee or detrimental to an employee's performance. Section 6(1) has been the subject of interpretation by the courts in the *JWN v Securex*,[12] *PO v Board of Trustees*,[13] *CAS v CS Limited*[14] and *SRM v GSS (K) Limited and Dominic Ooko* cases.[15] In these cases, the courts addressed diverse issues relating to sexual harassment, unfair dismissal, and contravention of constitutional rights relating to dignity and freedom from violence.

The adoption of the Constitution of Kenya in 2010 is viewed as entrenching 'an extensive, elaborate, and liberal Bill of Rights that seeks to promote the social, economic and political rights of Kenyans'.[16] Often, victims of sexual harassment are subjected to infringement of their rights to dignity, health, fair labour practices, and freedom from violence and torture (physical or psychological). The Bill of Rights provides mechanisms for the protection of these rights under Article 28 (right to dignity), Article 29 (freedom from violence and security of the person), Article 41 (right to fair labour practices), and Article 43 (right to health). Nevertheless, the pervasiveness of sexual harassment has continued in Kenya despite the introduction of the Sexual Offences Act, the Employment Act, and what has been lauded as a progressive Constitution which upholds fundamental human rights and freedoms.

In section that follows, I analyse the definition of sexual harassment, where I touch on US jurisprudence and how the concept of sexual harassment has evolved. I then focus on the laws specific to sexual harassment in Kenya by focusing the analysis on the Constitution, followed by the Sexual Offences Act and the Employment Act. Lastly, I examine provisions of the International Labour Organisation Convention No 190 for the Elimination of Violence and Harassment in the World of Work (ILO C190), which provides stronger protection of employees against sexual harassment. I then conclude with recommendations.

Definition and Concept of Sexual Harassment

The prohibition of sexual harassment as a sexual offence, an infringement of employee's rights, and a breach of personal and civil rights has received belated attention and inclusion under Kenya's legislative framework. However, this is not unique to Kenya. It was not until 1986 that the US Supreme Court pronounced in *Meritor Saving Bank FSB vs Vinson*[17] that sexual harassment is a violation of Title VII of the 1964 Civil Rights Act.[18] The Act prohibits discrimination on the basis of sex in the workplace. As noted by Sapiro and Campbell, the legal definition of sexual harassment evolved from *quid pro quo*[19] harassment relating to threats or benefits offered to coerce unwelcome sexual conduct. Sapiro and Campbell define sexual harassment as 'unwelcome sexual conduct that has the purpose or effect of unreasonably interfering with work performance or unwelcome sexual conduct that creates an intimidating, a hostile or offensive work environment'.[20] They also observe that the definition of sexual harassment has increasingly broadened from an initial focus on unwelcome sexual conduct to include 'verbal or non-verbal behaviour that is not explicitly about sexual relations, but which systematically demeans or insults people on the basis of their gender'.[21]

In her research, which traces the development of sexual harassment law, Reva Siegel[22] affirms that the concept of sexual harassment has evolved from subjecting employees to unwanted sexual advances at work to the recognition of sexual harassment as a discrimination based on sex. While Lee and Greenlaw also note the development of sexual harassment law, they advance the analysis that evolution has largely developed towards a specific type of sexual harassment; moving from *quid pro quo* to hostile environment-related sexual harassment.[23] Analysis of how sexual harassment has evolved in US jurisprudence is important as it enables the evaluation of the definition of sexual harassment under Kenyan law and the extent to which courts' interpretations have broadened its scope, as will be discussed in the section on Kenyan jurisprudence below.

Law on Sexual Harassment in Kenya

The laws on sexual harassment in Kenya are expressly set out in the Sexual Offences Act and the Employment Act. The Constitution of Kenya, especially in Chapter IV, also includes provisions which support protection from sexual harassment, including freedom of the security of the person[24] and right to dignity.[25] Over the years, emerging jurisprudence from the courts has proved to be a key component of development of the law on sexual harassment. Reasoned decisions from the courts, for instance *Board of Trustees*[26] and *Securex*,[27] have provided guidance on the standards to be adhered to, scope of prohibited behaviour, and appropriate sanctions for contravention of the law on sexual harassment. In the case of *Board of Trustees,*[28] the court described what kinds of physical behaviour constitute sexual harassment and broadened the concept of 'workplace' to include misconduct that occurs outside the formal workspace or offices. *Securex*[29] provides an interpretation of verbal and written harassment of a sexual nature which contravenes the provisions of section 6(1)(b) of the Employment Act. The courts' broad approach to interpretation of the workplace in *Board of Trustees* and extension of liability beyond *quid pro quo* and physical sexual harassment to include utterances of a sexual nature in *Securex*, is reflective of the evolving scope and definition of sexual harassment providing a wider ambit for redress.

The Constitution of Kenya, 2010

The Constitution of Kenya has a Bill of Rights in Chapter IV which provides for a broad range of rights. Article 19(2) of the Constitution provides that the purpose of recognising and protecting human rights and fundamental freedoms is to preserve the dignity of individuals and communities and to promote social justice and the realisation of the potential of all individuals. These concerns are at the core of the fight for safe workspaces and the elimination of sexual harassment. The Constitution has several provisions contained in the Bill of Rights that have a specific bearing on the protection of persons' rights from sexual harassment in the workplace.

Article 27 of the Constitution provides for freedom from discrimination. It protects every person from being discriminated against on various grounds, including gender or sex. Article 28 of the Constitution provides that every person has the right to inherent dignity and the right to have that dignity respected and protected. The Constitution also provides for freedom and security of the person and includes the right not to be subjected to any form of violence or torture in any manner, whether physical or psychological.[30] The inclusion of psychological torture is important, as sexual harassment cases are often overlooked where the aggressors' behaviour is non-physical. This is supported by Article 43 of the Constitution which provides that everyone is entitled to the highest attainable standard of health. The Health Act was enacted in 2017[31] to implement Article 43 by protecting, respecting, promoting, and fulfilling the health rights of all persons. Health is defined as the 'complete state of physical, mental and social wellbeing, not the absence of disease or infirmity'.[32] Article 41 provides for the right to fair labour practices and the right of the worker to enjoy reasonable working conditions in an environment that is free from sexual harassment.

In the cases I review in this chapter, the application of constitutional provisions as the basis for protection against sexual harassment was successfully invoked in *Securex*,[33] where the court found that the false accusations of a sexual nature directed towards the claimant by a supervisor at a parade amounted to a contravention of the claimant's right to dignity under Article 28 of the Constitution.

Sexual Offences Act

The offence of sexual harassment is articulated under section 23 of the Sexual Offences Act (SOA). It provides that:

> Any person, who being in a position of authority, or holding a public office, who persistently makes any sexual advances or requests which he or she knows, or has reasonable grounds to know, are unwelcome, is guilty of the offence of sexual harassment and shall be liable to imprisonment for a term of not less than three years or to a fine of not less than one hundred thousand shillings or to both.[34]

The three main elements of the offence of sexual harassment are: the act is committed by a person in a position of authority or holding public office, the act constitutes persistent sexual advances or requests, and the person accused of sexual harassment knows or has reasonable grounds to know that such sexual advances are unwelcome.

Person of Authority or Public Office Holder

Section 23(1) requires that the harasser is a person of authority or a person that holds a public office. The provision seeks to prohibit harassment behaviour facilitated by the power or influence that the harasser wields and the ability to use it to harass the victim by being a holder of a certain position or office. The assumption made in Section 23(1) is that a public office holder wields considerable power by virtue of the office. The focus here is on the person's influence rather than whether the harassment occurs in the public or private sector. Under Section 23(1), the harassment complained about need not have occurred in a formal workplace setting. It allows for liability to extend to relations beyond the workplace where the perpetrator and victim are not necessarily in an employer–employee relationship. Section 23(1) also requires that the sexual advances or requests be persistent. This means that a pattern of unwelcome sexual advances or requests from the offender to the victim must be established.

Actual or Reasonable Knowledge of Unwelcome Sexual Advances

For an offence of sexual harassment to be proved under the Section 23(1)(c), evidence must be provided to show that the offender knew or had reasonable knowledge that the sexual advances were unwelcome. Section 23(1)(c) includes both subjective and objective criteria in testing the knowledge of the offender on whether the sexual advances were welcome or not.

Intention, Effect, and Purpose of Unwelcome Sexual Advances

The Sexual Offences Act provides an opportunity to ask what the intention was behind the sexually harassing conduct – what was its purpose and what was its effect? To prove sexual harassment, it must be shown that the submission or rejection by the person to whom advances or requests are made is intended to be used as basis of employment or a decision relevant to the career of the alleged victim or a service due to a member of the public in the case of a public officer. It must also be shown that such advances or requests have the effect of interfering with the victim's work or educational performance or are creating an offensive working or learning environment for the alleged victim, or denial of a service due to the member of the public from a public officer.

For an aggressor to be culpable, it must also be shown under Section 23(2) of the Sexual Offences Act that the purpose of the unwelcome advances is to influence decisions relevant to career advancement or the employment of the person who was sexually harassed, or for purposes of offering favourable treatment in accessing public services. Submission to or rejection of the advances by the person who is sexually harassed is not a relevant factor in determining the culpability of the offender. The fact that the victim submits to the advances of the offender cannot be raised as a defence to the offence of sexual harassment. Under Section 23(2)(b) of the Sexual Offences Act, sexual advances or requests complained of must have three effects. The unwelcome advances must have the effect of interfering with the victim's work, create an offensive environment for a learner,[35] or result in the denial of public services by a public officer.

Employment Act

The Employment Act prohibits sexual harassment in Section 6. Accordingly, it is necessary to establish what constitutes the workplace, who is an employer and what agreements regulate the employer–employee relationship as set out in the Act. These are found in Section 2 of the Act and are discussed below. Terms including 'contract of services', 'employee', and 'employer' are relevant in understanding what the law defines as the 'workplace'.

Definitions

The term 'contract of services' refers to an oral or written agreement that allows one to employ or to serve as an employee for a period. A contract of service or an employment contract covers contracts of apprenticeship. An 'employee' is any person employed for wages or a salary and includes an apprentice and indentured learner. An 'employer' is 'any person, public body, firm, corporation or company who or which has entered into a contract of service to employ an individual and including the agent, foreman, manager or factor of such person, public body, firm, corporation or company'.[36]

Sexual Harassment

The Employment Act provides that an employee is sexually harassed if the employer of that employee, or a representative of that employer or a co-worker, directly or indirectly requests that employee for sexual intercourse, sexual contact, or any other form of sexual activity that contains an express or implied promise of preferential treatment in employment, threat of detrimental treatment in employment, or threat about the present or future employment status of the employee.[37] The Employment Act also states that sexual harassment occurs where the employer, representative of the employer, or co-worker uses words, whether written or spoken, of a sexual nature, uses visual material of a sexual nature, or shows physical behaviour of a sexual nature which directly or indirectly subjects the employee to behaviour that is unwelcome or offensive to that employee, and that by its nature has a detrimental effect on the employees' employment, job performance, or job satisfaction.[38]

This definition is progressive in several aspects. The law expands the ambit of the class of persons who may be liable for committing acts of sexual harassment to include representatives of the employer and co-workers. However, the limitation of the provision is that it fails to encompass all possible aggressors in a workplace, which may include suppliers, clients, public officers visiting the workplace, friends, and relatives of the employer. Such persons also have the ability to influence the employment status of the employee. Progressive models of a sexual harassment law should expand the definition further to include all these categories.

Secondly, Section 6(1) of the Employment Act does not tie the use of language or material of a sexual nature to the promises of preferential treatment in employment or threats of detrimental treatment in employment. This is a positive approach because sexual harassment can and does occur without promising or threatening the employment status of the person being harassed. This especially occurs amongst peers and co-workers. It is a good model to build on. Section 6(2) of the Employment Act also requires an entity with 20 or more employees to develop a sexual harassment policy in consultation with the employees. The policy is required to contain the following undertakings and statements:

- That every employee is entitled to employment that is free of sexual harassment;
- That the employer shall take steps to ensure that no employee is subjected to sexual harassment;
- That the employer shall take such disciplinary measures as the employer deems appropriate against any person under the employer's direction, who subjects any employee to sexual harassment;
- That the employer will explain how complaints of sexual harassment may be brought to the attention of the employer, and
- That the employer will not disclose the name of a complainant, or the circumstances related to the complaint to any person except where disclosure is necessary for the purpose of investigating the complaint or taking disciplinary measures in relation thereto.

The provision requiring a workplace sexual harassment policy is beneficial to employees as it nurtures an environment that promotes workplace safety and awareness of sexual harassment. It would be essential to require all workplaces to adopt a sexual harassment policy, including those with less than 20 employees, because all workers and employees have a right to equal protection before the law regardless of the size of their workplaces. The penalty of a fine for non-compliance with Section 6(2) is not adequate. Section 6(2) could be strengthened by non-retaliation policies requiring that workplace policies that provide mechanisms for the protection of victims after reporting, including provision of leave, psycho-social support, and counselling.

Kenyan Jurisprudence on Sexual Harassment

Jurisprudence on sexual harassment as a sexual offence under the Sexual Offences Act is limited.[39] This is likely because most of the jurisprudence has centred on the analysis of civil wrongs under Section 6 of the Employment Act. The following cases are analysed through several themes, including the scope of the meaning of sexual harassment, computation of liability for damages, and breach of constitutional rights.

Written or Spoken Language of a Sexual Nature

In the case of *JWN v Securex*,[40] the claimant sought a declaration that *Securex* (her former employer) had acted unfairly, unreasonably, and disregarded her human dignity by falsely disclosing allegations of a sexual nature concerning the claimant. The claimant worked for the respondent as a guard. During a parade attended by 39 other guards, the employer's supervisor announced that the claimant, while on duty, had been involved in a sexual escapade in a room at a shopping mall (her assigned station). He also announced that the incident had been captured on the security cameras in the shopping mall. The claimant's case was that the disclosure had been made without making any efforts to ascertain the veracity of the allegations, and that the public accusation was dehumanising and an infringement on the claimant's right to dignified treatment as provided under Article 28 of the Constitution.

After the accusation was made, the claimant was told to go home by the supervisor on the promise that she would be recalled. The claimant was not recalled as promised but was promptly replaced. The claimant asserted that she was unfairly and constructively dismissed from employment, and that the false allegations of a sexual nature subjected her to psychological torment and trauma. The claimant sought general damages for infringement of her right to dignity under Article 28 of the Constitution.

The court relied on Section 6(1)(b) of the Employment Act, which provides that an employee is sexually harassed if the employer or a representative of that employer or co-worker uses language, whether written or spoken, of a sexual nature. It held that the claimant had been sexually harassed by the employer within the meaning of Section 6(1)(b) of the Employment Act having been exposed to words of a sexual nature. The court also held that the claimant's inherent right to dignity under Article 28 of the Constitution had been violated through the false and embarrassing allegations made against the claimant in public. The court found that the false allegations had adversely affected the claimant and gave an award of Kshs 1,000,000/ as general damages. The court further ordered the company to pay Kshs 105,000/ for unfair termination of the claimant's contract of employment.

The court's decision in *JWN v Securex* relies on both constitutional and statutory provisions to protect the rights of the sexually harassed employee. The court's reasoning suggests that relating sexual harassment and public humiliation to a violation of the constitutional right to dignity and it paves way for further litigation of sexual harassment claims as a violation of rights of employees. Claims for violation of human rights under the Constitution will attract more damages along with awards for sexual harassment under the Employment Act and may act as a more significant deterrent. The court's interpretation of the accusation that the employee had engaged in sex at work amounted to words of a sexual nature within the meaning of Section 6 of the Employment Act and broadens the application of that section. Previous applications of the section had been limited to instances of physical behaviour of a sexual nature or when one nags another employee for sex.

Persistent Sexual Advances

In the case of *SRM v GSS (K) Limited and Dominic Ooko*,[41] the plaintiff sued the first respondent (former employer) and second respondent (former manager) for sexual harassment and unlawful termination. The manager had persistently commented on the plaintiff's bodily appearance and dressing despite warnings from the plaintiff to the respondent to refrain from doing so. The manager also persistently sought the employee's company for reasons other than those related to their work despite persistent rejection of the invitations, which led to the denial of an office driver. When the claimant reported the issue to her supervisor and managing director, she was referred to the manager and was directed to drop the complaint. Subsequently, audits and investigations of her performance were conducted, and the claimant was accused of neglecting duty.

The court found the employer and the manager jointly and separately liable for failing to prevent acts of sexual harassment. The court awarded the claimant a sum equivalent to two years' salary as damages for sexual harassment. In computing damages, the court applied the reasoning in the case of *GMV v Bank of Africa*[42] that sexual harassment should not be seen as another form of unlawful termination to award the claimant the equivalent of one year's salary. Courts have ordinarily applied Section 49(1)(c) of the Employment Act and computed damages for unlawful termination as the equivalent of the claimant's one-year salary. Section 49(1)(c) of the Employment Act provides that one of the remedies for unlawful termination is compensation 'equivalent of a number of months' wages or salary not exceeding twelve months based on the gross monthly wages or salary of the employee at the time of dismissal'. Courts have applied the remedy provided in Section 49(1)(c) for damages for unlawful termination in computing damages for sexual harassment. The court in *SRM* awarded twice the amount that has conventionally been awarded by other courts; that is, equivalent of the claimant's salary for two years.

Sexual Conduct of a Physical Nature

In the case of *PO v Board of Trustees*,[43] the claimant sued her former employer and her supervisor (second respondent) for compensation for sexual harassment. The claimant stated that she had been subjected to direct and indirect demands for sex by her supervisor. The supervisor's actions included implied preferential treatment regarding employment and threats about present and future employment status. The claimant adduced evidence of demands and threats after termination of employment. The claimant was also subjected to physical behaviour of a sexual nature during a business trip to attend a conference in South Africa. The supervisor had booked a single room for the two of them and the claimant opted to sleep on the floor. After the claimant rejected the sexual advances, the supervisor physically abused her. The claimant left South Africa and did not attend the conference. The claimant stated that the supervisor's behaviour was offensive, unwelcome, and had a profound effect on her employment and job satisfaction. After, the claimant rejected the supervisor's sexual advances repeatedly she was terminated.

The employer's defence that the events in South Africa were 'personal in nature' and not open to the court's interrogation was rejected. The court stated that 'conduct whether in Nairobi or a hotel room in Cape Town or at the sea near Greece would amount to gender-based violence against an employee'.[44] The court found that the defendant's actions amounted to sexual harassment and that the claimant was unfairly terminated. The court ordered general damages of Kshs 3,000,000/- for sexual harassment.

In the case of *CAS v CS Limited*,[45] the question before the court was whether the acts of a manager of the respondent company, which included touching the claimant's private parts and verbal utterances of a sexual nature, amounted to sexual harassment. The claimant sought declarations that the respondent was required to issue a policy statement on sexual harassment and that dismissal of the claimant was unlawful and unfair. The claimant also sought compensation for unfair dismissal and damages for sexual harassment. The claimant stated that she had been constantly physically and verbally abused by two managers of the company. The lack of a sexual harassment policy also created an environment which enabled the harassment. After lodging a sexual harassment complaint against her manager, the claimant sought and was granted sick leave. On her return to work, she was subjected to disciplinary action and then dismissed for absconding work. The claimant testified that she had been subjected to verbal utterances of a sexual nature and unwanted physical sexual advances, including touching her private parts. The court held that the dismissal of the claimant was unfair and unjustified,[46] and ordered damages equivalent to 12 month's salary for unfair dismissal.[47]

The respondent did not have a sexual harassment policy as stipulated by the law.[48] Whilst the court agreed with the testimony of the claimant, it did not make any pronouncement or give any reasons for not granting the claimant general damages for sexual harassment. It is unconventional for courts to deliberate on an issue raised by a claimant, affirm that the claim has been proven, and then not award compensation or any other remedy. In my view, the court avoided addressing the issue of sexual harassment directly and sanctioning it, instead focusing on compensating the claimant for unlawful dismissal from employment.

International Labour Organisation (ILO) Convention on Elimination of Violence and Harassment in the Workplace

Ratification

The ILO C190 was adopted by the Conference at its 190th session in Geneva on 21 June 2019.[49] The Convention has been ratified by Uruguay, Fiji, Namibia, Argentina, Ecuador, Somalia, Mauritius, Mexico, Canada, Peru, Barbados, Bahamas, Nigeria, Panama, United Kingdom, and Republic of Ireland.[50] As of this date, Kenya is yet to ratify the ILO C190. In its roadmap for advancing gender equality,[51] the Kenyan government committed to ratifying and implementing the ILO C190 by 2026.

I recommend that the Kenyan government honours its commitment to ratify ILO C190 and ensures this is accomplished before 2026. The new administration ushered in following the 2022 August national elections ought to revise prior timelines and ensure that there is immediate ratification and implementation for better protection of employees from sexual harassment. The reformulation of existing laws to bring forth more robust protection mechanisms for sexual harassment victims should form the basis of law reform. The key articles of the ILO C190 pertinent to sexual harassment and violence are discussed in the following section.

Articles of the Convention

The Convention grants member states the discretion to include gender-based violence and sexual harassment as a single law or to separate the two concepts.[52] Article 1 recognises that sexual harassment does not have to be persistent and can arise from a single incident. Article 1(a) defines 'violence and harassment' as 'behaviour or practices that result in physical, psychological, sexual or economic harm including gender-based violence and harassment', whether it is a 'single' act or a 'repeated' act. The Convention also broadens the notion of 'sexual harassment', as it provides a definition that includes sexual harassment as gender-based violence. Article 1(b) states that gender-based violence 'means violence and harassment directed at persons because of their sex or gender or affecting persons of a particular sex or gender disproportionately and includes sexual harassment'.

Article 2 broadens the scope of the application of the Convention beyond the traditional concept of 'work', which centred on formal and contractual engagements. Article 2 provides that the Convention applies in the protection of workers and other persons in the world of work, including employees as defined by national law and practice, as well as persons working irrespective of their contractual status; persons in training, including interns and apprentices; workers whose employment has been terminated; volunteers; jobseekers and job applicants; and individuals exercising the authority, duties, or responsibilities of an employer. Traditionally, categories of employment including job applicants or interns were not included in legal definitions as the focus was on the contractual status of an employee. Article 2(2) provides that the Convention applies to all sectors, whether private or public, both in the formal and informal economy, and extends to urban and rural areas.

Article 3 provides that sexual harassment applies to violence and harassment in the world of work occurring in the course of, linked with, or arising out of work. This includes violence and harassment that occurs: in the workplace, including public and private spaces; places where the worker is paid, takes a rest break or a meal, or uses sanitary, washing and changing facilities; during work-related trips, travel, training, events or social activities; through work-related communications, including those enabled by information and communication technologies; in employer-provided accommodation; and when commuting to and from work. Article 3 recognises workplaces that have not been traditionally captured in laws prohibiting sexual harassment. These include work-related trips, work-related social activities, lunch breaks, commutes to work, work-related communications, and employer-provided accommodation.

Article 9 of the Convention requires members to:

> adopt laws and regulations requiring employers to take appropriate steps commensurate with their degree of control to prevent violence and harassment in the world of work, including gender-based violence and harassment, and in particular, so far as is reasonably practicable . . . adopt and implement workplace policy on violence and harassment, identify and assess hazards and risks of workplace violence and harassment[53]

Article 9 of the Convention also provides that in addition to workplace policies on the prevention of sexual harassment, employers are required to have in place occupation and safety health measures to address violence and sexual harassment and the associated psycho-social risks. The Convention introduces positive benchmarks for member states concerning the regulation and protection of sexual harassment. It is necessary to urge more member states to ratify the Convention to adopt its progressive reforms.

Adequacy of Laws on Protection against Sexual Harassment

Broadening the Definition of Sexual Harassment

In the *Securex* case, the court made an interpretation of 'sexual harassment' that broadened its meaning and content. The court applied a meaning of sexual harassment wide enough to encompass the use of language of a sexual nature at the workplace, whether spoken or written, as amounting to sexual harassment. To the extent that Section 23(1) and Section 23(2)(b) of the Sexual Offences Act does not restrict the definition of sexual harassment to the workplace, it is commendable. Section 23(1) applies to 'any person in authority' or 'holder of a public office', while Section 23(2)(b) envisages sexual harassment may occur when accessing public services, employment, and educational institutions. Section 23(2)(b) provides that advances amount to sexual harassment if they have the effect of interfering with the victim's work, create an offensive learning environment, or result in the denial of public services by a public officer. It recognises that sexual harassment does occur outside the sphere of formal employment. Further, whereas traditional notions of sexual harassment have focused on physical harassment,[54] Section 6 of the Employment Act incorporates definitions which are broad enough to cover verbal and non-verbal forms of harassment. Though the Employment Act is limited to the formal workplace, Muthiani (2020) affirms this perspective that Section 6 provides an 'expansive' definition on what constitutes sexual harassment.[55]

However, Section 6 of the Act requires that sexual harassment must constitute 'persistent' acts of unwelcome sexual advances. The effect of the requirement for persistence poses a challenge for cases where victims have been subjected to harassment in a single instance or a one-off occurrence. The claim that unwelcome sexual advances must be persistent to constitute sexual harassment has not yet been raised as a ground of objection in cases brought before the courts in Kenya. However, this does not preclude respondents challenging claimants' account of sexual harassment for failure to meet the required threshold for persistence. The requirement for persistence of harassment under Section 6(1) of the Employment Act is discordant with the ILO position and will require a reformulation to strengthen legal mechanisms against sexual harassment. Article 1(a) of ILO C190 provides that sexual harassment occurs whether the behaviour is a single act or repeated acts. Therefore, the requirement of 'persistence' under Section 6(1) of the Employment Act should be removed, as it makes it difficult for the victim to prove sexual harassment.

Duty of Employer to Prevent Sexual Harassment

The courts have affirmed in the cases of *CAS* and *SRM* that the duty to prevent sexual harassment in the workplace rests on the employer. The employer is charged with formulating a sexual harassment policy and ensuring that all employees are informed of what it requires. The knowledge about a sexual harassment policy is not a preserve of the senior management. It is the duty of the employer to publish a policy statement on sexual harassment and avail it to all employees.

The courts have emphasised the importance of the formulation and dissemination of policy. In the *Securex* case, the lack of a policy statement by an employer was used by courts in apportioning liability on sexual harassment and was taken as an aggravation of the employer's liability. The courts now consider the formulation of a policy statement in apportioning liability in sexual harassment cases. This approach by the courts is commendable. However, as discussed in the following section, the sanction on employers for contravening the requirement for sexual harassment policy is far too lenient.

Damages

The damages awarded for sexual harassment and lack of development of a policy statement on sexual harassment are relatively low and may not achieve the intended punitive effect. In most cases, harassment damages were computed similarly to damages awarded for unfair dismissal. With the exception of the *Board of Trustees* case where the claimant was awarded Kshs 3,000,000/- as damages for sexual harassment, the awards have been quite low. The courts should draw from the approach adopted in *Board of Trustees* case. The penalty for non-compliance to the requirement of a policy statement under section 6 of the Employment Act is also relatively low, as it is set at Kshs 50,000/-. This should be raised and computed in tandem with turnover of the employer.

Beyond general damages granted for sexual harassment which are not adequate to compensate the victim for the loss suffered, other alternative remedial actions ought to be explored.[56] McLaughlin and Thomas propose that remedies should provide adequate compensation for health and economic costs. This would be achieved by increasing compensatory and punitive damages for sexual harassment cases to cover the cost for counselling to be borne by the harasser and the employer.[57]

Sexual Harassment as a Violation of Constitutional Rights

The concept of sexual harassment as an infringement of constitutional rights has not gained much traction in the reasoning of court decisions. Save for the *Securex* case, which recognised that sexual harassment infringed on the inherent dignity of the claimant under Article 28, courts have been reluctant to grant redress for sexual harassment based on constitutional provisions. In the *Securex* case, the court disagreed with the contention that the public humiliation and disclosure of language of a sexual nature led to the psychological torture of the claimant. Therefore, while the claimant succeeded on the right to dignity under Article 28, she failed on the issue that she suffered psychological torture as envisaged in Article 29 of the Constitution on the right to freedom from torture. Further, the understanding of what constitutes sexual harassment has not broadened enough to view sexual harassment as a form of discrimination under Article 27.

Analysis of the cases reviewed, including *Securex* and *CAS* vs *CS Limited*, does not reveal a pattern or recurrent theme to explain the low traction of upholding constitutional provisions in supporting the claims for sexual harassment before the courts.[58] In my view, it appears that from the perspective of advocates, the litigation strategy has been centred on seeking damages for unlawful dismissal and general damages for sexual harassment. It is only in the case of *Securex* where contravention of Articles 28 and 29 was raised along with sexual harassment and unfair dismissal. Therefore, advocates ought to encourage, as part of the litigation strategy, to include violation of constitutional rights when claiming for sexual harassment cases to strengthen protection and remedies for sexual harassment victims.

The Bill of Rights in the Constitution of Kenya is progressive, detailed, and forms the foundation for establishing cogent laws that address sexual harassment in the workplace. The Constitution can also be used to develop penal consequences for persons who engage in conduct amounting to sexual harassment. As discussed in this chapter, there is an urgent need to strengthen the laws on sexual harassment by basing them on the rights conferred by the Constitution under Article 28 (right to dignity), Article 29 (freedom from violence and right to security), Article 41 (right to fair labour practices), and Article 43 (right to health).

Conclusion

Over the last 10 years, the definition of sexual harassment and the acts that constitute it have been broadened with a positive implication on employee rights in Kenya. Court decisions including *Board of Trustees* and *Securex* have made pronouncements that expanded 'sexual harassment' to include acts that depict unwanted physical sexual behaviour and use of language of a sexual nature. However, some courts, as in the case of *CAS*, have been reluctant to sanction sexual offenders or to address sexual harassment directly, instead focusing on compensating victims for unlawful dismissal from employment, which unfortunately is the price victims pay for reporting sexual harassment. Further, the adoption of the provisions of the ILO C190 has exposed the inadequate protections availed under the Sexual Offences Act and the Employment Act. Broadening the definition of sexual harassment to include single acts of unwanted sexual advances, viewing sexual harassment as a form of violence, and recognising the psychological harm that it causes are progressive concepts of sexual harassment, which reforms I recommend should be adopted to strengthen and reformulate Kenya's legal framework on sexual harassment.

Notes

1 World Health Organisation *Violence against Women Prevalence Estimates, 2018: Global, Regional and National Prevalence Estimates for Intimate Partner Violence and for Non-partner Sexual Violence against Women* (World Health Organisation, 2021).
2 *Ibid.*
3 Chapter 63 of the Laws of Kenya.
4 Penal Code, Chapter XV.
5 Association for Women's Rights in Development 'Legislating against sexual violence: Interview with the Hon. Njoki Ndungu' (2007) 15/29 *Reproductive Health Matters* 149–154.

6 *Ibid* 149.
7 *Ibid*.
8 *Ibid*.
9 No 3 of 2006.
10 *Ibid*.
11 No 11 of 2007, Chapter 226 of the Laws of Kenya.
12 *JWN v Securex Agencies (K) Limited* [2018] eKLR.
13 *PO v Board of Trustees, AF and 2 Others* [2014] eKLR.
14 *CAS v CSS* [2016] eKLR.
15 *SRM v GSS (K) Limited and Dominic Ooko* [2017] eKLR.
16 B Sihanya 'Constitutional implementation in Kenya, 2010–2015: Challenges and prospects' FES Kenya Occasional Paper No 5, 3.
17 477 US 57 (1986).
18 Pub L 88–352, 78 Stat 241 (1964).
19 It refers to conduct where the harasser makes sexual advances and in return offers preferential treatment in the workplace or threatens the employee of detrimental effects.
20 V Sapiro and D Campbell 'Report on the 2017 APSA survey on sexual harassment at annual meetings' sexual harassment report' *Annual Political Science Association*, 2018, www.apsanet.org/reports (accessed on 2 June 2020).
21 *Ibid*.
22 R Siegel 'A short history of sexual harassment' in C Mackinnon and R Siegel (eds) *Directions in Sexual Harassment Law* (Yale University Press, 2003).
23 RD Lee and P Greenlaw 'The legal evolution of sexual harassment' (1995) 55/4 *Public Administration Review* 357, 364.
24 Constitution of Kenya, Art 29.
25 *Ibid* Art 28.
26 *PO v Board of Trustees* (n 13).
27 *JWN v Securex Agencies* (n 12).
28 *PO v Board of Trustees* (n 13).
29 *JWN v Securex Agencies* (n 12).
30 *Ibid*.
31 Health Act, Sect 3.
32 *Ibid*, Sect 2.
33 *JWN v Securex Agencies* (n 12).
34 One hundred thousand shillings is equivalent to $750.
35 Limiting application of the provisions of section 23 of Sexual Offences Act to a 'learner' is narrow in the sense that it leaves out culpability of other possible offenders in learning institutions including employees or co-workers.
36 A 'factor' is a special a type of agent, who is entrusted with goods by the principal with the authority to sell the goods.
37 Employment Act, Sect 6(1).
38 *Ibid*.
39 There is little literature or analysis available on why there is low reporting of criminal cases compared to reporting of employment and labour cases relating to sexual harassment. My observation is that criminal cases that receive attention are those considered to be a landmark judgment providing a fundamental shift in the criminal justice system, in particular Supreme Court decisions like *R v Francis Muruatetu* [2017] eKLR which declared a mandatory death sentence unconstitutional.
40 *JWN v Securex Agencies* (n 12).
41 *SRM v GSS (K) Limited and Dominic Ooko* [2017] eKLR.
42 *GMV v Bank of Africa Kenya Limited* [2013] Eklr.
43 *PO v Board of Trustees, AF and 2 Others* [2014] eKLR.

44 *Ibid* Para 31.
45 *CAS v CS Limited* [2016] eKLR.
46 *Ibid* 32.
47 *Ibid* 36.
48 *Ibid* 35.
49 International Labour Organisation (ILO) Violence and Harassment Convention (No 190, 2019).
50 ILO 'Latest ratifications and declarations' www.ilo.org/dyn/normlex/en/f?p=1000:11400:::NO:::
51 Republic of Kenya/ICRW 'Gender Equality Forum Kenya's Roadmap to for advancing gender equality and ending all forms of gender-based violence and FGM by 2026' 12.
52 ILO Convention 190, Art 1(2).
53 *Ibid* Art 9.
54 Sapiro and Campbell (n 21); Siegel (n 22).
55 L Muthiani 'Legal framework addressing sexual harassment and remedial processes' in *Focus Group Discussion* 1 (Online) (Africa End Sexual Harassment Initiative (AESHI), 2020).
56 H McLaughlin and C Thomas 'Costs v compensation: Legal and policy recommendations for addressing workplace sexual harassment' (2020) 14/8 *The Saint Louis University Journal of Health Law and Policy* 139, 148.
57 *Ibid* 159.
58 *Board of Trustees* case is omitted as the facts of the case occurred before the promulgation of Constitution in 2010.

References

Association for Women's Rights in Development 'Legislating against sexual violence: Interview with the Hon. Njoki Ndungu' (2007) 15/29 *Reproductive Health Matters* 149–154.

Board of Trustees 2010.

CAS v CS Limited [2016] eKLR.

Constitution of Kenya of 2010.

Employment Act No 11 of 2007, adopted on 22 October 2007.

GMV v Bank of Africa Kenya Limited [2013] Eklr.

International Labour Organisation 'Latest ratifications and declarations' www.ilo.org/dyn/normlex/en/f?p=1000:11400:::NO:::

International Labour Organisation (ILO) Violence and Harassment Convention (No 190, 2019).

JWN v Securex Agencies (K) Limited [2018] eKLR.

Laws of Kenya, Penal Code Chapter XV of 2010 (as revised).

R Lee and P Greenlaw 'The legal evolution of sexual harassment' (1995) 55/4 *Public Administration Review* 357–364.

H McLaughlin and C Thomas 'Costs v compensation: Legal and policy recommendations for addressing workplace sexual harassment' (2020) 14/8 *St Louis University Journal of Health Law and Policy* 139–162.

L Muthiani 'Legal framework addressing sexual harassment and remedial processes' *Focus Group Discussion* (Online) (Africa End Sexual Harassment Initiative (AESHI), 2020) 1.

PO v Board of Trustees, AF and 2 Others [2014] eKLR.

R v Francis Muruatetu [2017] eKLR.

Republic of Kenya/ICRW 'Gender Equality Forum Kenya's Roadmap to for advancing gender equality and ending all forms of gender-based violence and FGM by 2026'.

V Sapiro and D Campbell 'Report on the 2017 APSA survey on sexual harassment at annual meetings' in *Sexual Harassment Report* (Annual Political Science Association, 2018), www.apsanet.org/reports (accessed on 2 June 2020).

R Siegel 'A short history of sexual harassment' in C Mackinnon and R Siegel (eds) *Directions in Sexual Harassment Law* (Yale University Press, 2003).

B Sihanya '*Constitutional Implementation in Kenya, 2010–2015: Challenges and Prospects*' FES Kenya Occasional Paper No 5.

SRM v GSS (K) Limited and Dominic Ooko [2017] eKLR.

World Health Organisation *Violence against Women Prevalence Estimates, 2018: Global, Regional and National Prevalence Estimates for Intimate Partner Violence and for Non-partner Sexual Violence against Women* (World Health Organisation, 2021).

10 Sexual Harassment and the Law in Liberia

Veronica Fynn Bruey

Introduction and Historical Backdrop of Liberia

With the support of Kommunal, the Public Service International in collaboration with the National Health Workers Union of Liberia (NAHWUL) and the Civil Servants Union of Liberia (CSUL), the Sexual Harassment in Liberia project was launched in 2019. According to Martha C. Morris of the NAHWUL Women Wing,

> Liberian women have not known that sexual harassment was a serious issue to talk about. Even though they have been greatly affected, they have not been promoted or gotten the assignment that they deserve because bosses who were responsible to either you promote you because you deserve it or assign you, are the ones who have been the reason of the sexual harassment. Since we started the project . . . this have given a lot of women the courage to be able to stand up and talk about these challenges in the direction of sexual harassment. But before this project, women were so afraid to talk about it, it was even like a taboo.[1]

Herewith, three women recount their experiences:

Doris: Every time I will go to work from 2003–2018, at that workplace, I have been sexually harassed.

Irene: But then when he came, he saw me, he had nothing to do but to approach me [to make sexual advance]. I told him I am a Christian. I know that no many is supposed to have anything with a woman that he is not married to. So, he can't get that from me. After he and I went over and over and again, then I became a target for him.

Marie: I was sick and so they sent me to the hospital. So, I went to the hospital. I met this doctor who was supposed to see me. For each time I enter the place for not even stomach business, it is not even concerning down here, the fellow will allow me to get on the bed and then start to use his finger. So, I felt intimidated.

DOI: 10.4324/9781003373308-10

As a Liberian, I share many similar experiences with Doris, Irene, and Marie, having survived the ordeal of sexual harassment and sexual exploitation both as a young child, a vulnerable refugee living in Ghana, and a PhD researcher returning home to Liberia as an adult woman. For instance, sexual exploitation came in the form of a certain Mr X offering me a lift to school in exchange of going to his bedroom whilst his wife was at work. I also remember sexual harassment and exploitation in the form of a certain Mr XX, a key public servant responsible for approving refugee status in Ghana, demanding sex in favour of receiving a travel document to continue my education in Canada. Also recalling Mr XXX, a renowned public servant, university educator, and businessman who forcibly grabbed my jaw to kiss me when I asked for his assistance to conduct an interview on sexual violence in Liberia. It did not matter to him that I had regarded him as an elder and a mentor.

However, my experiences barely reflect the grim reality of the pervasiveness of sexual harassment in Liberia. In the last three decades, post-conflict Liberia has slowly been filling the gender inequality gap with a sustained focus on generalised violence against women. Herewith are major law, policy, and institutional frameworks that are integral to addressing sexual harassment in Liberia. The Comprehensive Peace Agreement between the government of Liberia and the Liberians United for Reconciliation and Democracy (LURD) and the Movement for Democracy in Liberia (MODEL) and Political Parties (CPA) 2003, the Rape Law of 2006, the Judicial Circuit Criminal Court Assizes 'E' (Special Court 'E') 2008, the Ministry of Justice's Sexual and Gender-based Violence Crimes Unit (SGBV Crimes Unit) 2009, the Truth and Reconciliation Commission (TRC) of 2009, the Liberia National Action Plan (LNAP) for the Implementation of the United Nations Security Council Resolution (UNSCR) 1325 2009 (Gender Based Violence Action Plan), the National Sexual and Reproductive Health Policy 2010, the National Gender Policy of 2010–2015, the Children's Act of 2011, the Liberia Education Reform Act (Education Law) of 2011, the Ministry of Gender, the Children and Social Protection (MoGCSP) of 2013, the Decent Work Act of 2015, the Sustainable Peace and Securing Development Liberia Peacebuilding Plan (Reconciliation Roadmap) of 2017, the Pro-Poor Agenda for Prosperity and Development (Pro-Poor Agenda) of 2018–2019, and the Domestic Violence Act of 2019.

It is worth noting that 71%, that is, 10 out of 14, of the key instruments just listed were created between 2006 and 2017 when former President Ellen Eugenia Johnson Sirleaf (President Johnson Sirleaf) was in office (2006–2012). The first democratically elected woman in Africa and the second Black African woman (along with Leymah Gbowee and Tawakkol Karman)[2] to win the Nobel Peace Prize (2011),[3] and the 24th president of Liberia, President Johnson Sirleaf out-performed the rest of her fellow male leaders, making significant milestones in the history of Liberia's post-war recovery.[4] She is also is an anomaly amongst her peers when it comes to fighting for women's rights legally, politically, socially, and economically. For example, 'without fear or favour', she enacted the first Rape Law in Liberia on 17 January 2006, a day after her inauguration.[5]

The nation-state of Liberia is Africa's oldest Republic, founded by former slave settlers from the United States in the 1800s. Declaring its independence on 16 July 1847, the former slave settlers sought refuge, freedom, and sovereignty as an independent state possessing all the rights, powers, and functions of democratic government. Unfortunately, 133 years after independence, political unrest culminating into a 14-year civil war resulted in the deaths of over 250,000 people and uprooted approximately 1.3 million people, with women and girls disproportionately affected.[6] The consequences of the civil conflict have indelible impacts on girls and women as rape, sexual violence, and sexual harassment were often used as weapons of war.[7] For instance, a study carried out by the Centre for Abused Women and Girls reports that Liberian girls and women between the ages of 10 and 36 years accounted for 80% of sexual abuse between 1990 and 1993.[8]

Efforts to curb violence against women, including declaring rape a national emergency,[9] have not lessened the scourge and has in a sense allowed sexual harassment to flourish. Drawing on theories of intersectionality and feminist-jurisprudence embodied within major regional and national law and social policy frameworks, I examine the history, state, and impact of sexual harassment to understand its persistence in public and private spaces. In the absence of evidence-based research, scant law, and meagre policy, I further assess the legal protection of girls and women against sexual harassment in Liberia.

Highlighting examples of the chronic situation of violence against women in schools (for example, sex for grades), the workplace (for example, lack of equal opportunity), and low reporting, I evaluate post-conflict Liberia's effort to create, implement, and deliver intervention programmes aimed at addressing sexual harassment. Contextualising the issue of sexual harassment within the broader sphere of violence against women before, during, and after the post-war necessitates employing an inference analysis to observe, predict, and conclude on the state of sexual harassment and the law in Liberia. In closing, I recommend the need for comprehensive, country-wide research to provide data-based evidence pointing to the severity of sexual harassment in Liberia. Such research should be used as a basis for law and policy reform, implementation, and intervention programmes, including ongoing awareness campaigns.

Theorising and Conceptualising Sexual Harassment

International Law

We live in a patriarchal, misogynistic, machismo, and masculine world. Period. Since 1945 when the United Nations (UN) was established as a 'feel good' mechanism to tame the inhumanity of European men's war, only

12% (47 out of 382) of women have led the top 33 multilateral institutions (mostly UN organisations).[10] Therefore, it comes as no surprise that the Convention on the Elimination of All Forms of Discrimination Against Women (CEDAW),'often described as the international bill of rights for women'[11] was adopted in 1979, more than three decades after the UN Charter was adopted in 1945. Specifically, for girls and children, the Convention on the Rights of the Child (CRC) 1990 was adopted on 20 November 1989 by UN General Assembly (UNGA) Resolution 44/25. Article 1 of the CEDAW broadly defines 'discrimination against women' to mean 'any distinction, exclusion, or restriction based on sex that hampers recognition, enjoyment, or exercise of women's equality, human rights and fundamental freedoms in the political, economic, social, cultural, civil or any other field'. On the other hand, Articles 19 and 34 of the CRC require member states to take all appropriate measures to protect the child from all forms of physical, mental violence, sexual abuse, and exploitation.

The word 'violence' (mentioned one time in the CRC) or the phrase 'violence against women' are not mentioned in the CEDAW or the CRC. However, 14 years after the adoption of the CEDAW, a long and hard women's rights campaign led to the CEDAW's Recommendation 19 in 1992, which was followed by the World Conference on Human Rights in Vienna.[12] Continuing advocacy on violence against women as a human right, the UN General Assembly proclaimed the Declaration on the Elimination of Violence Against Women (DEVAW) on 20 December 1993. Subsequently, on 4 March 1994, the Commission on Human Rights appointed a Special Rapporteur on Violence Against Women (VAW) to streamline women's rights into the United Nations human rights system.[13] Paragraph 6 of the Preamble to the DEVAW recognises that VAW is a manifestation of historically unequal power relations between men and women leading to men's domination over and discrimination against women, which prevents the full advancement of women since VAW is a crucial social mechanism that keeps women subordinated.

Although sexual harassment is not defined, Article 2(b) of the DEVAW includes sexual harassment prohibited at work, in educational institutions, and elsewhere as part of violence against women. To be clear, in both a post- and pre-conflict Liberia, sexual violence takes many forms: rape, sexual slavery, trafficking, forced pregnancy, sexual exploitation, forced abortion, sexual slavery, femicide, harmful traditional practices, and sexual harassment.[14] Sexual and gender-based violence in conflict can also take the form of sexual slavery, sexual harassment, femicide, and harmful traditional practices.[15] Article 4(d-f) of the DEVAW encourages the development of penal, civil, or other administrative sanctions, as well as preventative approaches to eliminate violence against women. Whilst the DEVAW is not legally binding, the CEDAW and the CRC have a binding effect on state parties. For instance, they are responsible for taking appropriate measures to eliminate discrimination against women and protect girls from sexual abuse/exploitation.[16] State parties must also pay particular attention to equality under the law in governance, politics, education, healthcare, the workplace, and in all other areas of public and social life.

Liberia ratified the CEDAW by accession on 17 July 1984. Liberia also signed and ratified the CRC on 26 April 1990 and 4 June 1993, respectively. Liberia is legally bound by the provisions of both the CEDAW and the CRC. This implies that Liberia is obliged to periodically report[17] to the CEDAW[18] and the CRC[19] Committees regarding steps taken to implement the treaties. It is the only mechanism put in place to monitor and ensure that states parties identify barriers to gender equality, child protection, and are continuously implementing measures to address VAW and sexual abuse/exploitation (in armed conflict). Since 1984 when Liberia acceded to the CEDAW, only two periodic reports have been submitted to the CEDAW Committee – a combination of the initial, second, third, fourth, fifth, and sixth reports in 2008[20] and the seventh and eighth reports in 2014.[21] Similarly, since 1990, Liberia has only submitted two periodic reports to the CRC Committee – the initial report in 2002[22] and the second, third, fourth, and fifth reports in 2011.[23] Both of the CEDAW and the last two sets of the CRC periodic reports were tendered during President Johnson Sirleaf's regime.

Held between 4 to 15 September 1995 in Beijing, China, the Fourth World Conference on Women was held under the theme 'Action for Equality, Development and Peace'. The resulting Beijing Declaration and Platform for Action 1995 has evolved into a pan African agenda for women's empowerment aimed at accelerating implementation of the Nairobi Forward-looking Strategies for the Advancement of Women. This will be achieved by removing obstacles to women's active participation in all spheres of public and private life through a full and equal share in economic, social, cultural, and political decision-making. The Beijing Platform for Action affirms Paragraph 178 of the DEVAW. It recognises sexual harassment as a form of violence against women and discrimination, and calls on the government to enact and enforce laws on sexual harassment. Employers must also develop anti-harassment policies and adopt prevention strategies. The then minister of Planning and Economic Affairs, Honourable Amelia A. Ward, represented and delivered a statement pointing out the effect of the civil war on women advancement in Liberia. She reiterated the unparalleled struggle of women in Liberia:

> Most of the women remain in difficult circumstances in many of our developing countries, including Liberia. They are illiterate and earn little or no income; they are over-burdened by work both inside and outside the home. They do not own or inherit property, have little or no control over the circumstances of their lives and are overlooked or even forgotten in the process of planning. They are women who till the rice fields and vegetable gardens, labour the whole day under the hot sun behind the market stalls, carrying their babies on their backs. They walk for hours to collect firewood and water for the household and go through the agony of bearing many children only to see them dying of diseases and starvation.[24]

Pledging Liberia's cooperation to uphold the Beijing Platform for Action, Minister Ward (a strong women's rights advocate who helped establish the Ministry of Gender, Children and Social Protection) emphasised that, 'the Liberian society remains a male-dominated one even though women constitute more than 50 per cent of Liberia's human resources and perform 68 per cent of all productive activities in the subsistence agricultural sector'.[25] Achieving the Beijing Platform for Action to make Liberian women full partners with men in the social, economic, and political realms means working in an environment free from sexual harassment and is therefore critical for Liberia.

Regional Instruments

At the regional level, the African Charter on the Rights and Welfare of the Child (African Children Charter) 1990 does not explicitly mention sexual harassment. However, Article 27 (a)(b) and (c) of the African Children Charter obliges state parties to protect the child from all forms of sexual exploitation and sexual abuse to prevent inducement, coercion, or encouragement in any sexual activities such as prostitution and pornography or performances with materials. Liberia signed the African Children Charter on 14 May 1992, ratified it on 1 August 2007, and deposited it on 15 July 2003 when President Sirleaf was in office. Liberia, therefore, has obligations under this charter to prevent both sexual harassment and the sexual exploitation of children. Educational institutions and informal sector work contexts can become hotspots for sexual harassment involving children and therefore this charter holds significance for Liberia.

Similarly, Liberia signed, ratified, and deposited the Maputo Protocol on 16 December 2003, 14 December 2007, and 15 July 2008. The Protocol to the African Charter on Human and Peoples' Rights on the Rights of Women in Africa[26] (Maputo Protocol) advocates for the elimination of all forms of discrimination against women in all spheres of education and training. Sexual harassment is referenced twice in all its 32 articles urging its eradication from schools and recognising its negative impact mental health.[27]

Sub-Regional Tools

Liberia became a founding member of the Economic Community of West African States (ECOWAS) when it signed the Lagos Treaty on 28 May 1975. The aim of the 15-member community is to promote cooperation, economic integration, and political stability. The ECOWAS played an instrumental role in resolving Liberia's civil war and by helping to restore peace, significantly contributed to curbing violence against girls and women. Two major events are relevant. First, though implicated in several human rights violations including rape, sexual harassment, and violence against girls and women, the ECOWAS Monitoring Group's (ECOMOG) 3000-men military intervention helped secure peace and constitutional order in Liberia.[28] Second, the CPA developed under the auspices of the ECOWAS Peace Process for Liberia was the final peace agreement that formally ended the Liberian civil war. Article XIII of the CPA called for an establishment of the Truth and Reconciliation Commission and Article XXXI urged the National Transitional Government of Liberia (NTGL) to pay particular attention to the issue of vulnerable groups including children, women, the elderly, and the disabled who have been severely affected by the conflict.[29]

More recently, ECOWAS is in the process of developing a policy on sexual harassment in the workplace and in educational institutions. Led by the ECOWAS Gender Development Centre (EGDC), Strategic Plan 2023–2027 under the theme 'Gender Equality and the Empowerment of Women and Girls: An Imperative for the Achievement of Sustainable Development and Effective Regional Integration in West Africa' is being drafted and validated by Ministers responsible for Gender and Women Affairs from ECOWAS member states.[30] Without release of the document, it is hard to assess the extent to which sexual harassment is included.

Domestic Law and Policy: Apathy or Complacency?

Sexual harassment in Liberia is shrouded in a history of slavery, colonial violence, violent conflict, political vengeance, social class/elitism, rural-urban inequalities, legal blasphemy, and overall abject poverty where the girl child is the quintessential object of injustice. Exported out of Africa as human cargos to the Americas for nearly three centuries, dehumanised descendants of African slaves returned to Africa in the 1820s to create the modern state of Liberia. Rape, floggings, hard labour, starvation, and death were their lot. Denied access to education, health, and all other social services, former slave returnees were undoubtedly traumatised by the horrific experience.

Of the 14,996 former returnees, 56% were males, 42% females, and 0.4% infants. Twelve percent (n=1,833) were freeborn, 15% (n=2,188) were freed, 39% (n=5,894) were emancipated, 1% (n=197) were purchased, and 32% (n=4,884) were unknown.[31] This is the stock that declared independence from the American Colonisation Society in 1847 under a constitution drafted and signed by 12 of them (all men).[32] This uneducated and traumatised elite group of men created an oligarchy, ruling Liberia for 133 years (1847–1980) as a one-party state. The Constitution of Liberia 1847 is masculinised. For instance, the constitution provides in Article 1(1) that 'all men are born equally free', granting every male citizen of 21 years of age who possessed real estate the right of suffrage, as stated in Article 11. Former slave returnee women were granted the right to vote in 1945 and indigenous women in 1946, more than a century after the first constitution granted men the right to vote. The revised Constitution of 1986 is demasculinised as it provides in Article 11(a) that 'all persons are born free equally', providing equal protection under the law for all persons as contained in article 11(c). Between 1847 and 2018, a total of 24 presidents, 23 of whom were males and one female, have been democratically elected. Not a single law, policy, or case law on sexual harassment in schools and/or the workplace was ever put into place until 2015, when the Decent Work Act was enacted during President Johnson Sirleaf's leadership. The failure to address the ever-present issue of sexual harassment suggests that the government is either apathetic or complacent.[33]

A consideration of the substantive provisions of the law, policy, and institutional framework in Liberia is important to not only understand but also assess the severity and extreme lack of reporting on sexual harassment. As there is very little direct focus on sexual harassment in particular, a brief overview of the substantive portion of the law, policy, and institutional framework set up to respond to violence against women infers an indirect response to sexual harassment. One significant law is Section 14.70(1–3) of the Rape Law, which expands the definition of rape to include penetration (however slight) of objects other than the penis. While the Rape Law does not explicitly provide for sexual harassment, it is relevant to the extent that any sexual harassment of employees and school-going children or students in tertiary institutions will obviously be covered in instances of rape.

In compliance with UNSCR 1325, the Women and Children Protection Services (WACPS) of the Liberia National Police[34] has set up 61 units to investigate sex and gender-based violence (SGBV) crimes across the country.[35] Since its establishment in 2009, the SGBV Crimes has only eight prosecutors assigned to the 15 counties.[36] Between July 2011 and January 2014, the Special Court 'E' received and documented 169 cases, but was only able to prosecute 35, of which 24 defendants were convicted and sentenced, ten acquitted, and one hung verdict.[37] From 2016 to 2019, 464 cases were received by the Special Court 'E', of which 274 were convicted, however 448 indictments are outstanding in a backlog of new cases.[38] The TRC report (2009) broke new ground as the first extensive public account of gross human rights violations.[39] Recommendations of the TRC, including the prosecution of those who committed war crimes and crimes against humanity, are yet to be implemented.

The Children's Law of 2011 grants to every child, as stated in Article 3(21)(1), the right to be protected from sexual abuse and exploitation, including prostitution and pornography; prohibits sexual molestation, as stated in section 16(10); permits service providers, parents, and the community to report sexual and other forms of abuse to the police, as provided for in Article V(4)(4); identifies a sexually abuse child to be in a situation of special vulnerability, as noted in Article VII(1.2)(u); and obligates the employer of a child protection officer to refrain from using language that may harass, abuse, sexually provoke, demean, and humiliate the child, as stipulated in Article III, (2)(g) and (h). If the very caregiver like family members, teachers, and protection officers are the ones harassing girls and children, how could reporting possibly be done? With no reporting, a low prosecution track record, and outright failure of institutions to address sexual crimes against girls and women, what hope is there for a meaningful law, policy, and institutional response to sexual harassment?

Prospects may lie in an institution, a law, and a policy. First, the Ministry of Gender, Children and Social Protection (MoGCSP) was created by an Executive Instrument 1 (E.I. 1) in January 2013 with the primary objective to create policy, coordinate, monitor, and evaluate gender, children and social protection issues within the context of the national development agenda. The MoGCSP's Division of Sexual and Gender-based Violence under the Gender Department has been instrumental in establishing much of the laws and institutions previously listed. To this end, there is no reason to doubt that MoGCSP is well equipped to initiate a policy focused on sexual harassment in Liberia, particularly in schools and the workplace. Second, is the Decent Work Act 2015, which repeals the Labour (Practices) Law 1956. This is the first law in Liberia to define and prohibit sexual harassment in the workplace. Section 2.8(b)(i) and (ii) defines sexual harassment as:

> sexual conduct, which is unwelcome, unreasonable, or offensive to the recipient, and which occurs in circumstances where a person's rejection of, or submission to, such conduct is used explicitly or implicitly as a basis for a decision which affects that person's job; or [a] conduct that creates an intimidating, hostile or humiliating working environment for the person that is subject to that conduct.

It is only a matter of time before we will know the efficacy of the Decent Work Act regarding reporting and prosecution of cases against sexual harassment in Liberia. Third, is a replacement of the outdated (2010–2015) National Gender Policy with a new one.[40] This is an opportunity for Liberia to insert and emphasise a strong response to sexual harassment, especially in schools and the workplace. It is reasonable to perceive Liberia's violent colonial history through the lenses of Frantz Fanon's, where there is no liberation without violence,[41] and Paulo Freire's lamentation of the oppressed becoming the oppressor.[42] The DEVAW history affirms the theoretical scaffolding of intersectionality.[43] To be clear, girls as students and women as employers stand at the crossroad of vulnerabilities to sexual harassment. Their identity as daughters, sisters, (single) mothers, and aunties demands their role as child-bearers, caregivers, and breadwinners. In Liberia, girls and women are less educated, teenage pregnancy is high, and child marriage is high. All these intersecting factors are exacerbated for girls and women living in relatively poor rural/indigenous communities with little or no access to health, education, and amenities.

The situation is compounded for those with disability, the elderly, teenage mothers, and single mothers which increases their vulnerability to sexual harassment in school, in the marketplace, while fetching water, or searching for firewood. Apart from the law (statutes) and policy discussed here, feminist jurisprudence (mainly judge-made law or case law)[44] on sexual harassment is non-existent in Liberia. Notwithstanding, further elaboration on these theories apart from what is already presented is beyond the scope of this chapter. However, the following two case examples contextualise the concepts in real life situation.

Case Examples

Workplace Inequality for Women

Article 18 of the Liberian Constitution 1986 provides that all Liberian citizens have equal opportunity for work and employment and are entitled to equal pay for equal work (Article 18). As previously noted, in Liberia, sexual harassment in the workplace prevents women from having equal access to work and equal pay compared to their male counterparts. On 3 December 2021, the National Health Workers Union of Liberia and Liberia Civil Servant Association released a joint press statement to the Ministry of Labor in commemoration of 16 days of activism against sexual harassment in the workplace.[45] Holding signs and placards which read, 'enough is enough', Sarah Scott Borvor delivered a 'petition statement against gender and sexual harassment in the world of work' to Liberia's Assistant Minister for Manpower and Development. It reads (in part),

> [w]e are here today to let you know about the agony of gender and sexual harassments we are suffering daily in the world of work that can no longer be swept under the carpet. Many of our colleagues have either left their job quietly or just do not have any pleasure to go to work simply because of harassment . . . stop [emphatically]! this situation is so frustrating that there is no clear roadmap on how to get a redress, even if one is brave enough to take up the challenge to report the madness, especially from our line managers on the work floor. We do not only want gender and sexual harassment to be reported but also investigated fully and the perpetrator be named and shamed.[46]

Sexual harassment is so much part and parcel of the entrenched culture of violence against women that it has become normalised in the workplace.[47] Girls and women, especially those falling in the categories of teen mothers and single parents and with low levels of education, are often coerced into sexually compromising situations to keep their jobs, feed their children, or send them to school. Despite signing and ratifying several international instruments and despite women's persistent resistance and advocacy, sexual harassment runs rampant in Liberia with very few complaints being lodged. Furthermore, there is no statute apart from the Decent Work Act which focuses on sexual harassment only in the workplace, and the MoGCSP does not have a gender unit or a policy focused on addressing the sexual harassment nationally.

Sex for Grades

The Liberian Constitution 1986 provides equal access to educational opportunities and facilities for all Liberians with an emphasis placed on the elimination of illiteracy. When girls have lower or no access to education, they become vulnerable and fall prey to harrowing experiences, as in the *More Than Me* saga.[48] Sex for grades, 'a troubling nightmare'[49] in educational institutions, is rampant not just in Liberia but also other parts of West Africa. Usually 'swept under the carpet', as previously alluded to by Borvor, sex for grades gained global attention with BBC's undercover investigative documentary in Ghana and Nigeria.[50]

It is noteworthy that it is impossible to dissociate the extremely high prevalence of rape in schools with that of sexual harassment. Contrary to the popular belief that rape is committed by strangers, sexual harassment is the precursor to rape usually committed by teachers, schoolmates/classmates, and acquaintances. While this 'epidemic'[51] has not been documented or researched to this extent in Liberia, anecdotal news reporting[52] and a few scholarly publications[53] affirmed by the author's lived experience as a survivor of Liberia's war support Klubo's story (not her real name). In early February 2022, Klubo who was at the time a 14-year-old sixth grader at the Grace Heritage International School on GSA Road in Paynesville, Monrovia, and was ordered by her math teacher, Mr. Anthony Mulbah, to remain on campus when all the other students had gone home. He raped her in one of the classrooms and dared her to tell anyone. He repeated his act shortly after. Frightened, Klubo remained silent about the incidence until her parent realised that she was pregnant. In an interview, Klubo said about the rape:

> After school, I was trying to leave but he stopped me and waited for everyone to get outside. He then closed the door, held my mouth, took off my uniform and put me on the desk, and raped me . . . I am not good at math, so he said if I refused or reported him; he would not just harm me but also fail me. The raping took place twice on the school campus. The second one was on February 15, and on that day, many students were not on campus. When school came to close for the day, he waited for everybody to leave and then he started rubbing my skin, closed the door, and raped me on the desk again.[54]

Mr. Mulbah denied being responsible for the pregnancy and the school principal told Klubo 'to not come to school because it was disgraceful and shameful and other students will be mocking her'.[55] The last news report about the case stated that Mr. Mulbah was in police custody. It is noteworthy that one major challenge associated with prosecuting perpetrator of rape resulting from sexual harassment has to do with the inability of the medical/health system to conduct a paternity test. In one case, both the survivor and the perpetrator (in detention) had to wait until the child was born to determine whether the child was phenotypically white (the accused is a White Canadian). A very crude and unscientific method of evidence smeared with injustice all round.

Conclusions and Recommendations: A Way Forward

Without doubt, particularly during the regime for former President Ellen Johnson Sirleaf, Liberia has demonstrated its potential legal, institutional, and policy frameworks to address violence against women and overall gender inequality. However, the specific issue of sexual harassment as a form of sexual and gender-based violence, especially in schools and the workplace, has seen little response from the government. Moving forward, it is recommended that Liberia conduct a nationwide research study to assess the efficacy of intervention programs to address violence against women and establish base-rate information on the incidence and prevalence rates of sexual harassment. Findings and results from the study should be used to create evidence-based law, policy, and an institutional framework aimed at addressing sexual harassment in Liberia. Since the law is useless without proper implementation, for Liberia to honour its obligations under international, regional, and domestic law, it must first understand the nature and severity of sexual harassment.

Notes

1. Project: Sexual Harassment in Liberia (Directed by PSI global union, You Tube 2020), www.youtube.com/watch?v=wEKw3zvrka8 (accessed on 30 July 2023).
2. L Gbowee and CL Mithers *Mighty Be Our Powers: How Sisterhood, Prayer, and Sex Changed a Nation at Aar: A Memoir* (Beast Books, 2013); *Pray the Devil Back to Hell* (Directed by Gini Reticker and Abigail Disney, Fork Films 2008), www.forkfilms.net/pray-the-devil-back-to-hell/ (accessed on 27 February 2017).
3. 'Snapshot' www.nobelprize.org/nobel_prizes/peace/laureates/2011/ (accessed on 25 February 2017).
4. H Cooper *Madame President: The Extraordinary Journey of Ellen Johnson Sirleaf* (Simon & Schuster, 2017); P Scully *Ellen Johnson Sirleaf* (Ohio University Press, 2016); EJ Sirleaf, *This Child Will Be Great: Memoir of a Remarkable Life by Africa's First Woman President* (Harper, 2009).
5. EJ Sirleaf 'liberia's gender-based violence national action plan' (2007) 27 *Forced Migration Review* 34, 34.
6. VF Bruey 'African union agenda 2063: Aspiring for justice and the rule of law in Liberia' in A Onuora-Oguno, WO Egbewole and TE Kleven (eds) *Education Law, Strategic Policy, and Sustainable Development in Africa* (Springer Berlin Heidelberg, 2017) 226–227.
7. VF Bruey 'redefining women's roles in international and regional law: The case of pre- and post-war peacebuilding in Liberia' in S Shekhawat (ed) *Gender, Conflict, Peace, and UNSC Resolution 1325* (Lexington Books, 2018) 4.
8. Association of Female Lawyers in Liberia 'Hundreds of victims silently grieving' in M Turshen and C Twagiramariya (eds) *What Women Do in Wartime: Gender and Conflict in Africa* (Zed Books Ltd, 1998) 131.

9 Staff Reporter 'Liberia declares rape a national emergency after spike in cases' *Al Jazeera*, 12 September 2020, www.aljazeera.com/news/2020/9/12/liberia-declares-rape-a-national-emergency-after-spike-in-cases (accessed on 10 August 2023).
10 Group of Women Leaders Voices for Change and Inclusion 'Where are the women leaders?' (2023) *Group of Women Leaders Voices for Change and Inclusion* 1–3, https://gwlvoices.com/download/climate-justice/?wpdmdl=8839&refresh=64ad6ef31a5d51689087731 (accessed on 30 July 2023).
11 P Khanna, Z Kimmel and R Karkara 'Convention on the Elimination of All Forms of Discrimination Against Women (CEDAW) for Youth' *UN Women*, 2016, www.unwomen.org/en/digital-library/publications/2016/12/cedaw-for-youth (accessed on 30 July 2023).
12 The United Nations Special Rapporteur on Violence against Women, and its Causes and Consequences *15 Years of the United Nations Special Rapporteur on Violence Against Women, its Causes and Consequences* (Office of the United Nations High Commissioner for Human Rights, 2009) 3, www.ohchr.org/sites/default/files/Documents/Issues/Women/15YearReviewofVAWMandate.pdf.
13 *Ibid.*
14 Inter-Agency Standing Committee 'Guidelines for integrating gender-based violence interventions in humanitarian action: Reducing risk, promoting resilience and aiding recovery' *Inter-Agency Standing Committee*, 2015, file:///Users/veronicafynn/Desktop/IASC_GBV%20Guidelines%202015.pdf.
15 A Mohammed 'Ending violence against women and girls in the Sahel: Crucial for sustainable development' (2018) *Africa Renewal Online* 4, 5.
16 Liberia also signed the Optional Protocol to the Convention on the Rights of the Child on the involvement of children in armed conflict on 22 September 2004 given its postwar situation that left tens of thousands of children, especially girls traumatised by rape and other forms of sexual/gender violence.
17 States must report within one year of accession or ratification of CEDAW and thereafter every four years or when the Committee requests (Article 18).
18 The Committee on the Elimination of Discrimination against Women (CEDAW) is the body of independent experts that monitors implementation of the Convention on the Elimination of All Forms of Discrimination against Women. The CEDAW Committee consists of 23 experts on women's rights from around the world that meet twice a year in addition to issuing statements, information notes and announcements, and participating/organizing a variety of other events (see United Nations Human Rights Office of the High Commissioner 'Committee on the Elimination of Discrimination against Women' *OHCHR – CEDAW Committee*, 2023, www.ohchr.org/en/treaty-bodies/cedaw (accessed on 5 August 2023).
19 The Committee on the Rights of the Child (CRC) is the body of 18 independent experts that monitors implementation of the Convention on the Rights of the Child by its States parties. It also monitors implementation of the Optional Protocols to the Convention, on involvement of children in armed conflict and on the sale of children, child prostitution and child pornography. The committee meets three times a year and publishes its interpretation of the human rights provisions as general comments on thematic issues. (see United Nations Human Rights Office of the High Commissioner 'Committee on the rights of the child' *OHCHR*, 2023, www.ohchr.org/en/treaty-bodies/crc (accessed on 5 August 2023).
20 Government of Liberia 'Consideration of reports submitted by states parties under article 18 of the convention on the elimination of all forms of discrimination against women – Liberia' (Committee on the Elimination and Discrimination against Women 2008) United Nations CEDAW/C/LBR/6, https://tbinternet.ohchr.org/_layouts/15/treatybodyexternal/Download.aspx?symbolno=CEDAW%2FC%2FLBR%2F6&Lang=en.

21 Government of Liberia 'Consideration of reports submitted by states parties under article 18 of the convention on the elimination of all forms of discrimination against women – Liberia' (Committee on the Elimination and Discrimination against Women 2014) United Nations CEDAW/C/LBR/8, https://tbinternet.ohchr.org/_layouts/15/TreatyBodyExternal/Download.aspx?symbolno=CEDAW%2FC%2FLBR%2F7-8&Lang=en.
22 Government of Liberia 'Consideration of reports submitted by states parties under article 44 of the convention initial report of states parties due in 1995 – Liberia' (Committee on the Convention on the Rights of the Child 2002) United Nations CRC/C/28/Add, https://tbinternet.ohchr.org/_layouts/15/treatybodyexternal/Download.aspx?symbolno=CRC%2FC%2F28%2FAdd.21&Lang=en.
23 Government of Liberia 'Consideration of reports submitted by states parties under article 44 of the convention combined second, third and fourth periodic reports of states parties due in 2009 – Liberia' (Committee on the Convention on the Rights of the Child 2011) United Nations CRC/C/LBR/2–4, https://tbinternet.ohchr.org/_layouts/15/treatybodyexternal/Download.aspx?symbolno=CRC%2FC%2FLBR%2F2-4&Lang=en.
24 AA Ward 'Fourth world conference on women, Beijing 1995: Statement by governments' www.un.org/womenwatch/daw/beijing/govstatements.html (accessed on 6 August 2023).
25 *Ibid.*
26 Maputo Protocol, art 12(1)(a).
27 Ibid, Article 12(1)(c) and Article 12(1)(d).
28 H Howe 'Lessons of Liberia: ECOMOG and regional peacekeeping' (1996) 21 *International Security* 145; 'Timeline: A history of ECOWAS military interventions in three decades' *Al Jazeera* Doha, Qatar, 1 August 2023, www.aljazeera.com/news/2023/8/1/timeline-a-history-of-ecowas-military-interventions-in-three-decades (accessed on 7 August 2023); L Gberie 'ECOMOG: The story of a heroic failure' (2003) 102 *African Affairs* 14.
29 T Jaye 'Liberia: Setting priorities for post-conflict reconstruction' (2003) 1 *Journal of Security Sector Management* 1; DA Bekoe 'Toward a theory of peace agreement implementation: The case of Liberia' (2003) 38 *Journal of Asian and African Studies* 256.
30 D Inaju-Challydoff 'Adoption of the EGDC strategic plan 2023–2027 at the Centre of a Meeting of Ministers Responsible for Gender and Women Affairs of ECOWAS Member States in Accra, Ghana. Economic Community of West African States (ECOWAS)' https://ecowas.int/adoption-of-the-egdc-strategic-plan-2023–2027-at-the-centre-of-a-meeting-of-ministers-responsible-for-gender-and-women-affairs-of-ecowas-member-states-in-accra-ghana/ (accessed on 6 August 2023).
31 VF Bruey 'Systematic gender violence and the rule of law: Aboriginal communities in Australia and Post-War Liberia' (PhD Thesis, The Australian National University 2016) 284–285.
32 CA Cassell *Liberia: History of the First African Republic* (Fountainhead Publishers, 1970) 137. The signers of the Liberia Declaration of Independence were twelve Afro-American settler men: Samuel Benedict, Elijah Johnson, Hilary Teage, Beverly R Wilson, JR Gripon and John Naustehlau Lewis for Montserrado County; John Day, Anthony W. Gardiner, Amos Herring, and Ephraim Titler for Grand Bassa County; and Jacob Prout and Richard E Murray for Sinoe County.
33 GK Kieh and DH Railey 'Women, sexual harassment and employment opportunity in Liberia' (1993) XVIII *Liberian Studies Journal* 189, 189–190; JS Guseh, 'Sexual harassment in Liberia: A review' (1994) 19 *Liberian Studies Journal* 183, 183–188.

34 Government of Liberia 'National report submitted in accordance with paragraph 5 of the Annex to Human Rights Council Resolution 16/21: Liberia' (Human Rights Council 2015) Human Rights Council Universal Period Review A/HRC/WG.6/22/LBR/1 para 48, www.ohchr.org/en/hr-bodies/upr/lr-index.
35 *Ibid.*
36 Government of Liberia 'National Report Submitted in Accordance with Paragraph 5 of the Annex to Human Rights Council Resolution 16/21; Liberia (n 34) para 49.
37 Bruey (n 29) 197.
38 Government of Liberia 'National report submitted in accordance with paragraph 5 of the Annex to Human Rights Council Resolution 16/21: Liberia' (Human Rights Council 2020) Human Rights Council Universal Period Review A/HRC/WG.6/36/LBR/1 9, www.ohchr.org/en/hr-bodies/upr/lr-index.
39 Truth and Reconciliation Commission of Liberia 'TRC Final Reconciliation Initiatives County Consultations and National Reconciliation Conference' (Truth and Reconciliation Commission 2009) Government Report.
40 The Government of Liberia created a Gender Policy and Action Plan 2021–2025 for the Liberian Ministry of National Defense and the Armed Forces of Liberia, https://mod.gov.lr/wp-content/uploads/2023/05/MOD_AFL-ActionPlan-Fin-PRINT-Rev-1.pdf.
41 F Fanon *Toward the African Revolution: Political Essays* (H Chevalier tr, Grove Press, 1967) 237; Bruey (n 29) 45.
42 P Freire *Pedagogy of the Oppressed* (30th Anniversary, Continuum International, 2005) 44.
43 K Crenshaw 'Mapping the margins: Intersectionality, identity politics, and violence against women of colour' (1991) 43 *Stanford Law Review* 1241; K Crenshaw 'What is intersectionality?' *You Tube*, 2018, www.youtube.com/watch?v=ViDtnfQ9FHc (accessed on 19 March 2020); N Lykke *Feminist Studies: A Guide to Intersectional Theory, Methodology and Writing* (Routledge, 2010); SV Knudsen 'Intersectionality – A theoretical inspiration in the analysis of minority cultures and identities in textbooks' (2006) Private Document. Intersectionality addresses the multiple ways in which race, gender, class, and the law interact to shape Indigenous girls and women's experiences of violence.
44 VF Bruey 'Indigenous women and international law' in *Research Handbook on Feminist Engagement with International Law* (Edward Elgar, 2019); B Hooks *Ain't I A Woman: Black Women and Feminism* (South End Press, 1981); PH Collins *Black Feminist Thought: Knowledge, Consciousness, and the Politics of Empowerment* (Routledge, 2009); B Hooks *Feminism is for Everybody: Passionate Politics* (South End Press, 2000); TC Okeke, USB Anyaehie and CCK Ezenyeaku 'An overview of female genital mutilation in Nigeria' (2012) 2 *Annals of Medical and Health Sciences Research* 70; S Tamale 'Legal voice: Challenges and prospects in the documentation of African legal feminism' (2011) 15 *Feminist Africa* 1. Feminist Jurisprudence suggests that the law (both statutes and judge made law) is comparable to a torsion spring whereby the same law that liberates girls and women from social injustices is also responsible for their discrimination and subjugation.
45 'NAHWUL, CSAL petition gov't to stop sexual harassment' *Daily Observer*, 9 December 2021, www.liberianobserver.com/nahwul-csal-petition-govt-stop-sexual-harassment (accessed on 30 July 2023; Public Service International 'Sexual Harassment in Liberia' *Newsroom*, 1 January 2019, https://publicservices.international/resources/projects/sexual-harassment-in-liberia?id=11545&lang=en (accessed on 30 July 2023).
46 Project: Sexual Harassment in Liberia (n 1); Public Service International 'Raising awareness on sexual harassment in Liberia' *Newsroom*, 3 February 2020, https://

publicservices.international/resources/news/raising-awareness-on-sexual-harassment-in-liberia-?id=10564&lang=en (accessed on 30 July 2023.
47 W Williams 'Liberia's working women plagued by sexual assault and harassment' *Front Page Africa*, https://newnarratives.org/stories/liberias-working-women-plagued-by-sexual-assault-and-harassment/.
48 F Young 'Unprotected' *ProPublica* (Monrovia, Liberia), 11 October 2018, https://features.propublica.org/liberia/unprotected-more-than-me-katie-meyler-liberia-sexual-exploitation/ (accessed on 26 July 2023); F Young 'More than me shuts down' *ProPublica*, 27 June 2019, www.propublica.org/article/more-than-me-shuts-down (accessed on 11 August 2023); A Higgins, 'How the 'white-savior industrial complex' Failed Liberia's girls' *Vox*, 24 October 2018, www.vox.com/future-perfect/2018/10/24/17995536/liberia-girls-more-than-me-katie-meyler (accessed on 11 August 2023).
49 Staff Reporter 'Medica Liberia increases effort to end sexual abuse and exploitation' *Front Page Africa*, 13 May 2022, https://frontpageafricaonline.com/news/medica-liberia-increases-effort-to-end-sexual-abuse-and-exploitation/ (accessed on 25 July 2023).
50 *Sex for Grades: Undercover inside Nigerian and Ghanaian Universities – BBC Africa Eye Documentary* (Directed by BBC News Africa, 2019), www.youtube.com/watch?v=we-F0Gi0Lqs (accessed on 11 August 2023).
51 M Zebedee and S Shahid 'Liberia's "Sex4Grades" epidemic is ruining children's lives' *Time Magazine*, https://time.com/4282516/liberias-sex4grades-epidemic/ (accessed on 11 August 2023).
52 Staff Reporter 'Education Minister Soni, what are you doing about rape in liberian schools?' *Daily Observer*, 3 May 2022, www.liberianobserver.com/education-minister-soni-what-are-you-doing-about-rape-liberian-schools (accessed on 25 July 2023); TS Mehnpaine 'Liberia: 14-Yr-Old allegedly impregnated by Math Teacher' *Liberian Daily Observer*, 2 February 2022, www.liberianobserver.com/liberia-14-yr-old-allegedly-impregnated-math-teacher (accessed on 11 August 2023); D Edwards 'A terrible failure to protect school girls in Liberia' *Africa's a Country*, 10 September 2018, https://africasacountry.com/2018/10/a-terrible-failure-to-protect-school-girls-in-liberia (accessed on 26 July 2023).
53 K Dahn 'Sex and bribery for better grades: Academic dishonesty in Liberia' (2008) 58 *Journal of Philosophy and History of Education* 46; JL Postmus et al 'Examining gender based violence and abuse among Liberian school students in four counties: An exploratory study' (2015) 44 *Child Abuse and Neglect* 76; JJ Steiner et al 'Sexual violence of liberian school age students: An investigation of perpetration, gender, and forms of abuse' (2018) 30 *Journal of Child Sexual Abuse* 21; C Dorph and A Sjögren '"A Window of opportunity": A qualitative study about "sex for grades" as social navigation in Liberian Universities' (Master of Science, Lund University, 2014).
54 Mehnpaine (n 52).
55 *Ibid.*

References

C Abayomi. *Liberia: History of the First African Republic* (Fountainhead Publishers, 1970).

Association of Female Lawyers in Liberia 'Hundreds of victims silently grieving' in M Turshen and C Twagiramariya (eds) *What Women do in Wartime: Gender and Conflict in Africa* (Zed Books Ltd, 1998).

D Bekoe 'Toward a theory of peace agreement implementation: The case of Liberia' (2003) 38/2–3 *Journal of Asian and African Studies* 256–294.

V Bruey 'African Union Agenda 2063: Aspiring for justice and the rule of law in Liberia' in A Onuora-Oguno, W Egbewole and T Kleven (eds) *Education Law, Strategic Policy, and Sustainable Development in Africa* (Springer Berlin Heidelberg, 2017).

V Bruey 'Redefining women's roles in international and regional law: The case of pre- and post-war peacebuilding in Liberia' in S Shekhawat (ed) *Gender, Conflict, Peace, and UNSC Resolution 1325* (Lexington Books, 2018).

V Bruey 'Systematic gender violence and the rule of law: Aboriginal communities in Australia and Post-War Liberia' (PhD Thesis, Australian National University 2016).

K Crenshaw 'Mapping the margins: Intersectionality, identity politics, and violence against women of colour' (1991) 43/6 *Stanford Law Review* 1241–1299.

K Crenshaw 'What is intersectionality?' *YouTube*, 2018, www.youtube.com/watch?v=ViDtnfQ9FHc (accessed on 19 March 2020).

H Cooper *Madame President: The Extraordinary Journey of Ellen Johnson Sirleaf* (Simon and Schuster, 2017).

K Dahn 'Sex and bribery for better grades: Academic dishonesty in Liberia' (2008) 58 *Journal of Philosophy and History of Education* 46–50.

C Dorph and A Sjögren ' "A window of opportunity": A qualitative study about "sex for grades" as social navigation in Liberian Universities' (Master of Science, Lund University 2014).

D Edwards 'A terrible failure to protect schoolgirls in Liberia' *Africa's a Country*, 10 September 2018, https://africasacountry.com/2018/10/a-terrible-failure-to-protect-school-girls-in-liberia (accessed on 26 July 2023).

F Fanon *Toward the African Revolution: Political Essays*, H Chevalier trans (Grove Press 1967).

P Freire *Pedagogy of the Oppressed* (Continuum International, 2005).

L Gberie 'ECOMOG: The story of a heroic failure' (2003) 102/406 *African Affairs* 147–154.

Government of Liberia 'Consideration of reports submitted by states parties under Article 44 of the convention combined second, third and fourth periodic reports of states parties due in 2009 – Liberia' *(Committee on the Convention on the Rights of the Child 2011) United Nations CRC/C/LBR/2–4*, https://tbinternet.ohchr.org/_layouts/15/treatybodyexternal/Download.aspx?symbolno=CRC%2FC%2FLBR%2F2-4&Lang=en.

Government of Liberia 'Consideration of reports submitted by states parties under Article 44 of the convention initial report of states parties due in 1995 – Liberia' *(Committee on the Convention on the Rights of the Child 2002) United Nations CRC/C/28/Add.21*, https://tbinternet.ohchr.org/_layouts/15/treatybodyexternal/Download.aspx?symbolno=CRC%2FC%2F28%2FAdd.21&Lang=en.

Government of Liberia 'Consideration of reports submitted by states parties under Article 18 of the convention on the elimination of all forms of discrimination against women – Liberia' *(Committee on the Elimination and Discrimination against Women 2008) United Nations CEDAW/C/LBR/6*, https://tbinternet.ohchr.org/_layouts/15/treatybodyexternal/Download.aspx?symbolno=CEDAW%2FC%2FLBR%2F6&Lang=en.

Government of Liberia 'Consideration of reports submitted by states parties under Article 18 of the convention on the elimination of all forms of discrimination against women – Liberia' *(Committee on the Elimination and Discrimination against Women 2014) United Nations CEDAW/C/LBR/8*, https://tbinternet.ohchr.org/_layouts/15/TreatyBodyExternal/Download.aspx?symbolno=CEDAW%2FC%2FLBR%2F7-8&Lang=en.

Government of Liberia 'National report submitted in accordance with paragraph 5 of the Annex to Human Rights Council Resolution 16/21: Liberia' *(Human Rights Council 2015) Human Rights Council Universal Period Review A/HRC/WG.6/22/LBR/1*, www.ohchr.org/en/hr-bodies/upr/lr-index.

Government of Liberia 'National report submitted in accordance with paragraph 5 of the Annex to Human Rights Council Resolution 16/21: Liberia' *(Human Rights Council 2020) Human Rights Council Universal Period Review A/HRC/WG.6/36/LBR/1*, www.ohchr.org/en/hr-bodies/upr/lr-index.

Group of Women Leaders Voices for Change and Inclusion 'Where are the women leaders?' *Group of Women Leaders Voices for Change and Inclusion*, 2023, https://gwlvoices.com/download/climate-justice/?wpdmdl=8839&refresh=64ad6ef31a5d51689087731 (accessed on 30 July 2023).

A Higgins 'How the "white-savior industrial complex' failed Liberia's girls' *Vox*, 24 October 2018, www.vox.com/future-perfect/2018/10/24/17995536/liberia-girls-more-than-me-katie-meyler (accessed on 11 August 2023).

B Hooks *Ain't I a Woman: Black Women and Feminism* (South End Press, 1981).

B Hooks *Feminism is for Everybody: Passionate Politics* (South End Press, 2000).

H Howe 'Lessons of Liberia: ECOMOG and regional peacekeeping' (1996) 21/3 *International Security* 145–176.

D Inaju-Challydoff 'Adoption of the EGDC strategic plan 2023–2027 at the Centre of a Meeting of Ministers Responsible for Gender and Women Affairs of ECOWAS Member States in Accra, Ghana. Economic Community of West African States (ECOWAS)', https://ecowas.int/adoption-of-the-egdc-strategic-plan-2023–2027-at-the-centre-of-a-meeting-of-ministers-responsible-for-gender-and-women-affairs-of-ecowas-member-states-in-accra-ghana/ (accessed on 6 August 2023).

11 Sexual Harassment in the Nigerian Media Environment

Juliana Taiwo-Obalonye

Introduction

In this chapter, I interrogate the dynamics of sexual harassment in the media in Nigeria. I assess the cumulative impact of sexual harassment on victims' productivity at work owing to career goals that are impaired resulting in underperformance and a toxic work environment. I further provide an assessment of the institutional weaknesses of the media regulatory organ, professional associations, and media organisations which contribute to deepening the impunity within the industry where female journalists across the various media platforms (print, broadcast, and digital media) are mostly affected.[1] I then proceed to profile a flagship professional practice by the Nigerian Bar Association,[2] a professional body of legal practitioners that developed a workplace sexual harassment policy for legal professionals and judicial workers in Nigeria. I also consider whether media organisations have mechanisms for reporting sexual harassment.

In this chapter, I detail specific cases relating to incidents of sexual harassment and note how against that backdrop both editorial[3] and non-editorial[4] staff complain of unsafe work environments, an absence of institutional mechanisms for seeking redress, and lack of protection for victims.[5] Often, perpetrators of sexual harassment are mostly male bosses or senior staff and, in some instances, colleagues exercising power and control over victims who are cowed and hushed into silence. Ijeoma Okere notes that 'Sexual harassment is believed to be rampant in Nigerian newsrooms, but many go unreported'.[6] In Nigeria, as in other African countries, there is paucity of public information about it.[7] However, ongoing surveys and interviews with survivors will aid the process of developing evidence-based data to showcase the prevalence of sexual harassment and potential interventions.

To bridge the gap in data on sexual harassment, the World Association of News Publishers-IFRA aptly responded by a survey of five countries in Africa seeking to know the prevalence rate of sexual harassment within the media.[8] It stated the objective of their survey was to include providing verifiable data for benchmarking measurable change in sexual harassment in the media.[9] The 'Data is a benchmark for measuring change. It enables assessment of the

DOI: 10.4324/9781003373308-11

impact of initiatives to improve the management of sexual harassment and, ultimately, newsroom safety, factors that directly impact equality'.[10] More importantly, data from survey by WAN-IFRA indicated that sexual harassment in the newsrooms is prevalent and requires a concerted effort to be eradicated.

It should be noted that 'Sexual harassment is a global societal problem, and WAN-IFRA views it as such. Evidence from this research shows that the culture of sexual harassment needs to change regardless of country'.[11] On the output of this initiative, WAN-IFRA states that 'This is the first time we have been able to draw on large-scale data to support the belief that it is prevalent everywhere and is a significant impediment to a healthy media industry, regardless of country or context'.[12]

I pose specific questions in this chapter; I ask how the challenge could be addressed in a sustainable manner, how to collectively create a safe work environment in the newsroom and whether there is any role regulatory authorities and professional unions, including the Nigeria Press Council,[13] National Broadcasting Commission,[14] Broadcast Organisation of Nigeria,[15] Nigerian Guild of Editors,[16] and Nigeria Union of Journalists[17] could play in taking joint efforts and actions in ensuring that media organizations adopt a policy manual on sexual harassment to protect workers.

An Overview of Sexual Harassment in Nigeria's Media Sector

In this section, I provide an overview of the prevailing culture of sexual harassment within media organisations using a reliance of surveys to strengthen my argument that this is an unaddressed problem in media. One online survey involving mostly journalists in Nigeria as respondents reaffirmed the harmful nature of sexual harassment, viewing it as a huge threat to the media industry. Of those surveyed, 34.4% of the respondents pointed towards the absence of an independent mechanism for seeking redress by victims of sexual harassment and expressed concern that perpetrators in the Nigerian media were not held to account.

Journalists will generally concede that sexual harassment ranks high on the list of crimes[18] committed with impunity against the media. According to a group of journalist's participating in an ActionAid Nigeria roundtable discussion, 'the harassment and impunity against journalists especially sexual harassment of female journalists will not end until perpetrators are investigated and punished accordingly organised'.[19] The event was in commemoration of the 2021 International Day of Impunity against Journalists.[20] Both the 1999 Constitution and the Criminal Code further note that sexual harassment is a crime punishable under the law in Nigeria.[21]

Yusuf Noah posits that sexual harassment is a key concern for most female employees in Nigeria, including those in the media industry.[22] A survey conducted by the author on sexual harassment in the Nigerian media sector indicates that 35% of journalists, mostly female, reported having been sexually harassed more than twice by their bosses, senior managers, and colleagues.[23] It is clear that sexual harassment in the media is pervasive, visible, and with insufficient deterrent measures to restrain or punish habitual offenders.

The Institutional Framework of the Nigerian Media Sector

In this subsection, I explain the various institutions that make up the media sector in Nigeria as well as their responsibilities in providing a professional standard of practice. The Nigerian media environment is dynamic and robust with an estimated 5,945 registered journalists nationally.[24] The media ownership structure includes professional journalists, businessmen, and politicians who establish media outlets to give visibility to partisan politics, economic, and ideological interests. The media house owners' control and influence national discourse. Of the estimated 100 newspapers and magazines in the print category, only a handful appear regularly on newsstands, while others are exclusively online publications. The Nigerian Press Council[25] regulates the print media,[26] whilst the National Broadcasting Commission (NBC)[27] regulates about 150 licensed public and independent broadcasting stations, radio, and television. The airwaves receive as much competition as the print media.[28] Additionally, the Nigerian Press Council regulates both the print and broadcast media.[29]

The Nigeria Union of Journalists (NUJ)[30] is the national professional body, having at least 5,945 registered practicing journalists.[31] It is worth stating that the exact data on journalists in Nigeria may be more than those in the NUJ official records. The consumers of online and social media contents in Nigeria have increased, propelled by the advent of digital communications in the early 2000, which led to expansion of the domestic information and communications technology (ICT) sector.[32] There is a plethora of media professional organisations recognised by the Nigeria Press Council Act.[33] The organisation represents various interests, including media owners, middle-level journalists, and editors. The list includes the Nigeria Union of Journalists,[34] the Nigerian Guild of Editors,[35] the Newspaper Proprietors Association of Nigeria, and the Broadcasting Organisation of Nigeria.[36]

The principle regulatory instrument for providing oversight on the media in Nigeria is the Nigerian Media Council Act of 1988.[37] The Act established the Nigerian Press Council, whose responsibilities include:

> to promote high professional standards for the press, and deal with complaints emanating from members of the public about the conduct of journalists in their professional capacity or complaints emanating from the press about the conduct o persons or organisations towards the press and for other matters connected thereto.[38]

The role of the media is reinforced in Section 22 on 'Obligation of Mass Media' of the 1999 Constitution of the Federal Republic of Nigeria, which states, *inter alia*,

> The press, radio, television, and other agencies of the mass media shall at all times be free to uphold the fundamental objectives contained in this chapter and uphold the responsibility and accountability of the Government to the people.[39]

Public Perceptions of the Media

Nigerian citizens have a positive perception about the media, as most of them see journalists as patriots who fight for the public interest on behalf of the oppressed, setting policy agenda for government, and holding the government to account. The media earned the moniker, 'the fourth estate of the realm', that takes over any cause for 'judication' in the court of public opinion, whenever the three arms of government – the executive, legislature, and judiciary – fail to resolve any matter. Often, journalists who are victims of sexual harassment have a negative impression of the media as pretentious and unwilling to address failings of the media. Although the media intervenes in matters of ethical practice in other professions by reporting misbehaviours, it has failed to intervene in regulating the bad behaviours of its members who commit sexual harassment. Unfortunately, the failure of the media to hold itself to account has led victims to believe that the media is responsible for the rising cases of sexual harassment within the industry. The proverbial cliché 'Physician heal thyself'[40] is a fitting epitaph in this regard. The media should muster the courage to undertake a house cleaning through internalised ethical practices within the media. As the maxim says, 'Caesar's wife must be above suspicion'.[41]

The Story of Rev Mother Esther Abimbola Ajayi and Key Lessons

Sexual harassment in the Nigerian media industry has existed for as long as there have been media houses in Nigeria. The story of Rev Mother Esther Abimbola Ajayi is illustrative.[42] She was sexually harassed by her boss in 1984 whilst working for the Nigerian Television Authority. She narrated in an interview to *Sun Newspapers* about how she ran out of his office, leaving her bag to escaped being raped.

> What led to my quitting the job was the action of one big man there then. I won't mention his name. He was my chief programme officer or producer then. One day, I went to his office, and he left his seat and advanced amorously towards me. I wondered what he was trying to do. Before you knew it, I had left my handbag and run out. Eventually, they

> brought it to me at the gate and that was how I ended my stay at NTA, Ibadan. What helped them to keep the programme running for a while was because I had recorded some of the episodes in advance. They tried talking to me to come back. I never did so because I asked myself: how would I face the man again? He was the one I was always reporting to as regards the programme.[43]

Rev Mother Ajayi resolved to leave the media organisation without reporting the incident to the management and, even if she had wanted to report, there was unlikely to be a gender-sensitive reporting mechanism or credible avenues for her to seek and access redress in 1984. Today, almost four decades later, not much has changed in the Nigerian media environment.

A report by junior investigative journalist Philip Obaji, under the caption, 'He told me to sit on his lap', the women enduring sexual harassment in Nigerian newsrooms' published by *Al Jazeera Journalism Review*,[44] highlights and reveals the depth and the magnitude of sexual harassment in the Nigerian media space.[45] The story focused on how the Nigerian female journalists interviewed by Obaji alleged their bosses sexually harassed them in the newsroom, which represents a common trend across the country. As expected for fear of intimidation and their safety, the victims asked that their real identities should not be disclosed. The female journalists shared their stories thus, as captured by Obaji:

> Female journalists suffer sexual harassment – and worse – on a daily basis in newsrooms in Nigeria. But for most, it's a case of 'put up and shut up' or lose your job. Just days after Pamela (not her real name) joined a prominent radio station in Abuja, Nigeria's capital city, last August, her immediate boss, the station's programme's director, called her to his office.[46]
>
> I just finished presenting a programme in the evening when he entered the studio and ordered me to his office'. When Pamela arrived at her boss' office half an hour later, she found him seated on his chair with a bottle of whiskey on his desk. Then came an embarrassing invitation from her boss the 26-year-old journalist says she never saw coming.[47]
>
> 'He looked straight at me and told me to come sit on his lap', she says. 'I told him straight away that I couldn't do that'. Pamela said her boss kept insisting but she turned him down each time he demanded she sit on his lap. 'When he saw that I wasn't ready to play along, he got up from his chair, put his hands around my waist and tried to hug me but I pushed him away and walked out of the office'.[48]

Pamela's boss never attempted to sexually assault her again after that incident, but his attitude towards her changed afterwards. 'He never said hello to me again and never approved any request I made to him that had to do with the programme I anchor'.[49] Pamela is not alone when it comes female journalists facing sexual harassment from their superiors or colleagues at work.[50]

The experience of journalists regarding sexual harassment in the newsroom is because of the absence of institutional frameworks that support credible reporting processes. As noted previously, in the online survey conducted, 34.4% of media workers indicated that media organisations in Nigeria did not have any staff policies on the prevention of sexual harassment or a reporting protocol for staff.[51] In addition, 35.3% of respondents admitted that they had been sexually harassed in the workplace, 17.9% respondents stated that they were aware of whistle-blowing policies for sexual harassment in the place they worked, 5.9% of the respondents stated that the predator was dismissed while 85.3% of respondents agreed that workplace jokes, conversations, and remarks exacerbated sexual harassment in the newsroom.[52] When there is no sense of fairness and justice, media workers find themselves vulnerable and with no recourse to justice.

In another study report released in February 2023, over 50% of journalists cited sexual harassment as a major safety concern.[53] I earlier recounted the example of the 1984 incident shared by Rev. Mother Esther Ajayi[54] where her boss, a producer at the state-owned Nigeria Television Authority (NTA) in Ibadan, harassed her and caused her to leave her job for fear of further victimisation by the offender who should have faced consequences. The fact that this incident was never reported, nor did the media organisation take any steps to investigate or hold the perpetrator accountable, underscores the institutional weaknesses of media organisations in Nigeria in dealing with the problem of sexual harassment. Rev Ajayi's story is a common thread in the daily grind of journalism in Nigeria as it is now being taken as a 'culture' that 'big men' within the Nigeria corporate environment can sexually harass women without any repercussions.

From the experiences of sexual harassment as told by victims, the consistent thread is that often, victims are coerced to resign from their jobs due to pressures from the predators, while impunity keeps growing every day. The problem of sexual harassment within the media industry is indicative of a wider societal problem reflected in high-level decision-making processes. For instance, since 2020, Nigeria's National Assembly has been unable to pass five critical pieces of gender legislation aimed at addressing sexual harassment across all sectors. Apart from the internal challenges faced by female journalists in relation to sexual harassment, a Nigerian journalist related her experience in the Report of State of Safety of Female Journalists in Nigeria, as follows:

> I have been in the practice for over a decade and the only sad experience I can relate to be a scheduled interview with a so-called reputable stakeholder in the trade union. While inserting my battery into the midget to have the interview after exchanging pleasantries, the next word he uttered was 'look my trouser zip', showing me his private part and the

need for me to pay attention to it if he will grant the interview. I immediately called off the interview and walked out of his office.[55]

The Nigerian Bar Associations' Sexual Harassment Policy

In a paper on sexual harassment within the legal profession ecosystem, Adetutu Aina-Pelemo *et al* asserts that sexual harassment is a major issue within professional workplaces and is also impacting the legal profession.[56] Seniors not only have the clout to 'silence' their victims, but also know all the loopholes there could be in the law books that they could take advantage of to escape punishment.[57] In response to the problem of sexual harassment the Nigerian Bar Association (NBA) took steps to address it through the development of a sexual harassment policy.[58] A high-level committee was established to draft the Nigerian Bar Association Sexual Harassment Policy and, as such, provided a professional model for other professional sectors in Nigeria, including the media industry.

As previously noted, this journey towards a sexual harassment policy began at the NBA annual general meeting of July 2019, which set up a committee to draft the 'Anti-Sexual Harassment Practice Code of Conduct' for the lawyers in Nigeria. At another event, the NBA conference in Port Harcourt, Rivers State, on 27 October 2021, the Nigerian Bar Association Women Forum collaborated with the NBA to finalize the policy document.[59] The then NBA national president, Olumide Akpata, presented and launched the 'Sexual Harassment Policy of Nigerian Bar Association'[60] containing the code of ethical behaviour on sexual harassment for lawyers in Nigeria. The policy document with 17 provisions seeks to address the perennial problem of sexual harassment and bullying within the legal profession and justice system in Nigeria.[61] Article 2 of the NBA sexual harassment policy sets the tone for conversation on the *raison d'être* for the policy and why the NBA undertook these efforts.

Article 2 of the policy document presents the purpose of the policy, which is to prevent and address the corporate issues of sexual harassment, to promote healthy, safe, productive, and conducive workplaces for Nigerian legal practitioners, as well as serve as a guide for employers to adopt an official policy and regulation on the subject matter.[62] Adetutu Pelemo disclosed that the NBA policy borrowed from extant laws on sexual harassment in Nigeria, although not codified in any singular document as legislation.[63] For instance, she noted, 'Article 3 of the NBASHP to include the following instruments: Nigerian Labour Law 2004, National Industrial Court Civil Procedure Rules 2017, Order 14 Rules 1(a) (b) (c) and (d), Violence Against Persons (Prohibition) Act 2015, Employees Compensation Act 2010'.[64] The example set by the legal profession through the NBA Sexual Harassment Policy code is unique and provides a solid example that needs to be embraced by the media in Nigeria.[65] The Nigerian Bar Associations' Sexual Harassment Policy defines sexual harassment in Article 5, *inter alia*:

> Sexual harassment is any sexual behavior that affects the dignity of women and men, which is considered unwanted, unacceptable, inappropriate, and offensive to the recipient and creates a hostile, intimidating, unstable, unconducive, or offensive work environment. It classifies sexual harassment in the workplace into four types physical conduct of a sexual nature, a verbal form of sexual harassment, a non-verbal form of sexual harassment and quid pro quo harassment.[66]

The definition of sexual harassment by the NBA Sexual Harassment Policy identifies both the form and substance of sexual harassment, including physical, verbal, non-verbal, and *quid pro quo*, and thus, it fits within the context of the discourse on the subject in the Nigeria media sector. It provides a pathway for media stakeholders in tackling the scourge through a multifaceted approach. It entails, first and foremost, a strong resolve to deal with the challenges of sexual harassment within the media sector; secondly, to embark on the sensitisation of journalists on the negative impact of sexual harassment on their capacity to deliver their services to the nation; and, thirdly, rebuild the integrity and credibility of the media institution as an accountability institution that disseminates public education via news, education, and entertainment to the public. More so, the media has a critical role to play in implementing self-regulation mechanisms in fostering a safe work environment.[67]

The NBA as a collective has demonstrated the commitment to stem the scourge of sexual harassment through the adoption of an anti-sexual harassment policy, which the media industry can replicate and use in regulating the behaviour of its members. An open conversation on sexual harassment within the media profession should happen urgently. The media needs to open the Pandora's Box as the NBA did, beginning with a public admittance of the fact that sexual harassment has had a negative impact on the legal profession and, hence, the resolve to find sustainable solutions to the problem, Aina-Pelemo argues for the adoption of the Nigerian Bar Association (NBA) Sexual Harassment Policy, a model document for professional bodies in Nigeria.[68] The logic is that if the media and, indeed, other professional groups in Nigeria replicate the 'Nigerian Bar Association Sexual Harassment Policy' as a form of self-regulation, it will easily enforce compliance via peer influence, shared values, and the protection of workers' rights.[69]

Global Effect of Sexual Harassment Perspectives in Nigeria's Media

An important perspective to the discourse on sexual harassment in the workplace was offered by the feminist scholar Catherine Mackinnon in her seminal work, *Sexual Harassment of Working Women: A Case of Sex Sexual Discrimination of Women*, in which she posits that:

> Sexual harassment may occur as a single encounter or as a series of incidents at work. It may place a sexual condition upon employment

> opportunities at a clearly defined threshold, such as hiring, retention, or advancement; or it may occur as a pervasive or continuing condition of the work environment. Extending along a continuum of severity and unwantedness, and depending upon the employment circumstances, examples include verbal sexual suggestions or jokes, constant leering or ogling, brushing against your body 'accidentally', a friendly pat, squeeze or pinch or arm against you, catching you alone for a quick kiss, the indecent proposition backed by the threat of losing your job, and forced sexual relations.[70]

I contend that sexual harassment at work is rooted in power relations within a traditional household setting, with the male exercising power and control over the female and, hence, the traits are transmuted to the workplace. The feminist bent that Mackinnon espouses aligns with the reality of sexual harassment within the media industry where women become the victims. Mackinnon identifies two categories of sexual harassment prevalent in the work explicitly, which places a social economic burden on women that finds expression through workplace harassment.[71] Reinforcing the key thesis that sexual harassment is the dynamics of power relations between women and men in the workplace, with women underrepresented, and, therefore, the presence of inequality in decision making places them at a disadvantaged position.

This is relevant for the Nigerian context and the ordeal suffered by female journalists in Nigerian power dynamics leading to abuse of power and is rooted in part to the fact that more men hold senior management and editorial positions than women. In fact, women in Nigeria's media are highly underrepresented, and, thus, exposed to harassment.[72] The 'Me Too movement' of 2017 had a profound impact on creating awareness of sexual harassment in Nigeria as a whole, but also in the media.[73] Professions went through a metamorphosis because of the Me-Too Movement, as it reverberated across various workplaces, including the media, legal, academic, non-profit and civic sectors, and the religious domain that are subject to accountability scrutiny.[74] The media sector globally also went through its own experience of the Me-Too Movement, resulting in resignations of top executives and senior media managers.[75]

Citizens now show interest in scrutinising how various professions respond to sexual harassment as well as how redress mechanisms set new bars in workplaces in Nigeria. With the NBA leading the way in 2021 following the launch of the Sexual Harassment Policy of Nigerian Bar Association, other professionals have followed suit, providing guidepost for 120,000 members of the NBA nationwide. With the NBA setting the precedent on putting in place an accountability mechanism on sexual harassment in the workplace, it makes sense for other professions to leverage this effort to ensure a safe workplace. Lending their voice to the issue of sexual harassment in the newsroom, Ms. Ladi Bala, president of the National Association of

Women Journalists (NAWOJ), the joint professional union of female journalists in Nigeria, notes that:

> Sexual harassment is a common issue that exist not only in the media space but in all aspects of our daily lives. It is disheartening that people hardly ever talk about it openly. Journalists, particularly women journalists, are not exempted from sexual harassment. It has become a norm within newsrooms across the country. Women are constantly exposed to verbal, emotional and sexual harassment both in the media and outside of it. Men often make advances at women, and often, it is the superiors who do this.[76]

They also provide the rationale on why women are reluctant in speaking out when sexually harassed in the workplace, which Bala identifies as fear and lack of secure job tenure, as well as casualisation as the major reasons for the silence.

> The challenge is that women are usually afraid to report the incidents officially due to fear of losing their jobs or being victimised as some of the women are often hired on a casual basis, and do not have permanent staff positions; this makes them vulnerable to harassment. People in newsrooms have a culture of engaging in conversations that put women in uncomfortable situations, leading to harassment. Unfortunately, media professionals are stigmatised, and there is a belief that women in the media are loose, easy-going, and of low virtue.[77]

Bala offers pathways for eradicating sexual harassment from newsrooms in Nigeria via a multi-pronged approach that advances the common interests of women journalists who form the greater ratio of victims. Her proposition is instructive.

> Curbing sexual harassment, women journalists need to build their capacity, improve their skills, and be more professional in discharge of their duties, while learning to keep their self-worth and not allow anyone to bully or intimidate them. By enhancing these qualities, they become more confident and know their worth, hence less easily toyed with.[78]

The NAWOJ president notes that the association will commence engagement with stakeholders in the media sector to canvas for the adoption of an institutional mechanism to address sexual harassment in the newsrooms in Nigeria.

> We will address this issue of sexual harassment of female journalists through advocacy with relevant stakeholders, recommending for every

> media organisation in Nigeria to have a shared policy on Sexual Harassment. This will give every victim of harassment the courage to seek redress. Until this policy is in place, sensitisation and advocacy remain the only way to ensure that women are protected in the newsroom.[79]

Identifying Additional Solutions

The risk and ever-looming threat of sexual harassment has been a hindrance to the career development of many female journalists.[80] As articulated in the previous sections, it remains a major concern for media workers in Nigeria.[81] The real challenge, however, is what steps are being taken to address the problem at the institutional level? What proactive measures could be taken by stakeholders and regulators to address the issue and ensure safe newsrooms in Nigeria? What role can the media regulatory authority play in ensuring appropriate sanctions? Human resources expert Carl Bosser suggests ways of handling incidents of sexual harassment, noting that every organisation needs to be proactive in providing psychosocial support to victims of workplace sexual harassment to encourage them speak out, and the need for openness and human resource offices to provide support and protection to victims.[82] He asserts that:

> Some organisations are careful about the issue, and they have a diversity management policy as a list of the best practices. Companies need to be transparent from the process of hiring to orientation and be more open to tackle sexual harassment at workplace. The issue should not be taken casually because this will make perpetrators think that it is okay, employers can start discussion around this issue and perhaps bring in a neutral counsellor since this is a very sensitive issue that employees can talk to and then give their feedback to the management for action thereby encouraging the victims to come out.[83]

I propose that media stakeholders including the NUJ, NGE, NPAN, BON, and NBC should draft and adopt the 'Media Workplace Code of Practice on Sexual Harassment' which will form the nucleus of a bill, say the 'Sexual Harassment and Media Workers Safety Bill', that the National Assembly can then deliberate on and eventually enact into law as a full legal national legislation to regulate safe media practices in Nigeria. Through sustained advocacy by media stakeholders in the National Assembly, the legislation will pass through legislative scrutiny, and be enacted into law. This will boost the confidence of workers in media institutions in the sense that such a legislation will provide a legal framework for punitive action against sexual predators. More importantly, it will provide a legal safeguard for handling cases of sexual harassment by media professionals in a timely manner and ensure that victims get justice and adequate compensation to victims and, also, further enhance the receding sanctity of the media environment as a paragon of ethical standard in the society.

I propose the establishment of an independent ombudsmen for journalists in Nigeria to investigate allegations of sexual harassment as a short-term strategy response to the challenge of sexual harassment. In my view, this proposition to set up an ombudsmen will strengthen dispensing of petitions by journalists who suffer from sexual harassment. An ombudsman can deliver and serve justice in a more sustainable manner, unlike an administrative body within a media organisation that may be subject to manipulation by the media owner, truncating the course of justice against victims of sexual harassment. Additionally, I propose that the National Assembly should enact a new legislation known as 'Sexual Harassment Against Media Workers (Prohibition), Safety and Related Matters Bill' to ensure safe newsrooms in Nigeria. This will, in my view, further strengthen efforts at making the newsroom safer. This legislation will be applicable across the country, giving that the media is listed on the exclusive list in the Constitution of Federal Republic of Nigeria 1999 which only the federal government of Nigeria can legislate on.[84]

Furthermore, I propose the establishment of a special fund to support victims of sexual harassment within the media for the following reasons: first, as compensation to victims of sexual harassment whose rights have been violated; second, to support medical care and access to psychosocial support that may be needed to heal; and, third, to fund research activities in finding the best ways towards the elimination of sexual harassment within the media.

Overall, it is clear that the media as an institution must take steps to support journalists who are sexually harassed and encourage the victims to 'speak out' and expose sexual predators through the naming and shaming option.[85] The United Nations adopted this strategy by putting pressure on violators of human rights conventions.[86] Several organisations and entities adopted the strategy and have been using it to put pressure on governments, entities, and powerful individuals to comply with good behaviours, conventions, and agreements. The media has leveraged this approach in calling out errant members to order through sanctions, following the example of the NBA in adopting a sexual harassment policy.

Universally, sexual harassment within the media environment is a major challenge that is attracting the attention of several organisations that embark on taking initiatives aimed at tackling the problem by providing information and data on the extent of the problem to society. Women in News, a media development programme of the World Association of News Publishers (WAN-IFRA), published an extensive study on sexual harassment within the media across eight African countries. The report interviewed women journalists to understand the phenomenon of sexual harassment. Data from Kenya is very instructive and germane to understanding the challenges faced by journalists in Nigeria with regards to sexual harassment.

> Eighty-three participants from Kenya completed the survey. Examining sexual harassment frequencies, for men 30% experienced verbal sexual

harassment and 15% physical sexual harassment. For women, 79% experienced verbal sexual harassment (55% five times or more) and 51% physical sexual harassment. One participant identified as gender non-conforming and reported experiencing verbal and physical sexual harassment one time. Only 29% chose to report, which resulted in action being taken in 54% of cases. The most common reasons for not reporting were being afraid it would negatively impact one's job (17.25%) and no reporting mechanisms available (13.1%). Action taken by media organisations was limited.[87]

Additionally, the Kenyan example as contained in the study provides perspective on the pattern of sexual harassment in the newsroom and an understanding of the dynamics of sexual harassment in the media in Africa, including Nigeria. The WANIFRA study notes thus:

> The challenge with reporting harassment in the newsroom as a woman is that the entire chain of command are men, and there are no clear structures on how to go about making such a complaint. I lost interest in the media industry because anytime I did not show interest to my editor, it was always a rough day for me. My stay there was hell. When my only female colleague left for another media house last October, my editor told me to be assured of her position; I needed to warm his bed. I quit after being harassed for 'running to HR'. I felt so helpless and had no one to go to and ended up being demoted. I am still affected five years later.[88]

Conclusion

There is compelling evidence of the reality of sexual harassment among media workers in Nigeria. What is surprising is that the media, which holds other sectors accountable, seems to have failed to hold itself to account. There is hardly any news coverage on sexual harassment within the media space. The failure of the media to hold itself to account with regards to naming and shaming of perpetrators within its ranks who sexually harass subordinate colleagues is a tragic part of the story of lack of accountability in the media sector. The media needs to be proactive in tackling incidents of sexual harassments in the newsrooms head-on and ensure that there is justice for every victim of sexual harassment that needs to be granted justice to serve as a demonstration of a renewed commitment to rid the sector of predators. Stakeholders in the Nigerian media sector need to take urgent steps in creating a framework that supports a safe workspace and accountability processes towards building a safe workplace for all journalists, both women and men. They need to ensure that newsrooms across Nigeria are safe and free from sexual harassment.

Recommendations

In this regard, I make the following recommendations:

- Set up an ombudsman within the Nigerian Press Council and Nigeria Union of Journalists who will be able to receive complaints for legal redress from media personnel, including complaints on sexual harassment.
- The formation of non-governmental organisations (NGOs) to protect the rights of workers and ensure the active involvement of trade unions in efforts meant to reduce the incidence of sexual harassment in the media work environment.
- The National Association of Women Journalists (NAWOJ), a union of women journalists working in Nigeria, should engage in advocacy for the adoption of an anti-sexual harassment workplace policy for media organisations in Nigeria to mitigate sexual harassments.
- As a regulator, the Nigerian Press Council and other professional unions in the sector, such as Newspaper Proprietors' Association of Nigeria (NPAN), Nigeria Guild of Editors (NGE), and Nigeria Union of Journalists (NUJ), should take the initiative to compel and mandate all media organisations to adopt a policy manual on sexual harassment that promotes a safe media work environment.
- The Nigerian Press Council (NPC) should send a bill on media safety and workplace and other connected matters to the National Assembly to support a safer media space in the country.
- There is a need for a mandatory inclusion of sexual and gender-based violence as prohibited behaviour in the staff manual of all media organisations in Nigeria.
- A special fund needs to be established to facilitate the process of dispensing justice to victims of sexual harassments in the media industry in Nigeria. Victims need to be encouraged to speak up and have support provided to them to ensure healing and from which proper compensation could be paid to them incidents of sexual harassment are established to have taken place.

Notes

1 I Okereke 'Lack of organisational policies, other factors encourage sexual harassment in Nigerian newsrooms' *Premium Times* (Abuja), 15 June 2022, www.premiumtimesng.com/news/top-news/537237-lack-of-organisational-policies-other-factors-encourage-sexual-harassment-in-nigerian-newsrooms.html.

2 The NBA is the statutory legal union for legal practitioners in Nigeria with 150,000 members nationwide; see Nigerian Bar Association – About Us, www.nigerianbar.org.ng/about_us#who-we-are (2023).

3 Editorial staff is a classification for journalists involved in news gathering, and editing, reporters, correspondents, producers, announcers, page planners, editors, columnists, photojournalists, and camera men.

4 Non-editorial are non-journalists working in a media organisation including, administration, finance, printers, engineers, administration, marketing, related activities.
5 Okereke (n 1).
6 *Ibid.*
7 C Ireton 'Sexual harassment in the media: The Africa report' World Association of News Publishers (WAN-IFRA) (Paris, 2023) 7, SexualHarassmentInTheMedia-Africa-English.pdf (womeninnews.org).
8 *Ibid.*
9 *Ibid.*
10 *Ibid.*
11 *Ibid.*
12 *Ibid.*
13 The Regulatory Agency for Media in Nigeria.
14 The Regulatory Agency for Broadcast Stations in Nigeria.
15 The Organisation of all Broadcasters in Nigeria.
16 National Union of Editors across media organisations in Nigeria.
17 National Union of all Journalists in Nigeria. It has offices in 36 states and Federal Capital Territory, Abuja.
18 Action4Justice Nigeria 'What does the law say about sexual harassment?' https://nigeria.action4justice.org/legal_areas/sexual-harassment-in-the-workplace/what-does-the-law-say-about-sexual-harassment/
19 V Nnakaike 'ActionAid urges security agencies to protect female journalists' *Businessday* (Lagos), 7 November 2021, https://businessday.ng/news/article/actionaid-urges-security-agencies-to-protect-female-journalists/.
20 *Ibid.*
21 Ibid. Action4Justice Nigeria.
22 Y Noah 'Experience of sexual harassment at work by female employees in a Nigerian work environment' www.krepublishers.com/02-Journals/JHE/JHE-30-0-000-10-Web/JHE-30-3-000-2010-Abst-PDF/JHE-30-3–179–10–1933-Yusuf-N/JHE-30–3–179–10–1933-Yusuf-N-Tt.pdf.
23 J Taiwo-Obalonye 'Survey to study incidents of sexual harassment among media workers in Nigeria' conducted between 5 and 7 May 2023. A randomised online survey using Google Sheet to collect responses from participants from media organisations in Nigeria.
24 Nigerian Union of Journalists 'NUJ Official Compendium' 2023, http://nuj.org.ng/compendium.phpIt.
25 Nigerian Press Council (2023) NPC Act, http://new.presscouncil.gov.ng/wp-content/uploads/2012/12/npc_law.pdf
26 *Ibid.*
27 National Broadcasting Commission, http://lawsofnigeria.placng.org/view2.php?sn=276.
28 J Zakari and A Adeyanju *African Media Development Initiatives: Nigeria Research Findings and Conclusions* (BBC World Service Trust, 2006) 15.
29 Nigeria Press Council (Abuja), Nigeria Press Council Act 1992 http://new.presscouncil.gov.ng/wp-content/uploads/2012/12/npc_law.pdf.
30 *Ibid.*
31 Nigerian Union of Journalist (n 24).
32 National Communications Commission Nigerian 'National broadband plan 2020–2025' (Abuja, 2020) 16, https://ncc.gov.ng/documents/880-nigerian-national-broadband-plan-2020–2025/file
33 Nigeria Press Council (n 25).
34 Nigeria Union of Journalists (n 24).

35 About NGE (2023), https://ngeditors.org.ng/about-us-2/.
36 Broadcasting Organisation of Nigeria (2023) 'About BON' (2023). https://bon.ng/history/
37 Policy and Legal Advocacy Centre, 'Nigerian Press Council Act', http://lawsofnigeria.placng.org/view2.php?sn=384.
38 *Ibid.*
39 The 1999 Constitution of Nigeria.
40 King James Version, Holy Bible: Luke 4:23, Life. Church/YouVersion, Edmond, Oklahoma, United States, www.bible.com/bible/1/LUK.4.23.KJV.
41 Farlex International 'The Free Dictionary' https://idioms.thefreedictionary.com/Caesar%27s+wife+must+be+above+suspicion.
42 Founder of Cherubim and Seraphim Church, and founder of Love of Christ Church, London, and notable religious leader in Nigeria.
43 J Taiwo-Obalonye 'Our first quarrel as couple: The inspiring story of Rev Mother Esther Ajayi and husband (2)' *The Sun Newspapers* (Lagos), 6 June 2020, https://sunnewsonline.com/our-first-quarrel-as-couple-the-inspiring-story-of-rev-mother-esther-ajayi-and-husband-2.
44 P Obaji Jnr 'He told me to sit on his lap: The women enduring sexual harassment in Nigerian newsrooms' *Al Jazeera Journalism Review*, March 2023, ttps://institute.aljazeera.net/en/ajr/article/2124.
45 An award-winning investigative reporter in Nigeria and correspondence of Daily Beast, a United States media publication, https://foreignpolicy.com/author/philip-obaji-jr/.
46 Obaji Jnr (n 44).
47 *Ibid.*
48 *Ibid.*
49 *Ibid.*
50 *Ibid.*
51 Taiwo-Obalonye (n 23).
52 *Ibid.*
53 Media Foundation for West Africa (MFWA) and International Press Centre (2023) Report: State of Safety of Female Journalists in Nigeria, www.mfwa.org/wp-content/uploads/2023/02/SAFETY-OF-FEMALE-JOURNALISTS-IN-WEST-AFRICA-NIGERIA-final-1.pdf 11.
54 Taiwo-Obalonye (n 23).
55 Report: State of Safety of Female Journalists in Nigeria (2023) 12.
56 A Aina-Pelemo et al 'Sexual harassment in the workplace: Case study of the Nigerian legal sector' (2019) *Journal of Law, Policy and Globalisation* 86.
57 The Guardian Newspapers 'NBA 2019: Focus on sexual harassment in the workplace' https://guardian.ng/guardian-woman/nba-2019-focus-on-sexual-harassment-in-the-workplace/.
58 Nigerian Bar Association Sexual Harassment Policy, Nigerian Bar Association: Creating a Safe Space for All (2021); Nigerian Bar Association *About Us*, www.nigerianbar.org.ng/about_us#who-we-are (2023).
59 Aina-Pelemo et al (n 56) 122–125.
60 *Ibid.*
61 *Ibid.*
62 *Ibid.*
63 *Ibid.*
64 *Ibid.*
65 *Ibid.*
66 Aina-Pelemo et al (n 56).
67 Okereke, J Premium Times (2022).

68 A Aina-Pelemo 'A review of the Nigerian bar association sexual harassment policy' (2021) 1 *International Journal of Law and Clinical Legal Education* 123.
69 *Ibid* 123.
70 CA Mackinnon *Harassment of Working Women: A Case of Sex Sexual Discrimination* (Yale University Press, 1979) 1–2.
71 *Ibid*, 31.
72 L Bala 'Key informant interview with the author' *Abuja*, 29 May 2023.
73 J Kantor and M Towhey 'Harvey Weinstein paid off sexual harassment accusers for decades' 5 October 2017, www.nytimes.com/2017/10/05/us/harvey-weinstein-harassment-allegations.html.
74 A Salaudeen 'In pursuit of justice: The women fighting against Nigeria's rape culture' *Afriquette*, www.afriquette.com/articles/women-fighting-against-nigeria-rape-culture.
75 A Barton and H Storm *Violence and Harassment against Women in the News Media: A Global Picture* (International News Safety Institute (INSI) and the International Women's Media Foundation (IWMF), 2006).
76 L Bala 'Key informant interview with the author'.
77 *Ibid.*
78 *Ibid.*
79 *Ibid.*
80 Report: State of Safety of Female Journalist in Nigeria (2023) 12.
81 Noah (n 22).
82 J Otieno 'The silent monster that is workplace sexual harassment' *The Citizen* (Dar Salam), 3 June 2021, www.thecitizen.co.tz/tanzania/news/national/the-silent-monster-that-is-workplace-sexual-harassment-2694986.
83 *Ibid.*
84 The Constitution of Federal Republic of Nigeria 1999, Sect 22, www.jonapwd.org/FRNconstitution.pdf.
85 G Heathcote 'Naming and shaming: Human rights accountability in security council resolution 1960' (2010) in on *Women, Peace, and Security Journal of Human Rights Practice Advance*, www.usip.org/sites/default/files/missing-peace/Naming-and-Shaming.pdf (access on 7 February 2012).
86 *Ibid.*
87 Ireton (n 7).
88 *Ibid.*

References

About NGE (2023), https://ngeditors.org.ng/about-us-2/.

Action4Justice Nigeria 'What does the law say about sexual harassment?' https://nigeria.action4justice.org/legal_areas/sexual-harassment-in-the-workplace/what-does-the-law-say-about-sexual-harassment/

A Aina-Pelemo 'A review of the Nigerian bar association sexual harassment policy' (2021) 1 *International Journal of Law and Clinical Legal Education* 123.

A Aina-Pelemo et al 'Sexual harassment in the workplace: Case study of the Nigerian legal sector' (2019) *Journal of Law, Policy and Globalisation* 86.

An award-winning investigative reporter in Nigeria and correspondence of Daily Beast, a United States media publication, https://foreignpolicy.com/author/philip-obaji-jr/.

L Bala 'Key informant interview with the author' *Abuja*, 29 May 2023.

A Barton and H Storm *Violence and Harassment against Women in the News Media: A Global Picture* (International News Safety Institute (INSI) and the International

Women's Media Foundation (IWMF), 2006). https://www.iwmf.org/resources/violence-and-harassment-against-women-in-the-news-media-a-global-picture/.

www.bible.com/bible/1/LUK.4.23.KJV.

Broadcasting Organisation of Nigeria (2023) 'About BON' 2023. https://bon.ng/history/

Farlex International 'The Free Dictionary' https://idioms.thefreedictionary.com/Caesar%27s+wife+must+be+above+suspicion.

Founder of Cherubim and Seraphim Church, and founder of Love of Christ Church, London, and notable religious leader in Nigeria.

G Heathcote 'Naming and shaming: Human rights accountability in security council resolution 1960' (2010) in on *Women, Peace, and Security Journal of Human Rights Practice Advance Access*, www.usip.org/sites/default/files/missing-peace/Naming-and-Shaming.pdf (access 7 February 2012).

C Ireton 'Sexual harassment in the media: The Africa report' World Association of News Publishers (WAN-IFRA)(Paris, 2023) 7 SexualHarassmentInTheMedia-Africa-English.pdf.

J Kantor and M Towhey 'Harvey Weinstein paid off sexual harassment accusers for decades' *African Union Agenda*, 5 October 2017, www.nytimes.com/2017/10/05/us/harvey-weinstein-harassment-allegations.html.

King James Version, Holy Bible: Luke 4:23, Life. Church/YouVersion, Edmond, Oklahoma, United States.

C Mackinnon *Sexual Harassment of Working Women: A Case of Sex Sexual Discrimination* (Yale University Press, 1979).

Media Foundation for West Africa (MFWA) & International Press Centre (2023) Report: State of Safety of Female Journalists in Nigeria www.mfwa.org/wp-content/uploads/2023/02/SAFETY-OF-FEMALE-JOURNALISTS-IN-WEST-AFRICA-NIGERIA-final-1.pdf 11.

National Broadcasting Commission, http://lawsofnigeria.placng.org/view2.php?sn=276.

National Communications Commission Nigerian *National Broadband Plan 2020–2025* (Abuja, 2020) 16, https://ncc.gov.ng/documents/880-nigerian-national-broadband-plan-2020–2025/file

Nigerian Bar Association – About Us, 2023, www.nigerianbar.org.ng/about_us#who-we-are.

Nigerian Bar Association Sexual Harassment Policy, Nigerian Bar Association: Creating a Safe Space for All (2021); Nigerian Bar Association *About Us*, 2023, www.nigerianbar.org.ng/about_us#who-we-are.

Nigeria Press Council (Abuja), Nigeria Press Council Act 1992, http://new.presscouncil.gov.ng/wp-content/uploads/2012/12/npc_law.pdf.

Nigerian Press Council (2023) NPC Act, http://new.presscouncil.gov.ng/wp-content/uploads/2012/12/npc_law.pdf

Nigerian Union of Journalists 'NUJ official compendium' 2023, http://nuj.org.ng/compendium.phpIt.

V Nnakaike 'ActionAid urges security agencies to protect female journalists' *Businessday*, *Lagos*, 7 November 2021, https://businessday.ng/news/article/actionaid-urges-security-agencies-to-protect-female-journalists/.

Y Noah 'Experience of sexual harassment at work by female employees in a Nigerian work environment' www.krepublishers.com/02-Journals/JHE/JHE-30-0-000-10-Web/JHE-30-3-000-2010-Abst-PDF/JHE-30-3-179-10-1933-Yusuf-N/JHE-30-3-179-10-1933-Yusuf-N-Tt.pdf.

P Obaji Jnr 'He told me to sit on his lap: The women enduring sexual harassment in Nigerian newsrooms' *Al Jazeera Journalism Review*, March 2023, https://institute.aljazeera.net/en/ajr/article/2124.

I Okereke 'Lack of organisational policies, other factors encourage sexual harassment in Nigerian newsrooms' *Premium Times, Abuja*, 15 June 2022, www.premiumtimesng.com/news/top-news/537237-lack-of-organisational-policies-other-factors-encourage-sexual-harassment-in-nigerian-newsrooms.html.

J Otieno 'The silent monster that is workplace sexual harassment' *The Citizen*, Dar Salam 3 June 2021, www.thecitizen.co.tz/tanzania/news/national/the-silent-monster-that-is-workplace-sexual-harassment-2694986.

Policy and Legal Advocacy Centre 'Nigerian Press Council Act', http://lawsofnigeria.placng.org/view2.php?sn=384.

Report: State of Safety of Female Journalist in Nigeria (2023) 12.

A Salaudeen 'In pursuit of justice: The women fighting against Nigeria's rape culture in Afriquette' (n.d.), www.afriquette.com/articles/women-fighting-against-nigeria-rape-culture.

J Taiwo-Obalonye 'Our first quarrel as couple: The inspiring story of Rev Mother Esther Ajayi and husband (2)' *The Sun Newspapers, Lagos*, 6 June 2020, https://sunnewsonline.com/our-first-quarrel-as-couple-the-inspiring-story-of-rev-mother-esther-ajayi-and-husband-2.

J Taiwo-Obalonye 'Survey to study incidents of sexual harassment among media workers in Nigeria' conducted between 5 and 7 May 2023. A randomised online survey using Google Sheet to collect responses from participants from media organisations in Nigeria.

The Constitution of Federal Republic of Nigeria 1999, Sect 22, www.jonapwd.org/FRNconstitution.pdf.

The Guardian Newspapers 'NBA 2019: Focus on sexual harassment in the workplace' https://guardian.ng/guardian-woman/nba-2019-focus-on-sexual-harassment-in-the-workplace/.

The NBA is the statutory legal union for legal practitioners in Nigeria with 150,000 members nationwide.

J Zakari and A Adeyanju *African Media Development Initiatives: Nigeria Research Findings and Conclusions* (BBC World Service Trust, 2006).

12 Sexual Harassment and the Law in Nigeria

Exploring the Existing Legal Landscape and Highlighting the Gaps in Legal and Institutional Frameworks

Oluwatoyin Adejonwo-Osho

Introduction

The offence of sexual harassment is a workplace concept applicable across multiple work sectors whether formal[1] or informal.[2] In Nigeria (a country with an estimated population of over 184 million people which accounts for about 47% of West Africa's population), sexual harassment is a scourge – persistent and pervasive. The primary source of law is the Constitution of the Federal Republic of Nigeria, and it is from this source that fundamental human rights pertaining to dignity[3] and freedom from discrimination[4] can be derived and litigated. Whilst the constitution provides a solid foundation for the enforcement of rights to protect against sexual harassment, specific and comprehensive laws are required to provide mechanisms for implementation and create categories of offences where required.

Only two out of the 36 states of the federation have laws specific to its prohibition, despite the widespread nature of sexual harassment in Nigeria. Furthermore, workplace policy on sexual harassment is not a common feature in many companies and organisations. In this chapter, I provide a detailed analysis of the state-specific sexual harassment laws and how they innovatively distinguish and highlight sexual harassment in the workplace from sexual harassment in educational settings. I articulate on how sexual harassment perpetuates power imbalances between the sexes in academic or employment settings. I also discuss how violations of fundamental constitutional rights as recognised by the Constitution of Nigeria has allowed victims of sexual harassment to seek redress in the National Industrial Court to enforce their fundamental human rights.

Sexual harassment is an unwelcome behaviour of a sexual nature that creates a hostile or offensive environment. The unwelcome behaviour includes unwelcome sexual advances, requests for sexual 'favours', and other verbal or physical conduct of a sexual nature.[5] According to the Convention on the Elimination of all Forms of Discrimination Against Women (CEDAW)'s General Recommendation, sexual harassment includes such unwelcome sexually determined behaviour as physical contact and advances, sexually coloured

DOI: 10.4324/9781003373308-12

remarks, showing pornography, and demands of a sexual nature whether by words or actions. Such conduct can be humiliating and may constitute a health and safety problem and it is discriminatory when the woman has reasonable grounds to believe that her objection would disadvantage her in connection with her employment, including recruitment or promotion, or when it creates a hostile working environment.[6] The key word is 'unwelcome behaviour', including sexual advances, request for sexual 'favours', and other visual, verbal, or physical conduct of a sexual nature.[7]

A notable drawback to eradicating sexual harassment in Nigeria is the predominant culture of patriarchy, the continued treatment of sex as a taboo, the culture of silence which emboldens perpetrators, fear of stigmatisation, a culture of shame and silence, and socio-economic vulnerability. Oyewunmi considers the social and cultural environment of the African society, especially its patriarchal relations and the traditional reticence of many African women.[8] She advocates that in addition to verbally assertive responses, conduct such as ignoring the perpetrator, walking away, or other conduct which can reasonably be construed as indicating a lack of interest ought to be interpreted as an indication that the overture is unwelcome.[9] Therefore, in patriarchal societies, a victim may consent or agree to certain conducts and actively participate even where the victim finds such conduct offensive and objectionable.

Global, regional, and national laws affirm sexual harassment as a violation of human rights and a form of discrimination and violence against women. These documents further provide standards and guidelines against sexual harassment, including from Africa, Latin America, and Europe.[10] The African Commission on Human and Peoples' Rights' 'Guidelines for Combating Sexual Violence and its Consequences' provides that sexual violence is not limited to physical violence and does not necessarily involve physical contact.[11] Sexual harassment can take various forms including looks, words, and physical contact of a sexual nature. Examples of sexual harassment are non-exhaustive. They include attempted or actual sexual assault, including rape; sharing or displaying sexually inappropriate images or videos in any format; sending sexually suggestive communications in any format; sharing sexual or lewd anecdotes or jokes; making inappropriate sexual gestures, such as pelvic thrusts; unwelcome touching, including pinching, patting, rubbing, or purposefully brushing up against another person; staring in a sexually suggestive manner; repeatedly asking a person for dates or asking for sex; rating a person's sexuality; making sexual comments about appearance, clothing, or body parts; name-calling or using slurs with a gender/sexual connotation; making derogatory or demeaning comments about someone's sexual orientation or gender identity.[12]

Sexual harassment occurs in the workplace and in a learning environment, including schools and university institutions. Sexual harassment in Nigeria also occurs in religious and political institutions, and cuts across social and legal relationships affecting broad categories of spaces.[13] This broad cross-cutting and multi-sectoral impact of sexual harassment is explicitly provided for in the Criminal Law of Edo State which has expanded the scope of sexual harassment environment beyond the workplace and educational space in Nigeria. In the light of this, the chapter will be presented in four parts covering 1) an introduction, 2) some statistics on sexual harassment in Nigeria, 3) the impact of culture on the perception of sexual harassment in Nigeria, and 4) an analysis of the current legal landscape, highlighting the gaps therein and the problems of implementation. I conclude that there is sufficient and accessible data to drive better policy and legal responses to sexual harassment through the legislation, state laws, and effective mechanisms to provide deterrence and protections against sexual harassment.

Statistics on Sexual Harassment in Nigeria

Existing and emerging data and statistics indicate a high prevalence of sexual harassment in the workplace and in both formal and informal settings. Both males and females can experience sexual harassment; however, women and girls in Nigeria are particularly vulnerable and exposed to sexual harassment in all spaces, whether it is in the privacy of their homes, in public spaces, in educational settings, online, or at their places of work.[14] For instance, studies on the prevalence, context, and impact of sexual harassment among employees working in diverse employment settings across multiple states in Nigeria indicate that 64% of participants in this study (259) had experienced one or more instances of sexual harassment. In addition, the study further reveals that heterosexual women aged between 18 and 30 who have never been married and worked at large organizations (with over 50 employees) were significantly more likely to experience sexual harassment compared to others.[15]

Several research studies have made an attempt to determine the prevalence of sexual harassment in the workplace through a sector-specific lens, such as banking;[16] teaching;[17] higher institutions of learning;[18] the public sector, including the civil service and public organizations;[19] medical;[20] and the legal profession.[21] In the banking sector, respondents consisting of 58% men and 54% women viewed sexual harassment as a challenge to the growth of Nigerian banking sector.[22] A case study of sexual harassment in the Nigerian legal sector reported that 68% of women participants were subjected to sexual harassment as compared to 32% of men that experienced same.[23]

In educational settings, particularly in the tertiary institutions, sexual harassment and misconduct is a significant problem. Several studies conducted at select universities and other higher educational institutions indicate that the categories of sexual harassment range from physically and verbally harassed behaviours to physically assaulted behaviours, with the perpetrators being faculty/staff. Interviews with 413 female students at the University of Port-Harcourt indicates that 47% had been subjected to sexual harassment.[24] According to Akiyode-Afolabi *et al*, nearly a quarter of women suffer from some form of sexual violence in their lifetime, but the number may be much higher in academia.[25] Owoaje and Olusola-Taiwo's study of the prevalence of sexual harassment of female graduates from various tertiary institutions in Nigeria determined that the 70% of the respondents had been sexually harassed, with the main perpetrators being male classmates and lecturers.[26] A 2019 documentary by the British Broadcasting Corporation's (BBC) *African Eyes* series titled 'Sex for Grades' also highlighted the prevalence of sexual harassment in select tertiary institutions in Nigeria and Ghana.[27]

The National Demographic Health Survey (NDHS)[28] recognises and provides data on several categories of women exposed to varying forms of gender-based violence. Available data from NDHS 2018 shows that violence against women is prevalent across geographical and demographic positions, affecting women of all ages, including young girls, women in rural and urban areas, women from different socio-economic stations, and women across the different geopolitical zones in Nigeria.[29] However, gaps remain in the NDHS categorisation; the data does not fully disaggregate the status of women and their experience of sexual harassment in the workplace and at educational institutions. Sexual violence has been subsumed under domestic violence or gender-based violence in the NDHS analyses so that it sometimes loses its distinctiveness. For instance, many forms of sexual violence are not 'domestic'. Various acts of sexual violence are reported in Nigerian communities, and some of the most common are incest, rape, sexual assault (including Intimate Partner Violence), and defilement. Sexual harassment, including inappropriate sexualised behaviour in the workplace and schools and groping in the marketplace, are prevalent but not reported as often.[30]

Impact of Culture on the Perception of Sexual Harassment in Nigeria

Nigeria has a diverse population of different dominant ethnic groups including the Hausa, Yoruba, and Igbo. One of the common threads amongst the culture of the dominant ethnic groups in Nigeria is the patriarchal structure of the society and the perceived superiority of the male child.[31]

> Nigeria is a male-dominated patriarchal society where the sexual harassment of women and female adolescents appears to be socially and culturally condoned, despite existing laws that prohibit harassment. Widespread sexual harassment is not unconnected from the culture of the people where women are objectified.[32]

Researchers attribute the culture of silence to a culture which frowns against open discussions of sexual conversations[33] and a weak legal framework to hold perpetrators accountable. Incidents of sexual harassment are often made light of by the relevant authorities in the workplace, and no serious action is usually taken against perpetrators, and, worse still, victims are often chastised for purportedly 'arousing the sexual drive of the harasser'.[34]

The predominant culture of patriarchy, the culture of silence which emboldens perpetrators, fear of stigmatisation, and a culture of shame and silence exacerbate the prevalence of sexual harassment in patriarchal societies.

The Current Legal Landscape

The Labour Act of 2004 is the principal legislation governing employment relations in Nigeria whose application extends to employees engaged under a contract of labour in both the private and the public sectors. However, it does not cover workplace sexual harassment. Prior to the constitutional amendment of 2010, there had been no recognition in Nigeria's Constitution of sexual harassment.[35] The courts have interpreted and victims have sought redress for sexual harassment through the rights guaranteed in the Fundamental Human Rights chapter of the Constitution 1999. The courts have relied on the interpretation of Sections 34, 35, 42, 254C(1)(f), (g), (h) and 254C(2) of the 1999 Constitution of the Federal Republic of Nigeria; and Articles 2, 5, 14, 15, and 19 of the African Charter on Human and People's Rights (Ratification and Enforcement) Act.[36]

Human rights are constitutionally guaranteed under Chapter IV of the 1999 Constitution. These rights are referred to as inalienable rights and include the right to life (Section 33), right to dignity (Section 34), right to personal liberty (Section 35), right to fair hearing (Section 36), right to privacy and family life (Section 37), right to freedom of thought conscience and religion (Section 38), right to freedom of expression and press (Section 39), right to peaceful assembly and association (Section 40), right to freedom of movement (Section 41), and right to freedom from discrimination (Section 42).

The intersection between human rights and sexual harassment is that it is a behaviour which invariably threatens the fundamental human rights of victims. Specifically, the right to dignity of a human person (Section 34) and the right to freedom from discrimination (Section 42). The list of fundamental human rights that may be violated by sexual harassment is endless and this is the confluence where sexual harassment is also a violation of fundamental human rights and consequently a breach of the constitution of Nigeria. The constitution provides adequate redress mechanisms for any violation of fundamental human rights and a clear procedure to seek enforcement.

As has been noted, labour laws in Nigeria do not make specific provisions for workplace sexual harassment. However, the 1999 Constitution confers on the National Industrial Court jurisdiction on matters connected with or pertaining to the application of any international convention, treaty, or protocol of which Nigeria has ratified relating to labour, employment, workplace, and industrial relations matters.[37] Further, to the third alteration to the constitution, Section 254 (1)(g) of the 1999 Constitution provides that the National Industrial Court (NIC) shall have exclusive jurisdiction with respect to disputes relating or connected with any dispute arising from discrimination or sexual harassment in the workplace. By virtue of this provision, the

NIC has exclusive jurisdiction in respect of sexual harassment disputes arising in the workplace.

Those drafting the 1999 Constitution thought the issue serious enough to protect against it under Section 42 of the 1999 Constitution as altered. Pursuant to that jurisdiction and in a bid to fill the void in the labour statutes in respect of workplace sexual harassment, the National Industrial Court Civil Procedure Rules 2017 provides direction in this regard. The National Industrial Court Civil Procedure Rules defines sexual harassment as:

> an unwanted, unpleasant, offensive, or threatening conduct of a sexual nature distinguished from sexual attention that is welcome and mutual. Sexual attention becomes sexual harassment if – (a) the behaviour is persistent, although a single incident or instance can constitute sexual harassment; and/or (b) the recipient has made it clear that the behaviour is considered offensive; and/or (c) the perpetrator should have known that the behaviour is regarded as unacceptable.[38]

Order 14 of the Rule creates four categories of acts that constitute workplace harassment, including physical conduct of a sexual nature, such unwanted contact ranging from touching to sexual assault, rape, strip search by or in the presence of the opposite sex, and further gestures that connote sexual harassment;[39] verbal sexual harassment, such as unwelcome innuendos, sexual advances, comments with sexual undertones, sexual jokes, and graphic comments about some one's body, unwanted and irrelevant enquiries about someone sexual life, unwanted whistling and any document, material, or exhibit that support the following claims;[40] a non-verbal form of sexual harassment that is unwelcomed gestures, indecent exposures, an unwelcome display of sexual images or pictures;[41] and *quid pro quo* harassment where an owner, employer, supervisor, manager, or co-employee undertakes or attempts to influence the process of employment, promotion, training, discipline, dismissal, or salary increments of an employee or job applicant in exchange for sexual favours.[42]

Nigeria recently became a party to the ILO Convention 190 on violence and harassment in the workplace (C190).[43] It provides a comprehensive definition on sexual harassment in the workplace[44] which can be used in the National Industrial Court of Nigeria. The National Industrial Court Civil Procedure Rules made pursuant to the exclusive jurisdiction granted to the National Industrial Court of Nigeria with respect to disputes relating or connected with any dispute arising from discrimination or sexual harassment in the workplace provides a clear definition and the categories of sexual harassment in the workplace. The constitution does not define what constitutes sexual harassment, however the National Industrial Court Civil Procedure Rules and the Convention Concerning the Elimination of Violence and Harassment in the World of Work, 2019 (ILO Convention 190), provide adequate guidance.[45] The clear guidance and definition of sexual harassment in the workplace provided by these documents will continue to provide the NIC with the required guidance to provide redress to victims of workplace sexual harassment.

The National Industrial Court Civil Procedure Rules and the provisions of ILO Convention 190 have therefore become particularly relevant to the development of sexual harassment laws in Nigeria because they contain a specific definition and create categories of what constitutes sexual harassment in contrast to the Constitution of Nigeria< which lacks a definition. Furthermore, the convention will form part of the legal landscape on sexual harassment without the need for domestication via the National Assembly. This is because the 1999 Constitution as amended confers on the National Industrial Court jurisdiction on matters connected with or pertaining to the application of any international convention, treaty, or protocol of which Nigeria has ratified relating to labour, employment, workplace, and industrial relations matters. This resolves the implementation challenges that other international conventions ratified by Nigeria but requiring domestication have had to contend with.[46]

The Employees' Compensation Act repeals the Workmen's Compensation Act and makes comprehensive provisions for payment of compensation to employees who suffer from occupational diseases or sustain injuries arising from accident at workplace or in the course of employment.[47] Section 8(1)(a) of the Act provides that an employee shall be entitled to compensation for mental stress not resulting from an injury for which the employee is otherwise entitled to compensation, only if the mental stress is an acute reaction to a sudden and unexpected traumatic event arising out of or in the course of the employee's employment.

Survivors of sexual harassment often attest to severe traumatic effects. A study consisting of 3,153 Danish social educators (females 79.3%) responding to the International Trauma Questionnaire (ITQ) and the Copenhagen Psychosocial Questionnaire II item on sexual harassment (COPSOQ) examined the effect of workplace sexual harassment on post-traumatic stress disorder (PTSD) symptoms.[48] The study found a correlation between exposure to workplace sexual harassment and PTSD symptoms. Harassment from a colleague/leader compared to a client was associated with higher levels of PTSD symptoms, although the difference was not statistically significant.

These findings suggest that sexual harassment, especially higher harassment frequency and harassment from a colleague or superior at a workplace, is associated with trauma and PTSD symptoms following exposure to workplace sexual harassment. However, it remains to be seen if an employee who is subjected to sexual harassment may be able to claim compensation for stress under this heading as long as the event happened in the course of work. Furthermore, it also remains to be seen how this provision will be interpreted and if it can be linked to sexual harassment that occurs in the workplace. According to Okpeku, because sexual harassment could be very traumatic it means that an employee who is subjected to such action may be able to claim compensation if the event happened in the course of work.[49]

Few states in Nigeria have laws that criminalise sexual harassment.[50] Lagos is the first state to have made a law focusing on protection of victims of sexual harassment with its Criminal Law of Lagos State. Section 264(2) of the Criminal Law of Lagos State creates a new offence of sexual harassment punishable with imprisonment for three years thus:

> Sexual harassment is unwelcome sexual advances, requests for sexual favours, and other visual, verbal or physical conduct of a sexual nature which when submitted to or rejected –
>
> (a) implicitly or explicitly affects a person's employment or educational opportunity or unreasonably interferes with a person's work or educational performance:
> (b) Implicitly or explicitly suggest that submission to or rejection of the conduct will be a factor in academic or employment decisions; or
> (c) creates an intimidating, hostile or offensive learning or working environment.

Similarly, the Criminal Law of Edo State 2022 creates an expanded scope for sexual harassment and takes the scope further than the Lagos state provision, The Criminal Law of Edo State provides:

> 219(1) Any person who sexually harasses another commits a felony and is liable on conviction to imprisonment for three (3) years.
>
> (2) Sexual harassment is unwelcome sexual advances, request for sexual 'favours', and other visual, verbal or physical conduct of a sexual nature by a person in authority, fiduciary relationship or position of trust or any other social relationship, which when submitted to or rejected-
>
> (a) implicitly or explicitly affects a person's employment or educational opportunity; unreasonably interferes with the person's work or educational performance; or impacts on the person's religious, political, social, or legal relationship.
> (b) implicitly or explicitly suggests that submission to or rejection of the conduct will be a factor in academic or employment decisions, or in relation to any other opportunities; or
> (c) creates an intimidating, hostile or offensive learning and working environment.

The Lagos state and Edo state laws provide a wide range and scope for the offense of sexual harassment and, in so doing, both laws are not subject to ambiguous or inequitable interpretations. The laws acknowledge that sexual harassment can occur in both an employment and educational setting. Importantly, the laws further acknowledge that sexual harassment can perpetuate power imbalances between the sexes in academic or employment settings. One significant ingredient of the offences created by both laws is that the sexual advances, requests for sexual favours, and other visual, verbal, or physical conduct of a sexual nature, which constitute sexual harassment are 'unwelcome'. The requirement of 'unwelcome' signifies a distinction between a mutually acceptable relationship and acts of sexual harassment.[51]

Edo state law provides further novel provisions and goes further than the Lagos state laws. It acknowledges that sexual harassment can be by a person in a fiduciary relationship or position of trust or any other social relationship to the victim. The law goes further by acknowledging that sexual harassment can impact on the victims religious, political, social, or legal relationship. Oyewunmi suggests that in interpreting the provisions on sexual harassment in Nigeria, the cultural environment, and the traditional reticence of many African women should be taken into consideration.[52] She argued that in addition to verbally assertive responses, conduct such as ignoring the perpetrator and walking away can reasonably be construed as indicating a lack of interest or to be interpreted as an indication that the overture is unwelcome.[53]

The Prevention, Prohibition and Redressal of Sexual Harassment in Tertiary Educational Institutions Bill, 2019, has a four-fold objective. It seeks to prohibit the offence of sexual harassment of students in tertiary institutions in Nigeria, criminalise the neglect or failure of administrative officers in addressing complaints of sexual harassment within a specified time, it creates a strict liability offence by removing the defence of consent, and it seeks to promote the fiduciary relationship between students and educators in tertiary institutions in Nigeria.[54] Stakeholders highlight the special relationship between students and educators, which is anchored on the doctrine of *loco parentis*.

Critics of the bill highlight the fact that it targets only the educators in tertiary institutions, and it excludes sexual harassment in primary schools, secondary schools, and workplaces. Critics of the bill further highlight the fact that it fails to take into cognisance the provisions of other extant laws with specific references to the Criminal Code Act; the Penal Code; Child Rights Act; Trafficking in Persons (Prohibition) Enforcement and Administration Act, 2015; and the Violence Against Persons (Prohibition) Act, 2015, which adequately deals with issues of sexual offences. The danger of this argument is that sexual harassment will become conflated with and subsumed under other forms of SGBV violence. Consequently, legislature has a duty to, through legislation, establish the framework for effectively addressing sexual harassment in tertiary institutions. This is pertinent especially in a situation where many tertiary institutions in Nigeria do not have sexual harassment policies and guidelines.[55]

Highlight of Cases on Sexual Harassment in the Workplace

In the case of *Ejike Maduka v Microsoft and Ors*,[56] the court held the perpetrator liable for sexual harassment and the employer was also held vicariously liable for the acts of sexual harassment perpetrated against its employee. Mrs. Maduka, a former employee of Microsoft Nigeria Ltd, sued her former employer together with its parent company, Microsoft Corporations, for wrongful termination of employment on the ground that she refused to succumb to the sexual advances of her boss, the chief executive officer of the company. She also sought other relief, including a declaration that the termination of her employment amounted to an infringement of her rights to dignity and freedom from discrimination. The court found that the respondent sexually harassed Mrs. Maduka and some other women workers in the office against their will despite their protests.

The court held that the sexual harassment of Mrs. Maduka was an infringement of her fundamental right to dignity of human person and freedom from discrimination.[57] The court further held that the inaction and silence of Microsoft Nigeria and Microsoft Corporation when the complaint was made on 12 August 2015 suggested that both companies tolerated and ratified the acts of the chief executive officer. Accordingly, both companies were held liable in damages for not taking the utmost care to ensure that the employees fundamental right to freedom from discrimination and degrading treatment in the workplace was not violated.[58] The applicant instituted her action under the Fundamental Human Right Enforcement Procedure Rules, praying the NICN to declare that the termination of her employment for her refusal to succumb to the sexual advances of her employer constituted a flagrant infringement on her right to dignity of person and freedom from discrimination as guaranteed by Sections 34 and 42 of the Constitution of Federal Republic of Nigeria, 1999 (as amended), and Sections 15 and 19 of the African Charter on Human and Peoples Right (Ratification and Enforcement) Act.

In the case of *Pastor Abimbola Patricia Yakubu v Financial Reporting Council of Nigeria*,[59] the claimant was employed by the first defendant, then known as the Nigerian Accounting Standard Board. In the year 2010, she was redeployed to the executive office directly presided over by the second defendant wherein she reported and worked directly with him. The applicant contends that while working with the second defendant, she was, at various times, subjected to incessant seductive, infidel, and sensuous compliments and gestures. That on her continuous rebuff, he resorted to unnecessarily harassing her. The court held that the termination of the claimant's employment simply because she refused to succumb to sexual harassment from second defendant constituted a violation of her human dignity and freedom from discrimination, as protected by the African Charter on Human and Peoples' Rights (Ratification and Enforcement) Act, and against the claimant's fundamental human rights under the 1999 Constitution, as amended.

Conclusion

The problem of sexual harassment is a multifaceted and complex issue that demands urgent and comprehensive action. This chapter has analysed the current legislative framework for protection against sexual harassment in Nigeria. It is evident that sexual harassment not only undermines the dignity and well-being of individuals, but also erodes the foundations of a fair and inclusive work environment. Effective legal and institutional frameworks are imperatives for deterring and addressing sexual harassment cases. However, this requires a collaborative approach among legislators, enforcement agencies, and organisations. Efforts to combat sexual harassment must extend beyond legislations to effective regulating and implementation. Education and awareness campaigns are crucial in helping individuals recognise inappropriate behaviours, understand their rights, and feel empowered to report incidents without fear of stigmatisation and retaliation. An effective legal mechanism, including dedicated legislation and an effective deterrence and implementation structure, will play a vital role in addressing sexual harassment cases.

Employers and tertiary institutions must actively promote a safe and open reporting system, ensuring confidentiality and a fair investigation process. Employers must prioritise gender sensitivity training, promote women to leadership positions, and cultivate an atmosphere of inclusivity where every employee's voice is valued. Furthermore, employers and tertiary institutions have the responsibility to protect employees and students in tertiary institutions from sexual harassment. In recent years, Nigeria has made efforts to address sexual harassment through legislation and legal frameworks. The analysis illustrates that there is an increased awareness of the prevalence of sexual harassment in the workplace and in tertiary institutions. The chapter highlights the emerging laws and policies in Lagos State and Edo State. It is hoped that other states will enact relevant laws and policies against sexual harassment.

Recommendations

I make the following recommendations to strengthen the response to sexual harassment in Nigeria:

- National legislation on sexual harassment, especially at the federal level and state laws. This will prevent a situation where sexual harassment will become conflated with and subsumed under other forms of GBV violence. Consequently, legislature has a duty to, through legislation, establish the framework for effectively addressing sexual harassment.
- NDHS categorisation and data should disaggregate the status of women and their experience of sexual harassment.

- Employers and tertiary institutions must establish a safe and open reporting system, ensuring confidentiality and a fair investigation process.
- Organisations registering with the Corporate Affairs Commission (CAC) should be mandated to have a sexual harassment policy as one of the requirements for its registration.
- Employers should be mandated to have policies and rules in their handbook and code of conduct expressly prohibiting sexual harassment.

Notes

1 Black's Law Dictionary defines formal sector as 'a group of people, usually employees, including recognised income sources for paying income taxes based on all 40-hour, regular wage jobs, https://thelawdictionary.org (assessed on 9 July 2023).

2 ILO 'Informal Economy and Atypical Forms of Employment' The term "informal economy" refers to all economic activities by workers and economic units that are – in law or in practice not covered or insufficiently covered by formal arrangements, www.ilo.org/actrav/areas/WCMS_DOC_ATR_ARE_INF_EN/lang–en/index.htm (assessed on 9 July 2023).

3 Sect 34 of the Constitution of the Federal Republic of Nigeria 1999 as amended.

4 *Ibid.*

5 UN 'What is Sexual Harassment' www.un.org/womenwatch/osagi/pdf/whatissh.pdf (assessed on 9 July 2023); see also UN Women 'Towards an end to sexual harassment: The urgency and nature of change in the era of #Metoo' www.unwomen.org/en/digital-library/publications/2018/11/towards-an-end-to-sexual-harassment (assessed on 9 July 2023).

6 CEDAW General Recommendation No 19, Article 11 paragraph 18 (11th Session, 1992), Violence against women, file:///C:/Users/MY%20PC/Downloads/INT_CEDAW_GEC_3731_E.pdf (assessed on 9 July 2023).

7 AO Bello *Essentials of Criminal Law in Nigeria* (University of Lags Press, 2022) 234.

8 AO Oyewunmi 'The criminalization of sexual harassment in Nigerian workplace: Is it an adequate response? (2012) 28/3 *International Journal of Comparative Labour Law and Industrial Relations* 387.

9 *Ibid.*

10 See the following regional Conventions: Global – The Convention on the Elimination of all Forms of Discrimination Against Women (CEDAW), www.ohchr.org/en/instruments-mechanisms/instruments/convention-elimination-all-forms-discrimination-against-women (assessed on 10 July 2023); Africa – Protocol to the African Charter on Human and Peoples' Rights on the Rights of Women in Africa (Maputo Protocol) adopted on 11 July 2003 African Union (entered into force on 25 November 2005), https://au.int/en/treaties/protocol-african-charter-human-and-peoples-rights-rights-women-africa (assessed on 10 July 2023); Latin America – Inter-American Convention on the Prevention, Punishment and Eradication of Violence Against Women (Convention of Belem do Para) adopted 1994, Organisation of American States (entered into force 5 March 1995), www.oas.org/en/mesecvi/docs/belemdopara-english.pdf (assessed on 10 July 2023); Europe – Council of Europe Convention on Preventing and Combating Violence against Women and Domestic Violence (Istanbul Convention) adopted 11 May 2011 (entered into force 1 August 2014), www.coe.int/en/web/gender-matters/council-of-europe-convention-on-preventing-and-combating-violence-against-women-and-domestic-violence (assessed on 10 July 2023).

11 The Guidelines on Combating Sexual Violence and its Consequences in Africa, https://achpr.au.int/en/node/848 (assessed on 10 July 2023).
12 UNHCR 'What is sexual exploitation, abuse and harassment?' www.unhcr.org/what-we-do/how-we-work/tackling-sexual-exploitation-abuse-and-harassment/what-sexual-exploitation (assessed on 10 July 2023).
13 Bello (n 7) 235.
14 O Ayeni and Stand to End Rape Initiative 'Examining the prevalence, context, and impact of workplace sexual harassment in Nigeria' (Stand to End Rape Initiative (STER), 2021), https://standtoendrape.org/statistics/ (assessed on 10 July 2023).
15 *Ibid.*
16 See FF Akinfala and Tunde Komolafe 'Sexual harassment as a predictor of organisational outcomes' (2017) 20/1 *African Journal for the Psychological Study of Social Issues* 60–73; A Alooma and S Atadiose 'Impact of target deposit mobilization on unethical issues and employee: Dissatisfaction in Nigerian banking sector' (2014) 4/10 *American International Journal of Contemporary Research* 120–132.
17 I Haruna et al 'Analysis of the causes and effects of sexual harassment on the performance of female employees in some selected organisations in Kogi State' (2016) 2/2 *International Journal of Democratic and Development Studies* 31–39.
18 See I Abe 'Defining and awareness of sexual harassment among selected university students in Lagos metropolis' (2012) 3/3 *Journal of Emerging Trends in Educational Research and Policy Studies* 212–218; M Mezie-Okoye and F Alamina 'Sexual violence among female undergraduates in a tertiary institution in Port Harcourt: Prevalence, Pattern, determinants and health consequences' (2014) 18/4 *African Journal of Reproductive Health* 79–85.
19 N Yusuf 'Experience of sexual harassment at work by female employees in a Nigerian work environment' (2010) 30/3 *Journal of Human Ecology* 179–186.
20 See O Abodunrin et al 'Prevalence and forms of violence against health care professionals in a South-Western city, Nigeria' (2014) 2/8 *Sky Journal of Medicine and Medical Sciences* 067–072; O Arulogun et al 'Experience of sexual harassment and coping strategies among students of the School of Nursing of a tertiary hospital in Southwest, Nigeria (2013) 5/4 *International Journal of Nursing and Midwifery* 70–75.
21 A Aina-Pelemo et al 'Sexual harassment in the workplace: Case study of the Nigerian legal sector' (2019) 86 *Journal of Law, Policy and Globalization* 123.
22 *Ibid*; see also S Bello 'Gender differences in perception of sexual harassment among Nigerian banks' employees' *Proceedings of ISER 29th International Conference*, UAE Dubai, 22 April 2016, 21–26.
23 Aina-Pelemo (n 21) 127.
24 Mezie-Okoye and Alamina (n 18) 79–85.
25 A Akiyode-Afolabi et al 'Harnessing student involvement: Perspectives from building infrastructure for sexual harassment prevention and response at the University of Lagos, Nigeria' (2022) 12/03075 *Journal of Global Health* 1–3.
26 E Owoaje and O Olusola-Taiwo 'Sexual harassment experiences of female graduates of Nigerian tertiary institutions' (2002) 30/4 *International Quarterly of Community Health Education* 337–348; see also Akiyode-Afolabi et al (n 25).
27 'Sex for grades: Undercover inside Nigerian and Ghanaian universities – BBC Africa Eye documentary' www.youtube.com/watch?v=we-F0Gi0Lqs.
28 NDHS 2018, National Population Commission and ICF International. Nigeria Demographic and Health Survey 2018. NPC, ICF, 2019.
29 See also NDHS 2008, National Population Commission and ICF International. Nigeria Demographic and Health Survey 2008. National Population Commission, ICF Macro, 2009. NDHS 2013, National Population Commission and ICF

International. Nigeria Demographic and Health Survey 2013. National Population Commission, ICF International, 2014.
30 O Ayeni and Stand to End Rape Initiative *Examining the Prevalence, Context, and Impact of Workplace Sexual Harassment in Nigeria*' (Stand to End Rape Initiative (STER), 2021), https://standtoendrape.org/statistics/.
31 Aina-Pelemo et al (n 21) 123.
32 A Arazeem Abdullahi et al 'Myth of the informal sector: A study on the sexual harassment of female adolescents in four motor garages in Ilorin, Nigeria' (2017) 16/6 *Perspectives on Global Development and Technology* 717–735.
33 Aina-Pelemo et al (n 21) 123; see also O Awosusi and F Ogundana 'Culture of silence and wave of sexual violence in Nigeria' (2015) 1/3 *AASCIT Journal of Education* 31–37.
34 Aina-Pelemo (n 21) 123.
35 Constitution of Nigeria 1999 (The third alteration to the Constitution of 2010).
36 See *Ejike Maduka v Microsoft* Unreported NICN/LA/492/2012.
37 See Sect 254(F)(1), of the Constitution of the Federal Republic of Nigeria, 1999 (as amended by the Third Alteration Act, 2010) and Section 36 of the National Industrial Court Act, 2006.
38 See Order 10 Rule 2 National Industrial Court of Nigeria (Civil Procedure) Rules, 2017
39 *Ibid* Rule (1)(a).
40 *Ibid* Rule (1)(b).
41 *Ibid* Rule (1)(c).
42 *Ibid* Rule (1)(d).
43 Nigeria submitted its articles of ratification of Ratification on the 8 November 2022. The Convention will enter into force for Nigeria on 8 November 2023, www.ilo.org/dyn/normlex/en/f?p=1000:11300:0::NO:11300:P11300_INSTRUMENT_ID:3999810
44 Adoption: Geneva, 108th ILC session (21 Jun 2019). Entry into force: 25 June 2021. www.ilo.org/dyn/normlex/en/f?p=NORMLEXPUB:12100:0::NO::P12100_ILO_CODE:C190
45 Infra footnote 1.
46 For example, the Convention for the Elimination of All Forms of Discrimination Against Women (CEDAW), which Nigeria ratified in 1985 but has not been domesticated as required by the Constitution for it to become part of our body of statutes. See also O Okpeku 'The world of work: What the law can do about sexual harassment' https://businessday.ng/news/legal-business/article/the-world-of-work-what-the-law-can-do-about-sexual-harassment/
47 Employee's Compensation Act, 2010 Laws of the Federation of Nigeria, www.ilo.org/dyn/natlex/natlex4.detail?p_lang=&p_isn=87608&p_classification=15.03
48 N Hansen et al 'Workplace sexual harassment increases the risk of PTSD symptoms with higher frequency and harassment coming from a colleague or leader as risk factors' (2022) 7/1 *Scandinavian Journal of Work and Organizational Psychology* 12; see also S Henin and L Black 'Understanding the long-term trauma of sexual assault patients' (2021) 2/4 *Journal of the American College of Emergency Physicians Open*.
49 O Okpeku 'The world of work: What the law can do about sexual harassment' https://businessday.ng/news/legal-business/article/the-world-of-work-what-the-law-can-do-about-sexual-harassment/. It is important to note the provisions of Section 8(2) of the Employees' Compensation Act which states that where the mental stress is caused as a result of the decision of the employer to change the work, the working conditions of work organisation in such a way as to unfairly exceed the work ability and capacity of the employee thereby leading to mental

stress, such situation shall be liable to compensation to the degree as may be determined under any regulation made by the Board.

50 See the Violence Against Persons (Prohibition) Act 2015 is an innovative anti-violence law for the Federal Capital Territory, Abuja, on Sexual and Gender-Based Violence (SGBV).

51 Oyewunmi (n 8) 387

52 *Ibid.*

53 *Ibid.*

54 https://placng.org/i/wp-content/uploads/2019/12/Senate-Committee-Report-on-Sexual-Harassment-in-Tertiary-Educational-Institutions-Prohibition-Bill-2016.pdf

55 See the 'University of Lagos policy on sexual harassment, sexual and romantic relationships' https://spessce.unilag.edu.ng/wp-content/uploads/2021/10/SEXUAL-HARRASMENT-UNILAG-COMMUNICATION-UNITS.pdf; see also the Lagos State University 'Policy on sexual abuse and gender-based violence 2022' https://lasu.edu.ng/home/downloadables/Policy%20on%20sexual%20abuse%20and%20gender-based%20violence_1680659829.pdf

56 Unreported NICN/LA/492/20120980–089.

57 *Ibid* 28.

58 Unreported NICN/LA/492/2012, 29.

59 Suit NO: NIC/LA/673/2013, www.nicnadr.gov.ng/judgement/details.php?id=6320.

References

I Abe 'Defining and awareness of sexual harassment among selected university students in lagos metropolis' (2012) 3/3 *Journal of Emerging Trends in Educational Research and Policy Studies* 212–218.

OL Abodunrin et al 'Prevalence and forms of violence against health care professionals in a South-Western city, Nigeria' (2014) 2/8 *Sky Journal of Medicine and Medical Sciences* 067–072.

African Commission on Human and Peoples' Rights 'The guidelines on combating sexual violence and its consequences in Africa' https://achpr.au.int/en/node/848.

AD Aina-Pelemo et al 'Sexual harassment in the workplace: Case study of the Nigerian legal sector' (2019) 86 *Journal of Legal Policy and Globalisation* 121–137.

O Ajai 'The balancing of interest in environmental law in Nigeria' in M Faure and W du Plessis (eds) *The Balancing of Interests in Environmental Law in Africa* (Pretoria University Law Press, 2011).

FF Akinfala and T Komolafe 'Sexual harassment as a predictor of organisational outcomes' (2017) 20/1 *African Journal for the Psychological Study of Social Issues* 60–73.

A Akiyode-Afolabi et al 'Harnessing student involvement: Perspectives from building infrastructure for sexual harassment prevention and response at the University of Lagos, Nigeria' (2022) 12/03075 *Journal of Global Health* 1–3.

AG Alooma and S Atadiose 'Impact of Target deposit mobilization on unethical issues and employee dissatisfaction in Nigerian banking sector' (2014) 4/10 *American International Journal of Contemporary Research* 120–132.

A Arazeem Abdullahi et al 'Myth of the informal sector: A study on the sexual harassment of female adolescents in four motor garages in Ilorin, Nigeria' (2017) 16/6 *Perspectives on Global Development and Technology* 717–735.

OS Arulogun and IK Omotosho 'Experience of sexual harassment and coping strategies among students of the School of Nursing of a tertiary hospital in Southwest, Nigeria' (2013) 5/4 *International Journal of Nursing and Midwifery* 70–75.

A Awosusi and F Ogundana 'Culture of silence and wave of sexual violence in Nigeria' (2015) 1/3 *AASCIT Journal of Education* 31–37.

O Ayeni O and Stand to End Rape Initiative *Examining the Prevalence, Context, and Impact of Workplace Sexual Harassment in Nigeria* (Stand to End Rape Initiative (STER), 2021), https://standtoendrape.org/statistics/.

AO Bello *Essentials of Criminal Law in Nigeria* (University of Lagos Press, 2022).

S Bello 'Gender differences in perception of sexual harassment among Nigerian banks' employees' *Proceedings of ISER 29th International Conference*, UAE Dubai, 22 April 2016, 21–26.

CEDAW General Recommendation No 19, Article 11 Paragraph 18 (11th Session, 1992), Violence against women, file:///C:/Users/MY%20PC/Downloads/INT_CEDAW_GEC_3731_E.pdf.

Convention Concerning the Elimination of Violence and Harassment in the World of Work, 2019 (ILO Convention No 190).

Convention on the Elimination of all Forms of Discrimination Against Women (CEDAW), www.ohchr.org/en/instruments-mechanisms/instruments/convention-elimination-all-forms-discrimination-against-women.

Council of Europe Convention on Preventing and Combating Violence against Women and Domestic Violence (Istanbul Convention) adopted on 11 May 2011 (entered into force on 1 August 2014).

N Hansen et al 'Workplace sexual harassment increases the risk of PTSD symptoms with higher frequency and harassment coming from a colleague or leader as risk factors' (2022) 7/1 *Scandinavian Journal of Work and Organizational Psychology* 12.

S Henin and L Black 'Understanding the long-term trauma of sexual assault patients' (2021) 2/4 *Journal of the American College of Emergency Physicians Open* 1–2.

H Idris et al 'Analysis of the causes and effects of sexual harassment on the performance of female employees in some selected organisations in Kogi State' (2016) 2/2 *International Journal of Democratic and Development Studies* 31–39.

Inter-American Convention on the Prevention, Punishment and Eradication of Violence Against Women (Convention of Belem do Para) adopted in 1994 by the Organisation of American States (entered into force on 5 March 1995).

M-M Mezie-Okoye and F Alamina 'Sexual violence among female undergraduates in a tertiary institution in Port Harcourt: Prevalence, pattern, determinants and health consequences' (2014) 18/4 *African Journal of Reproductive Health* 79–85.

NDHS 2018, National Population Commission and ICF International. Nigeria Demographic and Health Survey *2018. NPC, ICF, 2019.*

O Okpeku 'The World of Work: what the law can do about sexual harassment' https://businessday.ng/news/legal-business/article/the-world-of-work-what-the-law-can-do-about-sexual-harassment/.

E Owoaje and O Olusola-Taiwo 'Sexual harassment experiences of female graduates of Nigerian tertiary institutions' (2002) 30/4 *International Quarterly of Community Health Education* 337–348.

AO Oyewunmi 'The criminalization of sexual harassment in Nigerian workplace: Is it an adequate response?' (2012) 28/3 *International Journal of Comparative Labour Law and Industrial Relations* 365–394.

AO Oyewunmi 'The criminalization of Sexual harassment in Nigerian workplace: Is it an adequate response?' (2012) 28/3 *International Journal of Comparative Labour Law and Industrial Relations* 365–394.

Protocol to the African Charter on Human and Peoples' Rights on the Rights of Women in Africa (Maputo Protocol) adopted on 11 July 2003 African Union (entered into force on 25 November 2005),

The World Bank 'Nigeria overview' www.worldbank.org/en/country/nigeria.

United Nations 'What is sexual harassment' www.un.org/womenwatch/osagi/pdf/whatissh.pdf (assessed on 9 July 2023).

United Nations Hight Commission for Refugees 'What is sexual exploitation, abuse and harassment?' www.unhcr.org/what-we-do/how-we-work/tackling-sexual-exploitation-abuse-and-harassment/what-sexual-exploitation.

United Nations Women 'Towards an end to sexual harassment: The urgency and nature of change in the era of #Metoo' www.unwomen.org/en/digital-library/publications/2018/11/towards-an-end-to-sexual-harassment (assessed on 9 July 2023).

N Yusuf 'Experience of sexual harassment at work by female employees in a Nigerian work environment' (2010) 30/3 *Journal of Human Ecology* 179–186.

13 Mapping Future Directions in Addressing Sexual Harassment in Africa

Furaha-Joy Sekai Saungweme, Carol Chi Ngang and Graham Towl

In this concluding chapter, we provide some brief antecedence on how sexual harassment came to be known as a global problem of enormous adverse proportions, especially against women, including those in Africa, which motivated the research that resulted in the production of this book. Collectively, the chapters have gleaned comprehensively on the uncomfortable but necessary discussions relating to the far-reaching consequences of sexual harassment in Africa. Drawing from socio-cultural and economic realities as well as the law, this collaborative effort has successfully woven together a compendium of ideas from an African continental, country-specific, and comparative viewpoints on the question of sexual harassment in Africa. The chapters reflect an intellectual corpus of resilience and mobilisation drawn from academic discourses and grassroots activism. Ultimately, we see how each chapter singularly and collectively provides the prelude and catalyst on what must come next as a solution to this inexplicably persistent problem of sexual harassment across the continent of Africa.

From a global perspective, significant progress has been made since the days of Cornell University where, in the 1970s, a group of women brainstormed on the unfortunate phenomenon that had no name at the time. Through their efforts, it evolved into the legal concept of what we now understand to be sexual harassment.[1] The narrative on sexual harassment was escalated by the work of African American woman Tarana Burke[2] who, in 2006, began using the slogan 'MeToo' to help women who had been subjected to the societal scourge. Over a decade later in 2017, the #MeToo hashtag became a viral campaign propelled to greater heights of international visibility on the wings of celebrity-driven social media.

The #MeToo campaign, which took off in the United States, curiously coincided with a series of investigations into allegations of sexual harassment within key institutional structures across Africa. In 2018, under the direction of the chairperson of the African Union Commission, an investigation into allegations of sexual harassment was undertaken by a High-Level Committee (HLC).[3] Part of the findings of the investigative report highlighted the following observations:

DOI: 10.4324/9781003373308-13

> It is the finding of the Committee that incidents of sexual harassment exists in the Commission. This is established by the almost unanimous confirmation of the prevalence of this occurrence by interviewees appearing before the Committee. Evidence presented suggests that this form of harassment perpetuated by supervisors over female employees in their charge, especially, but not exclusively, during official missions outside the work station. The absence of a sexual exploitation and abuse policy compounds the adverse effects of this vice. The category of staff most vulnerable and exposed to this form of harassment are short-term staff, youth volunteers and interns. It would appear that the vulnerability of this category of staff is exploited on account of their insecurity of tenure. Senior departmental staff, who position themselves as 'gate-keepers' and 'king-makers', are well-positioned to make believable promises to young women that they will be offered contracts, are the identified perpetuators of this vice. Interviewees claim that these cases are not reported as this would be counter-productive to the victim, because there is no sexual harassment policy in the Commission, and therefore no dedicated, effective redress and protection mechanism available to victims or whistle-blowers. According to interviewees, the young women are exploited for sex in exchange for jobs.[4]

While the investigating committee categorised its findings into four areas – malpractices in human resource functions, corrupt/fraudulent practices, governance issues, and sexual harassment – it is worth emphasising that sexual harassment cuts across all the mentioned categories. It is easy to contend, therefore, that sexual harassment in addition to being an issue centring on gender and sex discrimination is also a governance issue that rears its ugly head in conditions of institutional malpractices.

During the same timeframe, allegations of rampant sexual harassment at South Africa's largest broadcaster, the South African Broadcasting Corporation (SABC), led to the establishment of a Commission of Inquiry to investigate the allegations.[5] In a briefing to the media, the chairperson of the commission, Barbara Watson, remarked as follows:

> We also found that a large proportion of people who came to see us was in the area of freelancers and what exacerbated the problem is the policy of the SABC around freelancers. Quite a lot of power is vested on one person or two people and because of that, it enables a predator who has all this power to then do as he or she pleases. The policy around the hiring and firing of freelancers has got to be relooked at urgently.[6]

Around the same period, it became clear that not even tertiary institutions were protected from the growing menace of sexual harassment. Makerere

University, a prestigious educational institution in Uganda, East Africa, established a committee to investigate the problem of sexual harassment within the institution.[7] The investigation led to a review of the Makerere University Policy and Regulations Against Sexual Harassment in 2018. Furthermore, upon the release of the report, the vice chancellor of Makerere University, Prof Barnabas Nawangwe, stated as follows to the media:

> Makerere University is the epitome of knowledge. The university is tasked to nurture and impart knowledge to people. It is expected that the people to whom we impart knowledge must be free from any impediment to learn. They should be free from any form of harassment. It is hard for a person to learn while facing sexual harassment. Sexual harassment is not only criminal but it is against human moral. It is the worst form of abuse against human dignity.[8]

These developments, among others, were undertaken across the African continent and motivated the formation of the Africa End Sexual Harassment Initiative (AESHI), which has continued to be influenced by other recent developments on the African continent and internationally. This book, which is an outcome of AESHI's commitment to curbing sexual harassment is indeed a product of the overarching influence and impact of global justice movements and the power of solidarity that cuts across class, race, and geographical boundaries.

It is important to also acknowledge the power of the feminist movement, which at its core is merely knitted around the simple concept that women's rights are, indeed, human rights. This is the echo that strikes a chord of resonance in each of the chapters in this book, ranging from legislative developments in Ethiopia, South Africa, and Kenya to clearly strung intersections of social responses to gender and violence highlighted in Liberia and the plight of women with disabilities in Tanzania, where the multiple forms of discrimination they encounter on a regular basis are highlighted.

A call to African governments to be more responsive to the problem of sexual harassment through requisite legislation among other measures is emphasised in Chapter 2, which embodies critical reflections on the question of equality in Africa. The author engaged in a robust assessment of the sustainable development goals, centring on gender inequality and thoughtfully building a case as to why sexual harassment infringes on the right to development. A continental response to sexual harassment touching on the African human rights system exposes the complexities of litigating before the African Court on Human and Peoples' Rights, and, particularly, on matters involving sexual violence. Whilst most of the litigation has not been specific to sexual harassment, the cases discussed are a valuable step closer towards litigating sexual harassment at the level of the African human rights system enforcement mechanisms. The Maputo Protocol is flagged in this chapter as an indispensable mechanism for redress when it comes to sexual violence. We believe that the Maputo Protocol is a strategic human rights instrument suitable for redressing the vexing problem of sexual harassment in all its (vile) forms in Africa.

The broad perspectives on sexual harassment gleaned through the various chapters in this book also intersect at the junction of individual state obligations. This means that questions of impunity and the political unwillingness to introduce legislative reforms and punitive measures for holding perpetrators of sexual harassment accountable is a contravention of the fundamental responsibility of African state governments towards their citizens. It is, indeed, an erosion of the concept of equality, which deliberately undermines a basic social contract and commitment to socio-economic rights because sexual harassment is as much a bread-and-butter issue as it is an issue that cuts across the legal norms that are shaped around sex and gender-based discrimination.

The singular stories of the brave survivors of sexual harassment that can be extrapolated from country-specific chapters, such as Uganda, is a stark reminder of how much further we still have to go. Similarly, the key lessons we learned from the story of Rev Mother Esther Abimbola Ajayi in the chapter addressing sexual harassment in Nigeria's media landscape whilst rooted in 1984 when the term sexual harassment was barely whispered resonates today. Rev Mother Ajayi's story is familiar regardless of the timespan and therein lies the challenge of future generations of feminists, lawyers, media practitioners, parliamentarians, and social justice activists in Africa. What comes next must be mirrored in the vision of justice, equity, and equality taking centre place at a regional level. This must be strengthened by a continental model law on sexual harassment developed by Africans for Africa. Whilst the specific legal content of what this law should look like is not settled, we can draw inspiration from existing and ongoing legislative efforts to address sexual harassment in selected jurisdictions and learn from the gaps and best practice benchmarks. For instance, the term sexual harassment may vary in definition, scope, and application. Most of the chapters in this book allude to the realities of the inconsistency in the legislative framework on what constitutes sexual harassment, identifying victims and perpetrators, the offensive conduct in question, classifying it as a civil or criminal act, and the workplace context within which it occurs.

It is our conviction that the African Union (AU) is well positioned to chart a path towards the harmonisation and standardisation of sexual harassment laws for its member states. The AU Commission has previously adopted a number of model laws, including the AU Model Law on the Protection of Cultural Property[9] and the AU Model Law on Access to Information for Africa.[10] The Southern African Development Community Parliamentary Forum (SADC-PF)[11] has similarly adopted a Model Law in 2016 addressing the problem of child marriages; namely, the Model Law on Eradicating Child Marriage and Protecting Children Already in Child Marriage.[12] A model law or legislation refers to 'a detailed set of standards on a particular issue, which are offered for the consideration of and adoption by, national legislators'.[13] Model laws are an established precedent imbedded in the African legal framework to which some academics have contributed to the drafting of some of the model laws, which have proceeded to gain greater acceptance and adoption at the national level.[14] The impact of the SADC model law is evidenced by member states within the SADC region responding positively to it by adopting national strategies and raising awareness about the problem of child marriages.[15]

Considering the nature of the problem that sexual harassment poses, an AU Model Law on Sexual Harassment just like those cited is likely to gain widespread acceptance and eventual incorporation into the domestic laws of every country on the African continent. There is ample evidence, as has extensively been discussed in the chapters of this book, to justify the need for a model law on sexual harassment in Africa. We are convinced that this book has only just lit the candle for further engagement and research on the subject, including concrete actions with respect to the legal reforms and programme initiatives that must come next.

Notes

1 S Cohen 'A brief history of sexual harassment in America before Anita Hill' *Times Magazine*, 11 April 2016, https://time.com/4286575/sexual-harassment-before-anita-hill/ (accessed on 2 September 2023).

2 T Burke, Founder 'Me too' https://metoomvmt.org/get-to-know-us/tarana-burke-founder/ (accessed on 2 September 2023).

3 African Union 'Outcome of the investigation of allegations of harassment against women and other institutional malpractices in the African Union Commission' *African Union*, 22 November 2018, https://au.int/en/pressreleases/20181122/outcome-investigation-allegations-harassment-against-women-and-other (accessed on 2 September 2023).

4 *Ibid.*

5 South African Broadcasting Corporation 'SABC Takes action against alleged perpetrators of sexual harassment' *South African Broadcasting Corporation*, 22 November 2018, www.sabc.co.za/sabc/sabc-takes-action-against-alleged-perpetrators-of-sexual-harassment/ (accessed on 2 September 2023).

6 N Kaza 'SABC releases sexual harassment inquiry findings' *FM 702*, 6 November 2018, https://702.co.za/articles/325991/sabc-releases-sexual-harassment-inquiry-findings (accessed on 2 September 2023).

7 N Proscovia 'Committee investigating sexual harassment at Makerere University presents the report to stakeholders for validation' *Makerere University*, 22 May 2018, https://news.mak.ac.ug/2018/05/committee-investigating-sexual-harassment-at-makerere-university-presents-the-report-to-stakeholders-for-validation/ (accessed on 2 September 2023).

8 *Ibid.*

9 African Union Model Law on The Protection of Cultural Property and Heritage Executive Council, Fortieth Ordinary Session 20 January–03 February 2022 Addis Ababa, Ethiopia EX.CL/1309(XL)d., https://archives.au.int/handle/123456789/10399#:~:text=The%20African%20Union%20Model%20Law%20on%20the%20Protection,on%20the%20protection%20of%20cultural%20property%20and%20heritage (accessed on 2 September 2023).

10 African Union Model Law on Access to Information for Africa, https://achpr.au.int/en/special-mechanisms-reports/model-law-access-information-africa-2013 (accessed on 2 September 2023).

11 The SADC PF was established by the SADC Summit of Heads of State on 8th September 1997, in accordance with Article 9(2) of the SADC Treaty.

12 SADC Parliamentary Forum 'Model Law on Eradicating Child Marriage and Protecting Children Already in Marriage' [Hereinafter 'SADC Model Law'] adopted on 3rd June 2016 at the 39th Plenary Assembly meeting in Swaziland; see also Girls Not Brides 'SADC parliamentarians adopt model law on eradicating child marriage' 4 June 2016, www.girlsnotbrides.org/sadc-model-law-child-marriage/ (accessed on 2 September 2023).

13 F Viljoen 'Model legislation and regional integration: Theory and practice of model legislation pertaining to HIV in the SADC' (2008) *De Jure* 384.

14 F Adeleke, 'The impact of the model law on access to information for Africa' in S Ololade (ed) *The Model Law on Access to Information for Africa and Other Regional Instruments: Soft Law and Human Rights in Africa* (Pretoria University Law Press, 2018).

15 A Olaborede and N Ndlovu 'Real law or cover up: Pros and cons of the SADC Model Law on Eradicating Child Marriage and Protecting Children Already in Marriage' (2020) 34/3 *Speculum Juris* 49.

References

F Adeleke 'The impact of the model law on access to information for Africa' in S Ololade (ed) *The Model Law on Access to Information for Africa and Other Regional Instruments: Soft Law and Human Rights in Africa* (Pretoria University Law Press, 2018).

African Union 'Outcome of the investigation of allegations of harassment against women and other institutional malpractices in the African Union Commission' *African Union*, 22 November 2018, https://au.int/en/pressreleases/20181122/outcome-investigation-allegations-harassment-against-women-and-other (accessed on 2 September 2023).

African Union Model Law on Access to Information for Africa, https://achpr.au.int/en/special-mechanisms-reports/model-law-access-information-africa-2013 (accessed on 2 September 2023).

African Union Model Law on The Protection of Cultural Property and Heritage Executive Council, Fortieth Ordinary Session 20 January–03 February 2022 Addis Ababa, Ethiopia EX.CL/1309(XL)d, https://archives.au.int/handle/123456789/10399#:~:text=The%20African%20Union%20Model%20Law%20on%20the%20Protection,on%20the%20protection%20of%20cultural%20property%20and-%20heritage (accessed on 2 September 2023).

Burke, Tarana Founder 'Me too' https://metoomvmt.org/get-to-know-us/tarana-burke-founder/ (accessed on 2 September 2023).

S Cohen 'A brief history of sexual harassment in America before Anita Hill' *Times Magazine*, 11 April 2016, https://time.com/4286575/sexual-harassment-before-anita-hill/ (accessed on 2 September 2023).

N Kaza 'SABC releases sexual harassment inquiry findings' *FM 702*, 6 November 2018, https://702.co.za/articles/325991/sabc-releases-sexual-harassment-inquiry-findings (accessed on 2 September 2023).

A Olaborede and N Ndlovu 'Real law or cover up: Pros and cons of the SADC Model Law on Eradicating Child Marriage and Protecting Children Already in Marriage' (2020) 34/3 *Speculum Juris* 49–60.

N Proscovia 'Committee investigating sexual harassment at Makerere University presents the report to stakeholders for validation' *Makerere University*, 22 May 2018, https://news.mak.ac.ug/2018/05/committee-investigating-sexual-harassment-at-makerere-university-presents-the-report-to-stakeholders-for-validation/ (accessed on 2 September 2023).

SADC Parliamentary Forum 'Model Law on Eradicating Child Marriage and Protecting Children Already in Marriage' [Hereinafter 'SADC Model Law'] adopted on 3rd June 2016 at the 39th Plenary Assembly meeting in Swaziland; see also Girls Not Brides 'SADC Parliamentarians Adopt Model Law on Eradicating Child Marriage' 4 June 2016, www.girlsnotbrides.org/sadc-model-law-child-marriage/ (accessed on 2 September 2023).

South African Broadcasting Corporation 'SABC Takes action against alleged perpetrators of sexual harassment' *South African Broadcasting Corporation*, 22 November 2018, www.sabc.co.za/sabc/sabc-takes-action-against-alleged-perpetrators-of-sexual-harassment/ (accessed on 2 September 2023).

The SADC PF was established by the SADC Summit of Heads of State on 8th September 1997, in accordance with Article 9(2) of the SADC Treaty.

F Viljoen 'Model legislation and regional integration: Theory and practice of model legislation pertaining to HIV in the SADC' (2008) *De Jure* 383–398.

Index

Note: Page numbers followed by "n" with numbers refer to notes.